NINE YEARS
ON THE
NORTH-WEST FRONTIER OF INDIA

NINE YEARS
ON THE
NORTH-WEST FRONTIER OF INDIA,
FROM 1854 TO 1863.

BY

LIEUT.- GENERAL SIR SYDNEY COTTON, K. C. B.

GYAN

Published by

Gyan Publishing House
5, Ansari Road
Daryaganj, New Delhi-110002
Phone: 011-47034999, 9811692060
E-mail: books@gyanbooks.com

Distribution Network
gyanbooks.com
India, USA, Canada, UK, Australia, France

ISBN: 978-81-212-8007-5 (PB)
First Published, 1868

2nd Impression 2023

Printed at: Gyan Press, Delhi.

NINE YEARS ON THE NORTH-WEST FRONTIER OF INDIA
Author: SYDNEY COTTON

NINE YEARS

ON THE

NORTH-WEST FRONTIER OF INDIA,

FROM 1854 TO 1863.

BY

LIEUT.-GENERAL SIR SYDNEY COTTON, K.C.B.

IN UTRAQUE FORTUNA PARATUS.

LONDON:
RICHARD BENTLEY, NEW BURLINGTON STREET.
1868.

INTRODUCTION.

In aspiring to the honour of appearing before the world as an historian, the author of this volume desires to record, in simple and unaffected terms, the events of a period of Indian history, which cannot fail to be interesting, if not generally in England, at all events amongst those of our Empire in India to whom the author is known, and with whom he may have been associated.

The author has an object in view also in thus appearing before the public.

Since his return to England from India, in 1863, his name has been publicly and frequently quoted as an advocate for certain Indian measures, so entirely at variance with fact, that he deems it expedient to record his sentiments on some questions of importance *in his own justification.*

At a recent agricultural gathering, a statement was made of this nature by one of the speakers in the author's presence, when he was unable to explain away the error, because the subjects, being unconnected with the object of the meeting, could not be entertained without annoyance to the company.

The author desires to make his statements as brief and as little personal as possible, and in order not to tire the patience of his readers (if he has any) he purposes to bring his narrative into as small a compass as he can, consistent with the object he has in view, in making known matters of public interest, which have hitherto, he thinks, been little thought of, or perhaps never heard of.

It is imperatively necessary, however, in the author's opinion, that the records of past events should be strictly truthful, and that whilst treating of matters without favour or affection, naught should be given in malice or bad feeling, and naught should be cast in oblivion, because the sacred memory of those who have passed away must not be trespassed upon, or the feelings of those remaining be meddled with. Facts are stubborn things, and history must lose its value and importance if from mistaken motives of delicacy its pages are incomplete. It is fair, and indeed necessary to explain, that the principal object which the author has in view, is to record facts of importance in such unmistakable terms, as are beyond the reach of cavil or contradiction, many of which have never as yet appeared in the open face of day, and which, by their disclosure, may serve to benefit the State, either as "solemn warnings" for the future, or as hopeful encouragement to those public functionaries, who, in the honest discharge of their duties, may be really desirous of arriving at just decisions in the disposal of their public functions.

The author claims to himself the privilege of being considered an experienced officer in Indian military affairs, and experienced almost beyond all precedent as to length of active service in all the Presidencies, extending over a period (off and on) of fifty-three years.

He served in the Madras Presidency for many years—in Burmah for a time, in the Bombay Presidency for many years, and in Scinde for a time; and in the Bengal Presidency, at two periods of his life, for a vast number of years, and in almost every station of the several Presidencies where European troops are located. He served in a regiment of Light Dragoons above ten years in the Carnatic and Mysore countries, and in the Ceded districts during the Pindaree war of 1816 and 1817, and on the staff of a general officer for two years at Bangalore, in Mysore; also in command of a station near Madras; and acted as Deputy Adjutant-General, and Deputy Quartermaster-General of the Royal forces at Madras; as Aide-de-camp to the Commander-in-Chief in India, and also as his Military Secretary. He served under Sir Charles Napier in the Scinde war. He commanded the field Brigade of Deesa, in the Bombay Presidency, and the Brigades of Umballah, Rawul Pindee, and Peshawur, in Bengal; and finally the North-West Frontier of India, with the Divisional command of Peshawur for many years.

Every description of force of the three arms of the service (native and European) of all caste and colour have been confided to his care; and as regards his claims to the favourable consideration of the public, the author cannot now do better than insert the copy of a letter of the late Marquis of Dalhousie, formerly Governor-General of India, addressed to himself, which was intended for publication :—

Edinburgh,
June 20th, 1856.

DEAR BRIGADIER COTTON,

Your letter of the 27th February did not reach Calcutta until after I had taken my departure, and it only lately has found me in England. You ask me to place on record at the Horse Guards my conviction that you are well qualified for command in India. Nothing would give me greater pleasure than to aid you in this object. But I fear that I cannot do so with effect in the way you have suggested, for I have no official standing on which I could address the Horse Guards regarding you, and I cannot pretend to the profession of any personal influence there.

I believe that I should render you more service by addressing yourself, and authorising you to make any use you please of what I am to say. During all the years I administered the Government of India, there was no military officer who commanded my confidence more fully than yourself, or who had earned it better.

Your command of the Frontier Force was satisfactory to me in the highest degree. I concurred, and more than concurred, with the Commander-in-Chief in regarding you as the man best fitted to hold that command, and which I considered to be the most important in India. If I had been able to carry into effect my wish to constitute the Frontier Force at Peshawur an entirely separate command, you are the man I should have selected to hold it. I could pay you no higher compliment than is implied in the statement I have just made. Looking, as I ever shall, to India with the keenest interest, I shall feel the highets satisfaction on public grounds if I should see you holding military command in that country, where your ability and experience have already rendered your service so valuable to the State.

Believe me to be,

Very faithfully yours,

(Signed) DALHOUSIE.

BRIGADIER COTTON.

CONTENTS.

CHAPTER IV.

CHAPTER V.

CHAPTER VI.

CHAPTER VII.

CHAPTER VIII.

CHAPTER IX.

CHAPTER X.

CHAPTER XI.

CHAPTER XII.

CHAPTER XIII.

CHAPTER XIV.

CHAPTER XV.

NINE YEARS

ON THE

NORTH-WEST FRONTIER OF INDIA.

CHAPTER I.

The Author's first appearance on the North-West frontier of India.

ON one intolerably hot day in the month of September, 1853, the author, being in temporary command of the Rawul Pindee forces, consisting of troops of the three arms, European and Native, was riding on his favourite camel, as was his custom, carefully superintending and inspecting works progressing for the use of the troops, when a mounted trooper, at a full gallop, overtook him, and delivered a despatch from the General Officer, then in command of the Peshawur Division, desiring him to proceed to Divisional Head Quarters without loss of time.

The Major General, at a personal interview, then informed the author that sad news had just reached him from the Frontier (Peshawur), that the British

Commissioner, (Colonel Mackeson), had been assassinated, and, according to the report he had received, the tribes in the surrounding hills, and the people of the border generally, were, in consequence, in such a state of excitement, as might necessitate the forward movement of the troops under the author's command. The Major-General, however, gave no orders at the time, but a few hours afterwards instructions were received for the march of the whole of the Rawul Pindee force to Peshawur, with the exception of such troops only as were absolutely necessary for the protection of the station, whilst a regiment of Native cavalry was ordered to Rawul Pindee, from Jhelum, to "back up," in case of need.

It is necessary here to explain the local circumstances under which the troops are, and were, placed in that part of the country.

The Peshawur Divisional Command extends from the river Jhelum to the Khyber Pass (the gate to Affghanistan and Central Asia) and its adjacent mountain ranges, and as may be observed by a glance at the map, the river Indus passes through the Command from north to south.

The great thoroughfare of the country from Lahore to that part of the frontier is through Jhelum; and by passing through Rawul Pindee, and crossing the Indus at Attock Peshawur is reached within a few miles of the Affghan Passes. The force at Rawul Pindee is in support of the frontier post of Peshawur; and is situated at the distance of one hundred miles from it, whilst the ferry of the Indus at Attock, on the line, is forty-four miles from Peshawur.

On the receipt of the order for the immediate despatch of the troops, the author, in communication with the civil authorities, used every exertion to obtain the necessary carriage for the material of his force, but even the baggage animals of the station (few, and quite insufficient in number) were away from the place under the existing orders of government, and cattle from the people of the country had to be hastily looked for elsewhere. The lieges, perhaps, are never very willing instruments in rendering assistance in such times of need; it therefore took four days and nights to procure even sufficient conveyance for a half supply of camp equipage, provisions, and munitions of war, with the commissariat.

The force was thus detained under such lamentable and ineffective arrangements, and the troops were unnecessarily exposed to heat and discomfiture, whilst the officers of the force were almost destitute, valuable lives being lost on the march, from apoplexy.

On the arrival of the troops on the left bank of the Indus, another almost insuperable difficulty presented itself, and with only seven country boats, which were accidentally procured, (and nothing better could be obtained), it took the force four days to cross the river. These boats are quite unsuited to the transport of camels, horses, and other animals, they are badly manned and rickety, and it must be remembered that this was, to all appearance, a great effort to meet an impending difficulty, ever likely to occur on a disturbed frontier.

As the author has an object in view just now, it is quite necessary to dwell on these facts. The force consisted of only six companies of European Infantry, a wing of a regiment of Native Infantry, and a regiment of Native Irregular Cavalry; but, small as the force was, with the utmost exertion that could be made under an apparently pressing emergency, *it took fourteen days to reach the frontier.*

First of all it must be conceded that the post of Rawul Pindee is too far distant from Peshawur to be a good and sufficient support, and secondly, it must be conceded that to be unable to move troops if required at a moment's notice (be they where they may), in such a newly acquired possession as the Punjaub, is dangerous to the interests of the State, although it is exactly what might be expected under civil rule.

On the arrival of the force at Peshawur, although the excitement had in a great measure passed away, and the necessity for such succour did not apparently exist, yet to those who know and understand such matters, it must be quite clear that the security of our frontier post, and the welfare of the troops, are in jeopardy under such arrangements, and besides, it must be manifest that, on the discovery of such difficulties, they should have been received as "solemn warnings" for the future. Matters, however, remained *in statu quo*, and the authorities were as unmindful of this as they always appear to be of "solemn warnings" of a like nature.

Sir Charles Napier, when Commander-in-Chief in India, opposed the measure of fixing a military cantonment at Rawul Pindee, without political or military object, and at so great a distance from the river Indus; but his remonstrances were not heeded, and Rawul Pindee exists still as a military post, having been greatly increased in dimensions of late years at a tremendous cost.

Rawul Pindee is a favourite station, and its salubrity, to a certain extent, might justify the measure, were it not for the long established fact that the climate of many parts of the Sind Saugor district is equally salubrious, and has been proved to be so, even up to the very bank of the Indus, where the author had for several years placed troops in cantonments, experimentally, under the sanction of Government.

During the many years that the author served in the East, and particularly during the latter part of his career, when the command of important forces and positions had been confided to him, he never ceased to expostulate with the authorities on the lamentable want of proper arrangements for the *instant action* of the troops. A false system of economy prevails, and the civil Government of the country, always apparently unmindful of its own necessities, allows masses of troops to remain in cantonments, without the means of moving. The reduction of our European forces in India has been frequently, and even now is loudly called for, and certainly might be safely effected under well organised arrangements for the troops. The author does not hesitate to state, that the military power of the Government might be immeasurably increased instead of diminished, on a considerable reduction in the military establishments—provided military instead of civil government prevailed in all our newly acquired possessions. In order to effect this, the great thoroughfares of the country, the passages of the great rivers, and the charge of all important positions, should be strictly under military, instead of under civil, control, and the native police, who now hold possession of the country, should be disarmed, and vastly reduced in strength, in order to place our possessions in security.

Every European and Native soldier in India should have the means of *instant action*, and not only that, but they should be seen by the people continually (when the season admits of it) in active movement throughout the country.

This is necessarily a hasty glance at the great evils at present and always prevailing in India from want of proper military organisation; and until a radical change is made, the country will be for ever in jeopardy. Something more than a few passing remarks of this nature, on so important a subject, are necessary to inform the reader, or perhaps to persuade him, of the frailty of our Government in India. It is known and understood by few, but the author, who devoted himself to the services of the State in all the Presidencies of India, extending over a period, on and off, of half a century, is desirous of publishing the result of his experience (as he hopes), for the benefit of the State; and during the progress of this little work, in many instances, facts will be recorded tending to prove the importance of the subject referred to.

But before returning to the camp of the author's force, which was for a time pitched on the outskirts of the Cantonment of Peshawur, (tranquillity apparently prevailing), it may be interesting to the reader to know the circumstances of Colonel Mackeson's death, and to peruse some other remarks and suggestions by the author, connected with it. The author was informed that the authorities at Peshawur were severely censured as "alarmists," for sending for the Rawul Pindee troops, but most unjustly so.

The author has long learned to consider and understand that we live in India, and more particularly on a disturbed frontier, like the Affghan border, continually, as it were, on a mine with a burning fuse ready for explosion, and well it would have been for the stability of our Indian Empire, if such a notion had never ceased to prevail with those in authority, and in the instance now referred to, to the author's certain knowledge, it wanted but little to cause a conflagration throughout the whole of the Peshawur frontier.

Colonel Mackeson, a bold and efficient officer, chivalrous in his feelings, and rightly judging the people within and beyond the border, was ever an advocate for resolute, immediate, and decisive measures. It ill suited such an officer tamely to submit to such indignities, inflicted upon the British Government, of which he was the representative. He well knew the character of the people he had been cast amongst, and he knew that imbecile and pusillanimous measures were not measures of humanity, but the reverse, always tending in the end to disaster and destruction. He knew that the natives of those parts were simply invited to revolt by acts of an apparently conciliatory nature, and that they imputed to British rulers cowardice and weakness in their acts of intended good-nature. With these views, Colonel Mackeson ruled the Frontier; he was greatly respected, but probably was dreaded by the fanatics of such a country.

In the city of Peshawur, at any hour of the day or night, an assassin may be procured for a few rupees, who would undertake, with the certainty of his own destruction, to murder any European functionary, because the act in itself, as is generally believed by these men, ensures to them their removal to Paradise; indeed, such is the general feeling of the fanatics of those countries towards the infidel, as the European is considered.

Sitting in the verandah of his bungalow (private residence), Colonel Mackeson was suddenly accosted by a native, who desired to be allowed to present a petition; the Colonel at first peremptorily refused to receive it at his private residence, and directed the man to attend the following morning at the Cutcherry or Court House, where all public business was transacted. The man, in true native style, fell down at the feet of the Commissioner, and, clasping his hands, very earnestly implored of him to read his petition, adding, that his family were deeply interested, and that the immediate orders of the Commissioner were required. Colonel Mackeson then took the paper, and commenced to read it, and being intent on its contents, the native suddenly sprung upon the Colonel, and plunged a dagger into his breast. He fell mortally wounded. The man was seized and hung, glorying in his deed of blood. Poor Mackeson died and was buried in the cantonment of Peshawur, in a position of security, as it was then discovered that large sums of money had been offered for his head, for exhibition at the Affghan capital.

It is well to dwell here for a few minutes on matters relating to this subject, and one of the most unaccountable of all public principles in which the high authorities of India indulge (as it always appeared to the author), is the desire to throw dust into the eyes of the world, by endeavouring to conceal from the public such matters as may tend to discover, or disclose, impending evils. The author never knew an instance in India, when such assassinations as poor Colonel Mackeson's had taken place, that it was acknowledged by the authorities that deep laid schemes were at the bottom—it was simply and solely the act of a fanatic and nothing more, and he who dared to state anything to the contrary was pronounced a "fool" or an "alarmist."

Assassinations have been frequent in those parts, and the poor missionaries have sometimes been the victims, but still there is nothing in it. Now the author declares that he scarcely ever knew an instance in which it could not have been discovered, had proper means been resorted to, that a deep-laid plot had originated the disaster, the assassin being simply and solely the instrument in the execution of it.

The death of Colonel Mackeson by the hands of the assassin was originated by the evil machinations of our enemies, the whole border of our territory were interested more or less in the transaction, and the origin of the deed might perhaps have been traced to Cabul itself, had it been considered advisable, but then war must have ensued, and money and blood must have been expended.

Colonel Mackeson was a sad loss, his policy was the best that had then been adopted on the North-West Frontier, although by no means in unison with the views and wishes of the distant Goverments of India.

It may be convenient at the moment to get rid of

an embarrassment on the principle that, "sufficient unto the day is the evil thereof," but to such miserable policy as this, may be traced all the great and most fearful evils and difficulties of the Empire.

Without looking too far back into ancient histor y we may refer to matter within the recollection of most, viz. : the unprepared state in which the British Frontier, then on the Sutlej, was found, when the Sikhs invaded the territory ; and the events preceding, and on the outbreak of the great mutiny in India, in 1857 ; and lastly, when we found ourselves involved in unexpected complications in the Umbeyla Pass, in 1863 ; on all of which occasions, as will be shewn herein, the British Empire of India stood on the very brink of destruction.

No apology is necessary from the author of these pages, when he brings such matters as these before the public, for consideration. He is a true patriot (as it is with private friendship), who openly informs the State, as he would his friend, of its failings, earnestly hoping that the result of his "Solemn Warnings," may be a complete change in its policy.

CHAPTER II.

Remarks on the nature of the Indian Government, on the North-West Frontier.—Feeling of the Border Tribes towards the Civil and Military Officers of the British Government respectively. —The existing necessity for making proper selections of officers with experience in Frontier Affairs, and with great energy, as Commanders of Frontier and adjacent Posts.—The subject of Commanders in general in India, being taken into consideration.

Now, as regards the North-West Frontier, the author's residence on that border of the Empire of India, of nine years, afforded him so very many opportunities of considering matters connected with the administration of affairs, that he can write with confidence on the subject. There are so very many highly objectionable arrangements, in the author's humble opinion, that it is scarcely possible to conceive how the British Government could have sustained itself in such a disturbed country, so long as it has done, and it will be the author's duty, during the progress of this little work, to adduce such instances as will infallibly prove the correctness of his opinions.

The late Marquis of Dalhousie, by much the most able, and right-minded of governors-general in latter times, had made up his mind to change the frontier systems, as may be observed by his Lordship's letter, a copy of which is inserted in the introduction to this work; but an unhappy difference of opinion that existed between the commander-in-chief and himself, together with cross-fire with the civilians, was fatal to the interests of the North-West Frontier. His contemplated changes were never, therefore, carried into effect.

One undivided authority, and that military, with full power to act always in minor matters, and always in cases of emergency, is essential to all frontier posts, but the military officer in command of Peshawur (it may be said) has no power whatever in political matters, nor can he meddle with the affairs of the district, beyond the immediate range of the frontier posts respectively, and worse even than that, the military authority, even such as it is, is subdivided, one portion of the force being under the order of the commander-in-chief of the army, and the other under the civil governor of the Punjaub. These sad inconsistencies tend to endless misunderstandings, and are the cause of all short-comings and disasters.

Civil government in such a country is, in truth, not only a stumbling block, but a manifest absurdity.

Constantly in intercourse with the people of the country, within, on, and beyond our border, the author gleaned intelligence to which few others were accessible. Strange as it may appear, the civil authorities of India are kept greatly in the dark by the designing natives about them; and whilst military men, who possess no political power nor influence, can obtain intelligence, the civilians cannot. War-like in their habits and pursuits, and indeed somewhat chivalrous in their feelings, the mountaineers, with the people of the adjacent countries, who are all mixed up together by marriage and otherwise, entertain a much higher respect for the soldier than for the civilian. The author feels quite confident of this, and it has frequently happened, when obtaining secret intelligence from the natives, that he has been warned by them that the civil authorities were not to be informed by whom the intelligence had been given. The natives, in fact, look with a very suspicious eye upon the civilians, and expect greater generosity from soldiers.

The general feeling of the natives is, that if unwelcome intelligence be given by them, they will be looked upon with the eye of suspicion, and to the civil authorities they dare not tell the truth if they would. The Burrah Sahib (as the high civilian is called) is a man whose every act must be considered infallible, a little Deity, who can do no wrong.

The mysteries of our position at Peshawur, the nightly intrusions of the hill people, and the means placed at the disposal of the military commander of the Frontier Force to avert such evils, will be referred to hereafter.

The intelligence, however, received either by civil or military officers from the natives, cannot be depended on simply by whisperings. They are deceitful to the core, and no one can judge of them except by duly weighing and considering all collateral circumstances connected with their reports; but in looking back to the many years passed by the author in high commands on the Peshawur Frontier, he can safely state, that the intelligence he had received from the natives, and had acted upon, was mainly confirmed by subsequent circumstances.

Previous to his quitting his command in 1862, the author was repeatedly informed by native gentlemen of Affghanistan and elsewhere, of the intended rising of the hill tribes on the border, which did afterwards take place in earnest in 1863. He was also informed that they only waited for the author's departure. The British government found it necessary, after endeavouring to avoid the enterprise, to send a force into the Umbeyla Pass to break up and destroy a confederacy which was for a second time becoming very dangerous to the peace and tranquillity of the frontier. Sir Neville Chamberlain, with an aggressive force, found himself in a defensive position in the Umbeyla Pass, maintaining that position with the utmost difficulty, with severe loss of life, and of prestige. In these pages will be found a record of the circumstances which led to that disastrous war, with a statement showing the "solemn or salutary warning" that was given by the author to the Government, before he quitted his command.

It must be quite fresh in the memory of most people, that the British Empire of India has been, during the last twenty-four years, repeatedly on the very brink of destruction, and at all times it will be clearly shown by the author where disasters and ruin impended, no other cause existed but the dangerous system of Government prevailing. We hastily run over great and extensive territories, we seize them with the sword and bayonet, and no sooner is the object accomplished, than we as hastily return the sword and bayonet into the scabbard, throwing our troops as useless logs into unhealthy quarters, and placing the Government of the country under a civil administration, with the subdued people as police in charge, and in possession of every thing. It has, however, been long since discovered, that although military rule must not be sanctioned, military officers, acting as civilians, are necessary to the existence of government in advanced positions; but those military officers with the police of the country, and with native troops in many places enrolled as their own, and under the civil government, carry out their measures entirely on non-military principles, excluding from all political power the high military functionaries of the districts of the army. It may be readily understood, therefore, how it happens that disasters are for ever occurring shaking to its very foundation the existence of our rule.

It may, and will be stated, no doubt, that military men might possibly be ill suited, as soldiers, to hold in political matters the reins of government (however good they may be), but surely it must be admitted that they could be at least trusted with the great thoroughfares of the country, the passages of the great rivers, and such like; and it must also be admitted that the European and native forces, *well blended*, must hold the country in greater security than a native police force scattered all over the empire as it is, and in very many cases far removed from the immediate observation of Europeans.

The author has frequently heard it stated by the civil authorities of India, that military men, if in power, would be for ever embroiling the country, for their own aggrandisement, in warlike enterprises; but such a notion is simply absurd; men in authority, whether they be soldiers or civilians, are equally responsible to the government for their acts, and soldiers would be as sensitive as civilians. It certainly cannot be expected that military officers from Europe, quite inexperienced in the affairs of the country, could discharge satisfactorily such duties as might be required of them. It requires years of tuition and experience; and the author does not hesitate to state, from his personal observation, that on the Peshawur Frontier in particular, the officer at the helm must have served an apprenticeship of many years, ere power can be safely placed in his hands. An intimate acquaintance with the Mullicks, and border chiefs, and people, is essentially necessary, and cannot be obtained without much fatigue, exposure, and trouble. It has frequently happened that officers fresh from Europe, simply on account of their rank and standing in the service, and perhaps from their social position in England, have been hastily sent to command on the various frontiers, and at the most important posts in the country. This is manifestly a serious error, for be it recollected, independent of local circumstances, that the troops composing the forces of the country are of the three arms of the service, and of all castes and colour, many with organization totally different from that which prevails in Europe. Without speaking disrespectfully of any particular individuals, who may, or may not, have had the necessary qualifications for active service in such a country, all have so much to learn, and to understand, that it must require a lengthened period to prepare them; and to this in a great measure may be attributed the feeling of the Government towards military rule in general. In order to command with success on such a frontier as Peshawur, great zeal and personal activity are required, with untiring perseverance, and, above all things, horsemanship, in which the higher officers of the army too frequently fail. A Commander-in-Chief of one of the Indian armies, a soldier in heart, took it into his head that he might improve the upper officers in this accomplishment. He even proposed to send them to equitation drill. There was something so monstrously ludicrous in this, that the scheme died a natural death. The author's plan is this, never to give a high command in India to an officer who cannot ride. Horsemanship is one of the most essential of all qualifications in such a country; and this being clearly understood, officers who could improve themselves in it would do so, whilst those who could not, having mistaken their profession, must seek occupation in some other branch of the public service. Owing to this, and to many other causes, may be attributed the lamentable occurrences that have from time to time been recorded of the short-comings of military men; but surely military men are not so much to be blamed as was the government of the country, which had shown itself to be so unmindful of the exigencies of the state, as to be indifferent to consequences when sanctioning the appointments of men to the several commands of the army.

That the Government of India, although it be civil, should have so dealt with the affairs of a mighty empire, even in regard to its most essential material, and in its most vulnerable points, would appear to be incredible, were it not that *long established systems* had blinded the eyes of the authorities to the ever impending dangers of the empire, and, as it were, by custom, had become unmindful of every thing, save the one and only object, viz., making provision for individuals.

As regards the North-west Frontier in particular, a general officer was at one time placed in command at the frontier post of Peshawur, who was quite unfit for any service whatever; and another officer, in command of the troops at Rawul Pindee, which are in support of the frontier post, who was broken down in health and constitution, and required an easy berth, with a good climate. The latter, *to the author's certain knowledge*, was informed, when he got the appointment, that he would have little or nothing to do, that he was near the Murree sanitarium, and that his command had been given to him as best suited to himself and family. Now the force at Rawul Pindee (it must be remembered) which is the main support to the frontier post of Peshawur, must ever be in readiness for "instant action." One of these officers had to surrender his command from incapacity, whilst the other passed away to his forefathers a few months after joining. These facts are so notorious, that it would seem to be scarcely necessary to refer to them.

At the termination of the great mutiny, when the reorganisation of the army was under consideration, amongst other very essential matters, the author, in a despatch dated June 11, 1858, strongly urged on the authorities the necessity that existed for amalgamating the services, in the following terms, viz. :—

"The amalgamation of the services is another measure of expediency, as well as of necessity, which should be at once resorted to, and the present is the most convenient opportunity for accomplishing it.

"The Crown of Great Britain has erected, under the name of Queen's and Company's services, a barrier, which is a stumbling block to all improvement, and causes embarrassment in carrying out measures of great public utility.

"In the reorganisation of the Indian Army, these

services should be blended without breaking faith with officers already in the army. The very feeling of jealousy which at present exists, even between brothers and relations, as well as countrymen engaged in the same duties, arising from this unnecessary and stupid distinction, is prejudicial to the interests, in a thousand ways, of the great Government under which we all are serving.

"It is scarcely to be understood how it has happened that the Crown of England should so long have permitted the existence of such a barrier, which to the nation at large is so highly prejudicial. India is, or ought to be, the great nursery or school of officers (Commanders and Staff) for the services of the Crown.

"The great field for the exercise of military talent, and ingenuity in officers and soldiers, is alone to be found in Her Majesty's Indian possessions, and to India, mainly, the Crown should look for officers of military experience in her European wars.

"It is too late to train and make officers when war breaks out in Europe, and can officers be formed and made efficient within the limits of Great Britain and her smaller colonies, where the three arms of the service *rarely or never, in the time of peace, come together in the field?* Certainly not. Hence, then I maintain, as regards 'European services,' that the interests of the Crown are not consulted, by the barrier which at present exists in regard to Indian officers; and that as regards 'Indian services,' it is necessary that all European officers serving in the same army should be placed on the same footing, and thereby made available in common, for all duties with the troops. In future engagements, therefore, all should enter on the same terms."

The exclusive privileges of the services (Queen's and Company's, as they were termed), had affected most seriously the arrangements for the selection of efficient military commanders. Certain commands were allotted to one service, and certain to the other, each service being supposed to have a fair share of the loaves and fishes. On a vacancy occurring, the selection could not be made of the officer best suited to the purpose, unless it so happened that he was of the same service as the officer who had caused the vacancy. If it was a Queen's officer's command in which the vacancy had occurred, the most eligible man in India of the Company's service was not ordinarily available, but reference had to be made in most cases to England, from whence an officer, without experience in Indian military affairs, was frequently received in due course.

Now, in an Indian command, as many people know, is included every arm of the service, corps consisting of Europeans and natives of all castes are mixed together, whose organization is totally different from each other, and no man can command such troops satisfactorily, who has not served amongst them all. However, the "hard and fast" rule generally disposed of the appointment, and the consequences were never heeded. Since the mutiny, scarcely any officers of the higher ranks, excepting general officers, are to be found in England who have not had some experience of India. Still, unless the qualifications are ably tested, and by that means encouragement is given to officers to qualify themselves for Indian service of a general nature, they never will be efficient, as very little experience is gained beyond the precincts of the barrack square of the regiment to which the officer belongs, in the usual or ordinary course of his proceedings.

Without divulging a State secret, the author here adverts to one solitary instance, during the time he held high commands in India, in which he was consulted by the higher powers, as to the qualifications for commands of officers serving under him. Sincerely desirous that the right man should find his way into the right place, the chief consulted the author, who gave his honest opinion on the subject referred to him. At the same time the author issued a "Confidential Memorandum" to his upper officers, warning them, that unless they took measures to warrant a recommendation, no recommendation would or could be given. This had the desired effect, the author having made up his mind, that were the power ever vested in him (come from whatever service or quarter he might), no man should ever, under ordinary circumstances, succeed to a command, who had not most fully qualified himself for it.

It is known to every one, that officers serving in

England, have frequently exchanged from one regiment to another, for the express purpose of going to India, and of succeeding to a high command in that country, which, by studying the Army List, they found they would be entitled to.

On their arrival in India, accordingly, a high command fell to their lot, these self-nominated officers having claimed it in virtue of seniority. This was a common occurrence. Now it is no reflection on any man to say, that on aspiring to a new dignity, time ought to be given to him to learn his duty, if he does not know it; but this most essential consideration is lost sight of almost, if not altogether.

To this may be advanced, that military commands in India are never disposed of by the Government of the country without the recommendation of the Commanders-in-Chief respectively of the local armies. This may or may not be true, but the established systems are (or were) of such a nature, that the Commanders-in-Chief could scarcely ever pursue any other course than what they did; non-military feelings prevail throughout, and the Government alone could set them aside altogether.

Having thus adverted to the subject of qualification of officers for commands in India, tending to account for the failures of military men at critical periods of its history, it may now be necessary to add, that so far from there being a dearth of good material in the British army, officers could be found, and without the slightest difficulty, in every branch of the service, eligible in all respects, not only to command troops under the most difficult and trying circumstances, but to take the reins of government in hand if required of them, but they must be encouraged to believe that they will be valued and estimated according to their merits, or they will not endeavour to qualify themselves. Officers of the army having once entertained such notions as these, would not be found as at present, killing time in frivolous and useless pursuits, but would devote themselves to the study of matters which they have now no anxiety to comprehend. It is sad to reflect on the numbers of military men of brilliant genius, who must have passed away, unknown almost, or unheard of, from want of opportunity of distinguishing themselves.

If the established systems, of India in particular, were essentially military instead of civil, a wide field would be open for the talents, and abilities of military men, and they would not be found wanting. It is the fashion of civilians to under-estimate the abilities of officers of the army.

The author tenders his advice honestly, as a "Solemn Warning," and assures the public in all sincerity, that unless very different systems have been adopted than those which prevailed in his time, our noble forces in India, cannot be in readiness for "instant action;" without which, the peace and well-being of the empire can never be secured.

CHAPTER III.

State of the station of Rawul Pindee after the Author and his force had quitted it.—Additional remarks on the Government of the Punjaub, and the North-West Frontier—Extraordinary and unsatisfactory state of the Cantonment of Peshawur and of the troops, which held that Frontier Post.—SPORTS OF THE FIELD.

THE author now proceeds to place on record the leading features of his services of nine years on the Frontier of British India, together with such relevant matters as must be set forth in support of his long established convictions, as to the erroneous systems prevailing in the administration of affairs generally of the British Empire in the East.

But before doing this, and somewhat in confirmation of what has already been stated in regard to the state of the frontier on the death of Colonel Mackeson, the author will briefly allude to the proceedings at Rawul Pindee after he and his force had quitted it.

Distant as Rawul Pindee is from Peshawur, the excitement on the Colonel's death had extended to it. Rawul Pindee, as above shewn, had been denuded of its troops, and the commander of the station, in his anxiety for its security, sent off (when too late) to the author, earnestly requesting his immediate return. Perhaps he was somewhat unnecessarily alarmed, but there is no doubt some reason existed for his uneasiness. The commissioner of the district was shot at on the road from Murree to Rawul Pindee, and indeed, excitement very generally prevailed. All this tends to prove that there was something more in the assassination of Colonel Mackeson than the individual act of an assassin.

Amongst the extraordinary anomalies of our rule in the East, there is none more objectionable, indeed, more extravagantly absurd, than the system of employing military officers in the civil services of the country. In advanced positions, bonâ fide civilians would be out of place altogether; and so, in order that civil government should prevail, the expedient is resorted to, of making men act as civilians, who are bonâ fide military men.

In order to maintain the civil administration, the army is thus drained of its very best materials, for no other reason in the world but to bolster up civil institutions. Even at a military post, like Peshawur, Colonels, Majors, Captains, and Lieutenants are found in civil employment, wholly unconnected with the commander of the frontier post, and the military establishments. This extraordinary expedient (for it is nothing more or nothing less) is, in its effects, suicidal in the extreme. Nevertheless it is quite confirmatory, as far as it goes, of the correctness of the author's remarks on Civil Government.

It fell to the author's lot, whilst holding the military authority of the frontier, to be associated with three military officers, acting as civilians, for whom he entertained the highest respect; and so it happened that the author, with a force of twenty or five-and-twenty thousand men under his command, (although entertaining such notions as are herein expressed) was always working in concert with the so-called civil authorities near him. It certainly might have been otherwise, because, *as regards army rank,* these acting civilians were immeasurably inferior to the author, and yet, in a manner, they were enabled, if they chose, by their position under the Civil Government which prevails over all, to lord it over a general officer of long standing in the service. It is highly in favour of the author's contemporaries, that no cross word ever passed between the author and these acting civilians. We saw, therefore, the very best that could be made of such an unnatural state of things.

From the very first moment that the author cast his eyes on the frontier, he condemned all measures connected with it, but all along he resolved in his own mind, that either he or the chief civil authority, (being a military man), ought to have been removed as a stumbling-block to the post. However that might have been arranged, there is one thing certain, (in the author's opinion), that the troops, and not the police under civil authority, should have held the country. It is quite manifest, that under the Government arrangements, everything had been done that could be done to cause disorder and embarrassment; and at a frontier post of great importance, by mixing up civil and military authorities, casting down the latter and exalting the former, until army rank had become (amongst military men) an inverted machine beyond comprehension, the whole concern was in a state of confusion. The truth is, that one individual authority, and that military, is essentially necessary to the interests of all frontier posts; and of all other countries in India, Peshawur is by much the most important. There is no man of common sense, who takes the trouble to consider this subject, who can possibly differ with the author in the opinions he has now expressed; at all events, if there should be one, he will be very liable to change his mind before he has waded through the contents of this volume.

During the long dark nights in winter, the demi-savages of the Khyber Pass, uncultivated ruffians, almost as naked as on the day they were born, quite unmolested visited the cantonment of Peshawur. They robbed and they plundered, and they got back (ninety-nine times out of one hundred) in safety to their mountain fastnesses; the whole ground between the military post and the hills being in the hands of the civil power. Not an outpost was allowed to the troops to cover their front, and the whole force might, at any time, in their beds, have had their throats cut by the predatory tribes of Central Asia, in thousands or tens of thousands.

The authority of the Military Commander of the

post of Peshawur was strictly limited to the boundary of his extensive cantonments, and here and there an outlying picket of cavalry (as it was called) was in a position, powerless to do good. These outlying pickets were nothing more than flank and front guards, saddled and ready to turn out.

The civil authorities had a police post of a Tusseldar, and twenty native policemen, three miles in front of cantonments at a place called Hurree Sing's Boooj, whose duty it was to warn the civil authorities of approaching danger. It was in the power of this illustrious functionary, (the Tusseldar), to give as much timely notice, or as little, as suited his own purpose, and in like manner, it was in the power of the European civil authorities to give as much notice to the Military Commander as they thought fit. The civil authorities are supposed to be in possession of all secret intelligence through the agency of natives about them; and after circumstances brought to light how little dependence ought to have been placed on their intelligence.

This inconceivable *mélange* of civil and military was never concocted by any other than a Civil Government, and it was by the blessings of Divine Providence alone, that vastly greater evils were averted than might have been reasonably expected.

The sentries were firing all night, in the dark, with little or no effect, whilst the nocturnal intruders were rushing to and fro; and once out of musket range, they had only to regain their hills at their leisure before the day dawned. Thus they carried off their spoils with impunity, becoming bolder and bolder, as success attended their enterprizes. Now there is a space of about ten miles intervening; and had a military post been established at Jumrood, as in the Sikh time, and had the frontier been under the military authority, by properly concerted signals, the Khyberrees never could have got back into their hills without molestation.

The nightly duties of the troops so uselessly expended, caused an immense amount of sickness, and certain it is, all these harassing duties might, by proper management, have been avoided; and the nocturnal visits of our neighbours might have been put a stop to.

The whole force was, at times, knocked down by this exposure to the night air, to the imminent danger of the frontier. It will be shown hereafter, that it was brought to an end, in a great measure, by a stratagem, and the sentries were removed by the author at last.

In the meantime it certainly may be fairly asked, "was there ever such a state of things prevailing before at a frontier post, excepting in British India?" The same system had prevailed several years before the author came to the frontier, and several years after he came, but before he assumed the command. However, as regards that, it was no fault of the Military Commander, who, no doubt, would have broken up the whole civil administration, if it had been in his power to do so—at least the author can speak for himself, in that respect, when he makes such an assertion.

It is against the prevailing systems, and not against the civil officers of Government, that these observations are made.

Colonel Sir Herbert Edwards, Major Hugh James, and Colonel Nicholson, were first rate officers, and they were the civil officers on the frontier, at that time. They all were men of great ability, but, unhappily for them, as well as for the state, they were civilians, and not soldiers, whilst so employed, and carrying out measures of civil government, wholly incompatible with military life. The author owes much to Sir Herbert Edwards, who supported him most ably in the great mutiny of 1857, as will be explained hereafter, and he has never ceased to lament that such a man should ever have been induced to turn the sword into a pen, and bring his talents and ability to bear on civil matters, away from the ranks of the army.

In order to explain more fully the views of the author on this subject, he will record in this volume his sentiments, as expressed in the year 1858, when called upon to suggest a scheme for the re-organisation of the Indian armies, or rather, when his opinion had been asked on that subject.

In a letter of his addressed to the chief of the staff of His Excellency the Commander-in-Chief, may be found the following words :—

"I would urgently recommend also, to the government, to abolish a system by which some of its best and most valuable military officers are excluded from the power to do good in their own profession by being locked up in Cutcherries and commissariat offices, and employed in the various civil services of the country.

"If the Government thinks that these officers, of whose valuable services the army is deprived, are, or ever can be, with all their talents, courage, and devotion, qualified to command troops (as they should be commanded) when brought out on a sudden emergency to serve with or lead them in the field, I, as an old soldier, can solemnly assure it, that they cannot be so.

"To have the entire confidence of the troops, and that natural influence so essential to military government, officers must be identified with their men, and must be associated with them in peace as well as in war. They must know well their wants, and enter warmly into their feelings, and so maintain discipline by paternal and friendly intercourse, rather than by perpetually turning to the clauses of the Mutiny Act.

"There is much more required of an officer than courage in battle. The admiration of the soldiers towards any man who is daring in battle will be gained, it is true, for the moment, but the general confidence in him must be wanting, if he be a stranger to the troops."

Let the army then have its own, and let the civil services of the country be otherwise provided for.

SPORTS OF THE FIELD.

Now as to the sports of the field in the north-west, there is no country in the world, probably, which affords the sportsman so little pastime as the Punjaub. The Sikhs were devoted to hawking, and destroyed all the small game of the country.

There are "Ooriall," or hill sheep, in the low ranges of hills bordering on the Sind Sagur district. A few royal tigers in the lower ranges of the Himalayahs; and bears in abundance on the same lower ranges when driven down by the snow from the upper ranges. "Obara," (bustard) snipes, wild ducks, and rock pigeons (being birds of passage), abound. Black and grey partridges, hares and chicore are scarce. But the very best sport in the world (in the author's opinion) has been recently introduced from Candahar to the Euzofzaie district by General Lumsden. Hawking and coursing ravine deer and antelopes is a noble sport.

Nothing can be more exciting or more beautiful than the combination of effort to kill deer by hawks and greyhounds. Neither dogs nor hawks can effect the object unless assisted by each other. Hawking is generally a dangerous amusement, because the game not being seen, the eye of the sportsman must be fixed in the air on the hawk, and at a rapid pace it is not very easy to recover the sight of the hawks if it be once lost; but where the dogs and hawks are combined, the pursued deer need never be lost sight of.

The process of this sport may be described as follows, and, as few Europeans have ever witnessed it, a description may be interesting.

A party of mounted gentlemen, with two or three old falconers on horses, with their hawks, and two or three brace of the best greyhounds, ride over the extensive plains till they come upon a herd of deer. As soon as the deer are seen, the master of the hunt manœuvres so as to get the game to leeward. If seen originally to windward, a wide sweep round, in order not to disturb the deer, is necessary, to have the weather-gauge. Hawks will not work to windward, if there be any strength in the breeze. The next thing to look out for is a single deer, if possible. The black buck is often found strayed away from the herd, and it is essentially necessary to get your game away from the flock. Should the hawks and dogs take after a different deer, there is not much hope of sport; neither the one nor the other can accomplish the object.

Supposing, then, that there is but one deer, and that the hawks and dogs are duly fixed on the game, pace is the next consideration. There is no use attempting the business unless the horse is a good one, fleet, and in training. The first burst is three miles at least at tip-top speed. The plains are open with only occasional ravines. During the hard gallop the hawks (generally three are slipped) continually pounce down towards the flying buck; dogs and horses all along at a respectful distance. The hawks make repeated efforts to strike the deer and repeatedly fail; at last one of them is seen with a flutter of his wings to fix itself on the top of the deer's head between the horns, and when firmly fixed he begins his work of destruction; he succeeds after a bit in injuring the unfortunate deer, and his pace begins to slacken. Dogs and horses then gradually gain upon the deer, and at last the dogs run in and complete the work which the hawk has so vigourously commenced.

The deer is killed, the horses are all but done up, and the sportsmen have had enough of it. It has been a glorious chase, full of the deepest interest, the repeated and unsuccessful descents of the several hawks on the game being indescribably beautiful.

The old falconers, who do not pretend to ride up to the dogs, gradually come up; and then the winning hawk is fed by cuts of choice pieces from the deer's head, whilst the hawks who have been thrown out, are made to look on and get nothing. The hawks generally come up at last, but sometimes they are lost for ever. It is said that when they tower too high at the outset, they are lost in the heavens, and are seen no more.

The season for this hawking is the winter, and the hawks are fresh every year. Since General Lumsden left Euzofzaie, it is supposed that the Candahar falconers and their hawks never make their appearance, as that noble officer and sportsman paid highly for this amusement. If there is such a sport now-a-days, the author strongly advises the traveller to work his way up to Hoti Murdau and take a look at it; but it is of no use his going if he cannot ride, and ride well, and if he be not right well mounted. Royal tigers are to be found, by looking for them, near Trait, between Rawul Pindee and Murree. Captain Colby, of the 98th, was killed by one of these; and the author met one, between one and two in the morning, who disputed the road with him, a mountain track, in which the tiger had placed himself. It was a dark, moonlight morning, and his horse suddenly stopped short, and no power could induce him to go on. The author had taken the tiger for the stump of a tree, when suddenly it moved, and he longed to have practised upon him with his revolver, but fortunately he could not get near enough.

The next day this tiger was found and killed by a party of sportsmen. No one need be surprised to find that men risk their lives in tiger shooting; it is, without exception, the most exciting of all earthly pastimes. The bears are savage only when they have young ones. The beautiful pheasants of the Himalayah are to be found in the lower ranges, but they afford little or no sport. If they take flight, they cross precipices where no one can attempt to follow them. For the pot, they may be taken in the low jungles by means of a small cock-dog, who "snaps" on finding them, and the birds simply rise to the lowest branches of trees, where they can be seen and shot. A man with his gun and dog, poking about, can often bag them in that manner, shooting them sitting in the lower branches of jungle trees. Of course there is no sport in that, but they eat well. There are plenty of wild hogs in the mountains, but there is no getting at them with the horse and spear. The author never saw, with the exception of a very few, any on the plains. They are excellent eating when you can get hold of them.

The old English sport of hunting has occasionally been introduced on the plains near the Indus, packs of hounds being imported from home; the jackall is substituted for the fox, and gives excellent sport.

CHAPTER IV.

The force under the author's command in the same order as it had arrived on the border from Rawul Pindee, now takes the field, and proceeds to the mouth of the Kohât Pass.—Circumstances recorded relative to the Pass.—Operations against the Affreedies in the Bori Valley.

THE force under the author's command, not being required, as at first expected, broke up from its ground of encampment in the Peshawur cantonment, and took the field under the instruction of the Chief Commissioner of the Punjaub. The force proceeded at first to the mouth of the Kohât Pass. The tribes in that Pass had rebelled, as they frequently did, against the British Government. There was a money transaction involved, subject to litigation and dispute. A sum of money was paid by the civil authorities to these Affreedie tribes for the use of their Pass, in order that British troops and subjects might be enabled to pass to and fro. They are for ever fighting against one another, and on one occasion, at a subsequent period, the author personally witnessed a hill fight not very far from the centre of the Pass. One tribe was fighting against another. They had quarrelled about a mulberry tree, and on visiting the scene of action with a young Affghan gentleman and an escort of cavalry, the author was informed that the fight had then lasted three days and three nights, and scarcely any number of men remained alive. The women were at their usual avocations, when the author and his party reached one of the hostile villages, and they appeared quite unconcerned about the whole affair. Their husbands, brothers, and fathers had been killed, and yet they were carrying their pots of water on their heads, spinning, &c., &c., as usual. They are quite accustomed to that kind of thing.

There is a "kotul"* in the Pass, very steep on all sides, where the author one day encountered twenty hill men unarmed, who demanded money of him. He told them that although the Government paid them money, he certainly would not, and pulling out his revolver, threatened them with lead instead of *silver*. On which he was allowed to pass on without molestation.

The Pass is an open, and not a very difficult one, and with very little expense, it would have been a simple matter for the British troops to have held it, as they certainly ought to do, and the people of the Pass had given ample provocation to justify our seizing it. The station and district of Kohât is at one end of the Pass, and the Peshawur district at the other. It was therefore necessary that the connecting line should not have been left to the caprice of the natives, and liable to interruption. The natives are for ever quarrelling, as before stated, amongst

* The key to, or most defensible hill in the Pass.

themselves; they quarrel over the money paid by the British Government for the use of their Pass, and whilst these matters are under discussion, they shut us out, it seems, altogether.

The dignity of the British Government is cast down by such unworthy measures as these, under a non-military system, which causes embarrassment with the loss of prestige. All this because it is cheaper to pay a few rupees, than to hold our own as soldiers ought to do.

On the occasion now referred to, the Pass had been closed against us, and the force was there to *threaten*; and then again the Affreedie tribes in the Bori Valley had committed depredations in our territory, and they had to be *threatened.* Bori is not far distant from the Kohât Pass, on the same range of hills, and in all likelihood there was a combination against us, all equally despising our rule, and showing their contempt for it by overt acts of hostility against the Crown and dignity of England. Some time after this, a detachment of the Kohât force was attacked by vastly superior numbers of the people of the Pass in a wanton and uncalled-for manner, tending to prove upon what erroneous principles our Government were acting.

The author's force was for some time encamped on the ground on which Fort Mackeson now stands, overlooking the entrance to the Bori Valley and Kohât Pass respectively, whilst the Chief Commissioner and his civilians were discussing the matters at issue, with these demi-savages, although summary punishment in both directions was the one thing needed, and the only thing. Of course no good came out of such discussion, and at last three columns of attack were organised, under the author's command, for the purpose of seizing the Pass at three different points. The treachery of natives is always at work, and some of our particular friends in camp, having hastily given intelligence of our intentions, the Pass was thrown open with the promise of better behaviour in future. With this declaration and assurance, the Chief Commissioner was satisfied, and thus terminated an inglorious military demonstration.

The people of the Kohât Pass had treated us with contempt, and trifled with us; they had put the British Government to trouble and expense, and had simply opened their Pass when they found they could not help themselves, and until it was convenient for them to close it again.

And now for the Bori Afreedies. What is to be done with them? The author, although commanding the force, was not admitted to the State Councils until the plan of operations, as it appeared, had been resolved upon. He was at last sent for, and a rough sketch of the Bori Valley and hills was shown to him. To be brief, it was resolved to "hammer the heads" of a set of scoundrels who had committed frequent depredations on the British territory, and whose heads ought to have been hammered long before.

The author here again thinks it necessary to state,

that it is against measures, and not against men, that he offers his observations; being of opinion from first to last, that had the Commandant of a frontier force of such magnitude as Peshawur been a free agent to redress the wrongs of the British Government, when or wheresoever they occurred, these demi-savages of the hills, knowing well the instant consequences of their transgressions, would have ceased to commit them. No system so injurious to all parties could have been adopted, as that which prevailed when treating with these men as civilized beings. The author in this instance was informed that the Bori people, amongst other high crimes and misdemeanors, had been called upon to surrender certain vagabonds (our enemies) who had taken refuge in their territory, being a set of rogues all together, combined with one common feeling of hostility to British rule. So at last it had become necessary to burn, destroy, and lay waste their villages, crops, and corn-stacks. It always appeared to the author, as he gained experience in the country, that these sad proceedings might have been greatly avoided by a different policy.

Here, as in other parts of the hills surrounding the valley, distress at times prevails to such an extent as to drive the hill people from their hills into the fertile plains below, for the purpose of robbing and plundering in order to exist; and we certainly might, and should have encouraged them to cultivate lands in our territory which are lying waste. When the author was leaving the frontier, he was informed that

Major James, the Commissioner of the district, entertained the same notions, and had recommended to Government that money might be granted to increase the irrigation of the valley for the express purpose of affording the hill people the opportunity of earning an honest livelihood, as their settling in our territory would give us, of course, ample hold on them. Dost Mahomed, of Affganistan, suggested this remedy to our civil authorities, to the author's knowledge, years before, and he always advocated the same measure, coupled with summary punishment, and "instant action" in all cases of aggression, which in no instance should have been avoided. Nothing, at all events, could be worse than the policy of allowing transgressions to be *summed up* until it became imperatively necessary to resort to a terrible chastisement.

With this prelude, the Bori Valley expedition must now be explained. Leaving sufficient troops in camp for its protection, the whole force marched out long before daylight, and after marching three or four miles, entered the hills by a steep, narrow, and difficult defile, under the direction of the Chief Commissioner, who accompanied the troops. No European force had ever before been in that part of the hills, and the country was little known. The force consisted of the following troops, viz., six companies of European Infantry, under the author's command; the Guide Corps, horse and foot; a regiment of Goorkah Infantry; a regiment of Hindustanee Infantry; a nine-pounder light field battery; the mountain train, with four three-pounders, and four twelve-pounder howitzers; a regiment of Native Irregular Cavalry, with some few other detachments, the whole force being under the command of one of Her Majesty's officers, who had come into camp a night or two previous to the engagement, and had superseded the author in command of it.

It was many hours ere the summit of the hills was attained which commands a view of the Bori Valley. Little or no opposition was made to the force in ascending the mountain; but it was manifest that the enemy had been made aware of our approach. In many directions on the distant hills surrounding the valley, could be seen bodies of matchlock-men approaching to assist in the defence. The delay and difficulties of the ascent of the mountain, and descent into the valley, had been so great, that it was near ten o'clock in the day before any operations could be commenced, and it was at first considered doubtful if any could be undertaken during that day, the troops being already much fatigued, and a long day's work was before them. However, after some consultation and rest for the men, the force progressed.

Nothing could be more beautiful than the scene which presented itself. Numerous villages are scattered through a long line of valley, each village having defensive towers, built of brick, towering above the houses, and very distinctly seen at a distance. As the force approached, they were densely manned with matchlock-men. These villages extend many miles, and are placed immediately at the foot of a long and precipitous mountain, which, in a military point of view, commands them.

The round towers in these villages are the pride of the mountaineers, and are a good defence in internal commotions, the tribes being continually at war with one another. Such towers, against European troops, are quite worthless, although the proprietors are quite aware of the advantage they have, in having such precipitous mountains overlooking them; inaccessible as they are to any but hill men accustomed to them.

On the first shot being fired, by a nine-pounder, the matchlock men abandoned the tower or towers, and the village, against which the shot had been directed, and, like monkeys, flew to the hill at the back; so that on the approach of our infantry, they could defend their village in masterly style, by pouring down a heavy fire on their assailants.

Before anything more could be done, it became necessary, therefore, to endeavour to take their hills from them, a work, not only of difficulty, but, with European soldiers, nearly impracticable. The Guide Corps, which consisted chiefly of hill men and such like, and the Goorkah regiment, also accustomed to hills, were let loose to skirmish, and sweep the mountain.

Owing to the nature of the obstructions, it was with the utmost difficulty that they got on the end of it, and there, being met by the Affreedies, a contest ensued, which to spectators in the valley was most interesting and exciting. Little or no progress was made for hours, and a fusilade was kept up, incessant and sharp. The mountaineers, bounding from rock to rock, and over precipices (having an intimate knowledge of the country), had manifestly the advantage, throwing their matchlocks across their backs, whilst ascending and descending steep places.

To take possession of these villages, and to destroy them, which was the object of our enterprise, was almost impossible, as we had soon discovered, and could only be accomplished by men creeping clandestinely into them, and setting fire to corn stacks which were in and about the houses, and then under cover of the smoke, the villages were approached from one to the other.

During the struggle on the mountain, numbers fell on both sides; and although the villages were damaged and partially destroyed, the towers were left standing and uninjured throughout—a more interesting spectacle than what has been faintly described here could not have been witnessed.

The author, with his European regiment, had received instructions to proceed to the extreme end of the Valley, out of the range of matchlock fire, (as he passed along) from the villages; and by commencing at the opposite end, to endeavour to burn a certain number of villages which had been indicated.

This was a rude war without strategy or skill, according to the ordinary acceptance of the terms, although developing a degree of natural tact and ingenuity on the part of the defenders which could not well have been conceived or expected, and the difficulties were not anticipated, certainly, when the work began. At all times, as the force passed on, the Affreedies re-occupied their towers, with incredible celerity.

The author, on arriving at the extreme end of the range of villages, found the hills at their back much less precipitous, and he was enabled to throw out two companies of his regiment in skirmishing order to occupy the Mountain. The enemy were too warmly engaged with the Guides and Goorkahs at the opposite end of the Valley, to hold the whole of the long ranges of hills, although they were hourly increasing in numbers, and could be seen in most directions coming over the mountains, attracted by the heavy fire of musketry. The artillery were of little use, although the author, in subsequent affairs of this nature (when the command of a force had been allotted to him), discovered the value of five and half inch mortars, which were conveyed on elephants.

Strange as it may appear, there is no beast of burden in the world that can beat an elephant in traversing precipitous mountains, and the author never went without these mortars on any future occasion.

The villages placed at the author's disposal proved to be the weakest points of the enemy's position, and had the force commenced its operations at that end of it, instead of at the other, the hills would have been much more easily cleared, and their villages more speedily destroyed. The Europeans, after completing the work allotted to them, laid down, awaiting further orders. A Staff Officer at length arrived with orders to recall the Europeans to the place from whence they had originally come. The "recall" of the skirmishers was at once sounded, and the troops fell in in quarter-distance column, with its rear near the walls of a burning village, at the end of the long range. The two companies of skirmishers had scarcely got into column when a fire of matchlocks through loopholes in the village walls, was opened upon them. The astonishment caused by this sudden and unexpected attack may well be imagined. The Europeans had been a couple of hours in and about the village, and not a sound had been heard, save the crackling of the burning town, indeed, not a native had been seen, and none were there, concealed or otherwise. The fact was that the hill men had been watching the skirmishers, and when they were recalled from the mountain-top, came down like deer into the village, under cover of the smoke, and re-occupied it, in very considerable force. Fortunately for the column, the loop-holes in the walls were so constructed, that the muzzles of the matchlocks could not be sufficiently depressed, and the shots mainly passed over the men's heads. One man only fell mortally wounded, and a few others slightly so, and certainly it was only by good luck that the butcher's bill was not a heavy one. The author, being on his horse, had bullets, like hail, whizzing past him, and one or more of the men in the column called out to him to dismount.

The troops were speedily moved nearer to the wall; and, their bayonets being fixed, about two hundred men rushed into the village, but the mountaineers had fled back as speedily as they had come down, and not one of them was disposed of.

The author freely admits the error he committed in withdrawing his Light Infantry until he had moved off his column into a place of security; and his only reason for it is, that neither he, nor any one else, could imagine that there was any living soul within reach, tending to prove that experience in this, as in all other matters in hill warfare, is the one thing needful.

This was the author's first adventure in the hills; and, before it came to a conclusion, he had learned lessons and received "solemn warnings," which, in after times, were of the utmost value to him. The principal harvest, however, of these mountaineers is looked for on the retreat of their enemy from their mountain fastnesses. It must be manifest that the hills, by which an enemy's force ascends, must be sooner or later descended, and as the agility of the mountaineers never fails, no sooner are their mountain tops evacuated by their enemy, than they reoccupy them, pouring down a deadly fire after their retreating foes, who are then not in a position to retaliate. The most dangerous and most difficult of these flying hill operations is, therefore, towards the conclusion of the work.

The day was far spent when the author, with his regiment, rejoined the main body of the force. There had been a discussion with the higher powers, civil and military, as to the route by which the force should retreat.

Retreat was imperatively necessary, and as speedily as possible. The troops had had no water nor provisions all day, except some biscuits in their havresacks. They had suffered much owing to the sad want of proper management.

In the villages which had been seized (and they were but few) some large chatties (earthenware pots) were found full of water, which were instantly destroyed to prevent the soldiers rushing to them.

Futtah Khan, a native chief and great friend of the author, as well as an able adviser in these extraordinary localities, recommended that these steps should be taken.

The demi savages of the hills are quite wide awake and quite wicked enough to poison their enemies. They well knew the distress that our troops must experience from want of water, and, wily as they are, would certainly not have left us a supply of the article we most needed, if they could have helped it. It was clear, therefore, the water might have been drugged. Futtah Khan had foreseen the difficulty of our enterprise, and of our position from first to last, and he knew that the retreat by the route that the force came into the hills would be dangerous for its return.

In the dusk of the evening, the descent from the mountain must be attended with fatal consequences, particularly with troops, jaded and fatigued as they were, and he had sent off emissaries to the opposite end of the valley to ask permission of a powerful tribe for the force to get back into the plain through their territory.

This tribe had in no way been concerned in the affairs of the day, and had kept aloof from interfering in the contest.

By the promise of payment of money, (the old scheme of our authorities), they had agreed to let our columns out quietly ; indeed, they promised us a safe passage through their territory, but there could be no certainty in it, and we had to be prepared for the worst.

To remain in the hills all night, would probably have been disastrous, and the old story of Sir Charles Napier and his nocturnal adventure in the Kôhat Pass, which had occurred some years before, was a "solemn warning" for us.

It was determined, therefore, to go through the friendly village, as we hoped it would turn out to be, leaving the Chief Commissioner to settle the pecuniary part of the transaction. In fact there was nothing else left for it, and all we had to do was to make our escape the best way we could.

One of the principal difficulties was to keep the men from firing on our newly acquired allies. No one could tell exactly where they were. There was firing going on in all directions almost, and we had to be cautious lest damage should be done, although unintentionally, to them. Any man being hit or hurt would have been a declaration of war, and we should have had our route at once blocked up by a very powerful tribe. The column of route was formed for the retreat, and proceeded with the European regiment in the centre.

The most valuable of all commodities in such a country, is, of course, the European, as he is the most costly; and besides, the death of one of them at the hands of the hill-men, is a great and glorious victory. The column proceeded slowly, its rear being covered by the Guides and Goorkahs. These are valuable troops, but the enemy, in such numbers, pressed so hard on the retreating column (as they are wont to do) that our skirmishers ran in continually, and two companies of Europeans were ordered out. The order was reluctantly given, and orders were flying about on pieces of paper, written by whom the author never knew, such as these—"For God's sake, send out the Europeans!"—and then again—"For God's sake, recall the Europeans!"

The author had no doubt whatever of the propriety of sending out the Europeans, and sent them, although the men were so tired that they could hardly crawl.

As the villages, at the mouth of the valley, became in sight, nothing could be more picturesque or beautiful than the *tout-ensemble.* There were no less than nineteen of the Boorjes, or round towers, built of brick, high above the level of the surrounding houses, all of which were unusually well built. The villages lay in a gorge of the mountains, and had stood there for ages. The towers were well manned with matchlock men, and all the low ranges of hills were covered in like manner. The sun had set, darkness very shortly after prevailing, and then was seen a stream of fire from a long line of our enemies, numbering thousands, who, in extended order, were following up our retreating columns, which the darkness exhibited as a brilliant display of fireworks. As our troops passed through and got clear of the villages, the fire and pursuit by the enemy began to cease, and we thanked our stars that we had escaped from a hornets' nest.

Now, the precarious nature of this retreat will be readily understood. It was certainly in the power of our temporary allies or friends to have turned against us, and they must have had wit enough to feel how completely we were in their power. Had they taken common cause against us, which was most natural, the whole force must have been annihilated, and our fate, in fact, had been hanging on a thread. These hill tribes, although frequently at war and fighting most desperately one with another, are married and intermarried here as elsewhere.

Consanguinity prevails throughout the mountains, extending even to the plains below. Nevertheless, brother against brother is for ever fighting, and we had no sort of security in the relative position of our friends and foes, besides which, the treacherous character of all these people rendered it more than probable that the whole might unite together, when, certainly, they had us completely in their power. I strongly felt all this, and understood it at the time, and was prepared for extremities.

Considering the predicament we were in, we have no right whatever to reflect on the conduct of the Civil Authorities for loosening the purse strings on the occasion; but still it is lamentable to think, that from gross mismanagement, we were driven to the necessity of resorting to such undignified transactions. We are, after all, not altogether a nation of shopkeepers.

Disreputable confusion no doubt had prevailed, and a considerable force of valuable troops had been placed in jeopardy by mismanagement. The confusion, arising from the mixture of civil and military authorities, both of which were giving orders, was one of the great evils, and in after times, when in command of troops in the field, the author never would sanction such interferences. But in this case, the Military Commander (a perfect stranger to hill warfare) was quite incompetent to the command, and the lesson taught by his incapacity, should have been a "solemn warning" for the future. Can anything be more preposterous than the systems prevailing, and still prevailing under British rule, by which men, simply from seniority, and without any necessary qualification whatever, can force themselves into positions, on which the fate of thousands, and the prestige of the Government, must depend? But so it is to this day. The author does not claim for himself any vast credit in this affair, as he was at that time as ignorant as others of mountain warfare, but his services had not been tested in the Bori Valley, beyond the sphere of his own regiment, for the conduct of which he received the recorded approbation of Government.

To him, the expedition had proved, as before alluded to, of the utmost value and importance, because he had been initiated, not only in a new line of military operations which few understand, but had seen the glaring evils of the existing systems. The interference of the Civil Authorities had, indeed, in this instance, been mainly the cause of the state of the troops, who had suffered such severe deprivations. The supplies had been placed on the elephants, and were proceeding with the column until they were ordered back by the Commissioner, lest they should get wounded under the fire of the enemy. There was an idea prevailing, and no doubt a correct one, that if hit and hurt, the elephants, who were moving in a narrow defile, would suddenly turn round and rush upon the force, carrying and destroying all before them. But the elephants and supplies, in the confusion, were never seen again, and hence the destitution of the force—arising from one authority not prevailing. The troops, towards morning, got back into camp with the utmost difficulty, owing to their extreme fatigue, and want of refreshments. Every few minutes during the night, the "halt" was sounded to prevent straggling and loss of men.

On the day after the hill fight in the Bori Valley, a large number of Affreedies of the hills (our enemies the day before, and fighting desperately against our troops) came unarmed into the camp, to obtain information as to the fate of some of their own kinsmen and friends, who had fallen *whilst fighting on our side.* This is thoroughly characteristic of these demi savages. They are blood-thirsty, and appear to fight for the sake of fighting, not caring with whom.

No doubt the Affreedies of Bori had received a lesson, notwithstanding the difficulty and delicacy of our position. They had seen that we could venture to pay them a visit if they misbehaved, and from the experience we had gained, we could hope to manage matters better another time.

The return of killed and wounded during these short operations was very considerable, chiefly amongst the native troops. In the author's regiment, one man only was killed, with a few wounded in the retreat, and elsewhere.

The force was now broken up, and returned into cantonment at Peshawur; the author remaining in command of his regiment.

CHAPTER V.

The Cantonment and Valley of Peshawur.—A description of the Frontier Posts.—The Climate of the Valley, together with such Remarks on the Military Occupation of the Country as are necessary in support of the Author's Opinions, his Statements, and his Suggestions.

HAVING seen everything done that could be done, for the health and comfort of the regiment under his command, the author began to speculate on the future ; and with the presentiment that he had much work before him (*trans Indus*), he lost no time in examining the cantonment of Peshawur, the great city adjacent to it, and the border of the territory generally ; or what is termed the North-West Frontier of India.

The regiment, then under the author's command, was one of the next on the roster for "home service." It had served its time in India, in Scinde, and in Bombay Presidency, and was about to finish its Indian career under the Bengal Government.

During the time the corps was at Rawul Pindee, from whence, it will be remembered, it was removed to Peshawur, its two Lieutenant Colonels (of which the author was the junior) were pulling hard against each other. The senior was anxious to avoid the frontier service, and the junior most anxious to ob-

To face Chapter V.

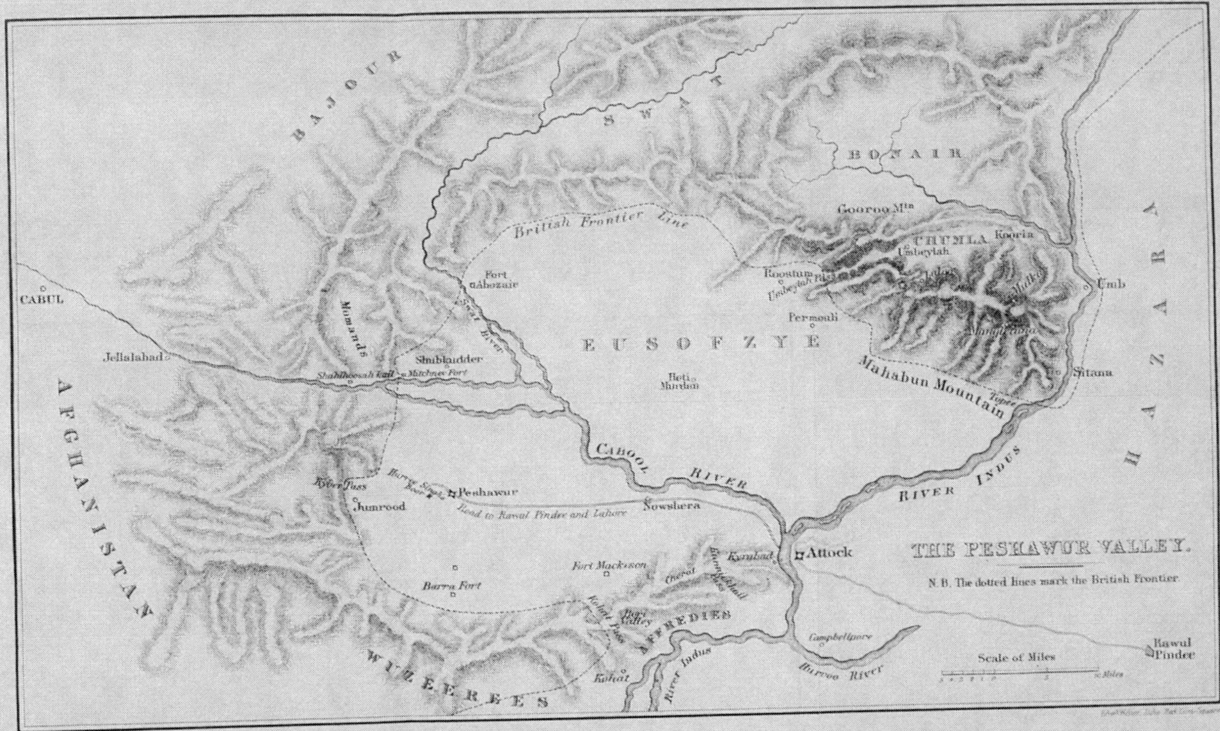

tain it. In the struggle, in all likelihood, the junior would have been beat, had not the death of poor Colonel Mackeson decided in his favour as before described. "It is an ill-wind that blows no one any good;" and so the violent death of a Commissioner proved to be a cast of dice for the author's benefit. He got his foot, at all events, into the stirrup, and he resolved, ere long, if possible, to be firmly seated in the saddle.

It is impossible sufficiently to condemn the authorities, who fixed upon the present site of the main frontier post in the Valley of Peshawur, containing so large a force as ten or twelve thousand men of the three arms, more or less. It is true, the city of Peshawur required to be carefully watched and guarded; it contains a community of discordant spirits from all Central Asia, of as bad a description as could be found in any city of its size in the known world. It is true also, that the Khyber Pass, within sight, is the gateway of Central Asia, and requires constant observation; and it is true, that our predecessors, the Sikhs, had always a strong force in and about the city.

Unhappily, as in most cases on our acquisition of territory, no pains had been taken to look carefully into matters in a military point of view, in order to ascertain the advantages and disadvantages of so important a military post.

The cantonment having been once commenced upon, it was gradually and inconsiderately augmented, enormous sums were expended, and the quarters for the troops became not only extensive, but were unnecessarily costly. To abandon a large portion of such a station, where millions of money had been expended (should it be found expedient) was next door to impracticable.

The author does not hesitate to state here, as he has for many years officially recorded, that the system of building costly and permanent barracks for our European and native soldiery in India, is the worst that could possibly be adopted. In nine cases out of ten we have taken root, as it were, in localities which have proved to be objectionable.

Nothing could be more unwise or injudicious, than the hasty decision that has been arrived at in such matters, and the permanent barracks are the source of great evil, and of endless embarrassment.

It never could have occurred to the ruling powers, that in newly acquired territories like the Punjaub and in our new lines of frontier, to fix at once upon permanent places for the troops, might be productive of the most serious embarrassment in the end.

The departments of the Government, and the high civil authorities, have all this in their own hands, or mainly so, and the latter have discovered, when too late, the serious errors that had been committed, the military authorities not being exempt from blame in these matters, although accessories only.

The author can never admit, and never did admit, that permanent barracks, even in well selected localities in these newly acquired territories, are advantageous to the troops. The temporary buildings of mud and thatch are vastly cooler, and are greatly preferred by the soldiers themselves. The temporary buildings will last seven years, and it is very desirable for the health of the troops, that the ground should be occasionally shifted. All that is really wanted, is a standing camp, covered in sufficiently (and no more) to save the troops from the effects of the climate. The Engineer department, taking a professional view of the question, as to which system should be preferred, decided, as well may be imagined, that puckah or permanent buildings would be the cheapest in the long run, and so the Government went head-long into the mischief.

Now, at this moment, in the Punjaub, and in the Cis-Sutlej territories, there are several most extensive permanent cantonments, which are not only of no value in a political point of view, but are positively injurious to the troops themselves. This is an admitted fact, some of these stations are unhealthy in the extreme, but they have cost millions of money, *and on that account only, cannot be abandoned.*

Of the number of these ill selected localities, Meean Meer, near the Punjaub capital, Sealkote, Rawul Pindee, Nowshera, Peshawur, Ferozepore, and Loodianah, may be selected as specimens.

Meean Meer was hastily fixed upon by a very hasty Commander-in-Chief, whose whole business was to do exactly what the author is now complaining of, and it has proved to be the very hot-bed of sickness. Sealkote is healthy, but, in a political point of view, is of no value whatever. Rawul Pindee, nominally the support to the frontier post of Peshawur, is very much too far distant; it is healthy and agreeable, and consequently popular. Nowshera, in which are a set of the very best built and finished barracks in the world, is not only unhealthy, but positively dangerous. On one occasion, the whole of the officers' quarters were washed away by a flood, which may occur again and again, and has often occurred before, as any one may observe who looks to the principal features of the surrounding country. Had the flood, above alluded to, been a little more extensive, and had it occurred in the night instead of in the day, a whole European regiment of a thousand men would have been annihilated.

Peshawur cantonment is probably one of the most unhealthy places in the world, and it contains quarters for three or four thousand European troops. A glance at the map of the Valley must convince the military reader that so large a force in such a place, without any due and proper support, must be considered in a false position. With enemies in front, on the right and left, and even on the right and left rear—in fact, nearly all round them, it must be manifest that the main body of the frontier force should never have been placed there. Had the author been enabled to carry out his own wishes, in regard to

Peshawur and Nowshera, many of the beautiful barracks in both places would long ago have been levelled with the ground.

The author has reason to believe that, after a severe struggle of years, the authorities have, at last, been satisfied that the main force of the frontier should be on the left bank of the Indus, and that a couple of thousand men only in an entrenched position, overlooking and overawing the city of Peshawur and the Khyber Pass, is all that is necessary for the security of that part of the frontier, provided a powerful force be kept in reserve in the very healthy climate of the Sind Sagur District, and in a well selected locality, as near to the left bank of the Indus as can be conveniently fixed upon. Connected with this arrangement, in order to secure the immediate reinforcement of the troops in position at Peshawur, (should occasion suddenly call for it), the author has long proposed to the Government the organization of a boat transport system, to be established on the Indus, with enrolled and experienced boatmen, for the immediate removal of troops across the river. These transport boats should be so disposed of, as to enable the military authorities to throw across the river at the several passages, at any moment, bodies of horse, foot, and artillery; and, to provide against the evil effects of climate, no troops should ever be located in the entrenched position, at Peshawur, more *than six months at a time;* the garrison of the Post being relieved from the parent or reserve force, on the left bank of the river, at regulated periods of short duration.

The tunnel, or rather proposed tunnel, at Attock has been hitherto fatal to the author's *projêt* in this latter respect. Nothing has been done, nor is likely to be done, about transport boats, so long as there is a prospect of passing troops across the river by tunnel. A rail and a tunnel, it is said, will provide for all our wants, but neither the one nor the other (if ever accomplished) could be depended on. The author feels convinced that every military man who knows the localities, must admit that to have the power (which up to the present time has not been obtained) of throwing troops across the Indus, *at all points,* instead of at one point only, at Attock, would be most desirable. Attock is commanded by hills, and there is a rapidity of current there, at times far exceeding that at the various other ordinary ferries and passages of the river, and here again the author repeats, at all points, because the strength and security of our frontier position must, under all circumstances, depend upon the relief and assistance that could be hastily afforded in times of need. The policy of the ruling powers has generally been to pooh, pooh, the "solemn warning" they have received, and the wholesome advice that has from time to time been given to them, and there is no position in British India which requires more careful attention than our North-West Frontier. It has been found to be so at all times, and it is very particularly so at this moment.

The narrative of the affairs at Peshawur in the year 1857 (when the empire was tottering to its foundation) which will appear in this volume, will be a convincing proof, if such be wanting, that the very life and soul of our Indian Empire is the prepared condition for active service, in which we may be found on that border. The "solemn warning" of the invasion of our territory by the Sikhs, who found us (wonderful indeed to relate) quite unprepared for the defence of our frontier (then the river Sutlej) and again the great mutiny of 1857, and even the minor affair in the Umbeyla Pass, have been lost sight of and disregarded.

The author, very soon after his arrival at Peshawur, found himself on his horse, or his camel, traversing the border of the British territory; he desired to qualify himself for the frontier command; and that qualification could only be attained with considerable trouble and exposure. Men may, and have, very unworthily, taken upon themselves the charge of so important a position, without having the least knowledge of the country, of the tribes surrounding the position, and other local circumstances.

The author, in making this, his first tour round the district, visited in the first instance the Kuttuck hill ranges, which extend to the right bank of the Indus at Khyrabad, and passing through the Khunny Khail Pass, surveyed it with a view to opening a passage for artillery and troops from Peshawur to the ferry of the Indus, near Camelpore, near to where the small Hurroo river falls into the main stream.

He visited Cheratt (in the Kuttuck Hills) which he afterwards proposed as a sanitarium for the troops of the Peshawur Valley, and which had been brought to his notice by the British Commissioner. He visited, as he passed along, the site of Fort Mackeson, and so went on to the mouths of the Kohat and Khyber Passes. He visited, *en route*, Fort Barra, and so on to Jumrood; but here the connecting link was wanting, as that Fort is unoccupied by British troops, and has been allowed to go to ruin. He then went on to Mitchnee, Shubkudder, Abazaie, Hoti Murdan, and along the Eusofzaie border to Topi, on the Indus, at which place is one of the principal ferries leading into the Hazara country.

It was not many weeks, therefore, after his arrival in the Peshawur country, that the author found himself in intimate acquaintance with the European and native commanders of these several outposts, and with very many Mullicks and chiefs of the different border tribes.

There is a great deal of good in all these positions. They have been generally fairly selected, and are of much value, and had the immediate front of the Peshawur cantonment, opposite to the Khyber Pass, been provided for at Jumrood, the outposts all round the valley would have been tolerably satisfactory; but where a military post was most needed (near or at Jumrood) there is none whatever, and the connecting link between the border outposts is thus broken. The civilians were afraid of the troops coming too close to the Khyberees, lest the peace of the border should be disturbed, thereby doubting their discipline.

There are a variety of passes, besides the Khyber Pass, leading into central Asia and elsewhere, from the valley of Peshawur. There is land and water communication by the Cabul river, and its banks, from Jellalabad to the Momund frontier by Shah Moosah Khail, and there is a pass leading from the Swat country to our frontier post at Abazie.

There are numerous other sheep, or goat tracks, by which the tribes of the hills come down on the plains in our possession to plunder and lay waste our property.

It is quite necessary, for the benefit of the State, that all power should be vested in one individual Commander. But at Hoti Murdan (strange to say) there is a force under the Kohat Commander's orders which cannot be interfered with by the Peshawur military authorities, and *vice versâ*, neither must meddle with the other, and hence endless difficulties and embarrassments arise. The late Lord Dalhousie, as before stated, had determined on removing these difficulties, and would have done so, had not the conflicting interests of the civil and military authorities prevented him. The author entertained great respect for the rival Chief of the Kohat force, and for the Government of the Punjaub; but he never ceased to condemn the prevailing system, and consequent confusion.

The author cannot now be suspected of any personal feelings in these matters; he has passed away, although he cannot help bearing in recollection the inconvenience he felt at the time; and he emphatically declares, as he has done over and over again before, that the pre-eminence of civil power in such newly-acquired territories as ours, is simply a crude absurdity, and dangerous in the extreme.

The jealousy of the Civil Government of the country, and its ascendancy over the military authorities, who are kept in an unnatural position in the background, are the source of all the evils and disasters which occur, which have occurred, and which will occur again and again, until England can change its policy towards its distant possessions, and towards such colonies as are inapplicable to the laws or institutions of the mother country.

The author does not hesitate to state that the Civil Government of India, as at present constituted, is a century or more in advance of that which such an immense empire can be prepared for. The late East India Company's monopoly died a natural death. It was wisely the policy of that Company not to extend its frontier; but force of circumstances drove it to the necessity of doing so, and at last (as far as the Company was concerned) the whole machinery went to pieces. The real fact is, that the civil government, which had been introduced by the East

India Company, was wholly unsuited to so newly an acquired empire of such magnitude; but it is stated that, owing to the old court of directors remaining in power under a different name, their erroneous systems of government have been perpetuated.

Before concluding the present chapter, the author must offer some other observations, for the perusal of his readers, in regard to the climate of the Peshawur country, the nature of which can only really be known and understood by those who have passed many years there.

Many officers and soldiers have passed away from Peshawur (even after two or three years residence there) without being much the wiser.

The climate is of that extraordinary nature, that moderately good health may prevail for a considerable time, save only that the extreme heat of the summer, which is always peculiarly distressing, must take its effects. It is not only the peculiar fever of the country which at times visits the valley and prostrates almost indiscriminately the strong and weak, but apoplexy to a fearful extent prevails, and so do cholera, ophthalmia, small-pox, and many other terrible diseases.

One of the most remarkable things connected with this subject, is the difference of opinion that prevails in regard to the nature of it. Some even declare that Peshawur is a healthy place, and the returns from hospitals at times may indeed almost justify such a conclusion, and this circumstance may be accounted for by some having only seen the valley of Peshawur in a temporarily healthy condition.

The high medical authorities, who periodically and hastily visit Peshawur in their tours of inspection, have done more mischief by their reports than can well be imagined, invariably almost pooh-poohing every thing that they had previously heard and were prepared to see.

Governors-General of India, Lieutenant-Governors of the Punjaub, Commanders-in-Chief, Inspectors-General of Hospital, *cum multis aliis*, who make flying visits periodically through the country, and who almost invariably travel for their own comfort's sake in the healthy and agreeable seasons of the year, are alike disinclined to believe that the climate of Peshawur is as bad as they have heard it represented.

Much mischief has been done by this ; and in allusion to these flying visits of these high functionaries, it is the author's firm belief, that more real mischief than good is generally done by them, so far as the real interests or welfare of the troops is concerned.

With all due respect to great men, who are placed in exalted positions, it may be truly stated that some of their visits to the out-stations of the army have proved to be not only tending to mischief, but ludicrous and absurd in the extreme. Men, although cast into high positions, are not infallible or omniscient. They are not under divine inspiration, and yet too frequently, with the experience of a few hours only, they presume to form opinions, which must be adopted as of greater value and importance than those of inferior officers who had formed them after years of anxiety, and on mature consideration.

The remarks made by these exalted individuals in passing through barracks and hospitals in the presence of the troops, are frequently not only puerile and absurd, but even tend to discontent. Soldiers are very shrewd fellows, and the moment an exalted officer opens his mouth in their presence, they measure the length of his foot. He little thinks it ; but they discover at once his knowledge or ignorance of military life.

One very eccentric Commander was wont to visit troops with the apparent object of discovering some fault or other in the issue of provisions. He continually pronounced good bread and meat bad, and bad bread and meat good, and so forth. His failings in this respect became quite notorious, inviting, as it were, discontent, and provoking discussions amongst a class of men who are ever ready to grumble. Stories fly about barracks after such visits, sometimes creating discontent, and sometimes merriment.

The author, throughout life, never ceased to lament over the strict line of demarcation which exists between officers and soldiers of the British army, and certainly the very little friendly intercourse that exists between them is remarkable. It is not so with any other army in the world ; but the author always took opportunities of conversing with his men, and often heard opinions and sentiments which were most useful to him.

Nothing can be worse in a Commander than to "pump" the men, and thereby obtain secret intelligence, in which some exalted individuals have been known unworthily to indulge; but conversations on matters connected with the health of the troops have frequently tended to much good, and are otherwise innocent. The remarks of the troops themselves on these periodical visits of high functionaries, are sometimes amusing in the extreme. These visits to the sick in hospital are positively crying evils. The great man, followed by his *brilliant staff*, numbering twenty or more, with their swords and spurs, indeed with everything but their horses, passes through the hospital, closely questioning even dying men as to the treatment they have received. Nothing can be more inconsiderate than this (however well intended), but it is the constant practice. On one particular occasion, under the author's own observation, a circumstance occurred which wounded his own feelings so much, that he cannot help referring to it. A dying soldier was closely questioned by the Chief as to the treatment he had received in hospital. The man said that he had had nothing that he could eat for several days, meaning that he had no appetite to eat. The Chief burst out into great wrath, entirely misunderstanding the poor man, and said, "I desire to be informed why this man has not been properly treated," and was proceeding in that strain, when the dying man made an effort to explain himself, being much exhausted and excited. The poor man died a few hours afterwards.

If the medical officers cannot be trusted, and if it in any way relieves the minds of the sick and dying men, when they find that the Head of the Army takes an interest in them, why should not the Chief proceed by himself without incumbrances, and quietly discharge his duty? There is so much ostentation in the whole affair, as it is done, that it is really lamentable. A poor man, at his last moment, is called upon, as it were, to complain, or otherwise, of the treatment he has received, probably against the friend who, in countless instances, *indeed almost invariably*, has nurtured him with the utmost care and solicitude. The author has frequently heard that soldiers, when called upon for complaints, have made them, simply to get rid of importunities, and the author verily believes it.

Some of these exalted individuals travel hastily through the country, and frequently in palanquins (a kind of locomotive box) by night. They cannot possibly see anything, and still they make elaborate reports. On one occasion, one exalted functionary, having passed, in the heat of the day, through the cantonment of Peshawur, stated in his official report that heaps of dirt were allowed to remain on the road-side, to the injury of the health of the troops, and the local authorities were called upon to account for such a dereliction of duty. The impetuous commander of the garrison became furious. He had ever considered his Station the pattern one of the country, and furiously exclaimed to his staff officer: "Send instantly, sir, for the Commanding Officer and Quarter-Master of the 140th, in whose lines these heaps of dirt are said to be, and I will speedily teach them that my cantonment shall not be brought into disrepute through their neglect."

A staff officer standing by quietly remarked that the so-called heaps of dirt could be no other than the macadamised stone which had been prepared by the district engineer, to repair the roads, and probably their dirty appearance had been caused by a recent dust storm, which could be productive of no evil whatever; and such turned out to be the case. Thousands of stories of this kind might be recorded, tending to prove the little that is gained by the visits of these high functionaries, and the author has only to hope that these remarks, serious or otherwise, may prove to be "solemn warnings" for the future.

It was always the intention of the author, had he succeeded in obtaining a new station on the left bank of the Indus, to throw up a mud entrenchment, with a ditch round his intended new position at Peshawur, by which would be enclosed the Artillery Barracks and lines, the temporary Church, the Artillery Hospital, the Residency, the Kutcherries and civil lines, the lines of the Native Cavalry Regiment close by, and the lines of two Native Infantry Regiments, with the Mackeson post, which latter commands the entrance to the city of Peshawur at three different points. The author intended to employ the troops in the cold season in throwing up this work, paying the men for the same, to avoid expense, and to practise the troops in the use of the spade and pickaxe.

The whole of the remainder of the cantonment should be pulled down, including the new church, which never ought to have been built where it now stands. The author did all he possibly could to prevent that church being built. It is always objectionable to pull down and remove a church after it has been consecrated; but it would be vastly more objectionable to allow it to remain outside the works, and removed from military protection, because the natives are sure to defile it, and desecrate the walls.

The author desires to draw particular attention to his proposals in these respects, because he has recently been led to understand that the Government of India have contemplated building a masonry or permanent Fort at Peshawur, at a heavy cost, which the author considers most objectionable.

Permanent forts, in hot climates, are injurious to the health of the troops, and require permanent garrisons to save them from being occupied by our enemies. They bind us to particular localities, which is always objectionable in unsettled and hastily acquired countries; and again, with an efficient force on the left bank of the Indus, troops in an entrenched position, at Peshawur, would easily be reinforced or relieved, in case of need. The cost of a masonry fort, too, would be a very useless outlay of money.

As before stated, the Engineers recommend permanent buildings in preference to temporary ones, as being cheapest in the long run, but that is simply a professional view of the question, and the Engineers are not called upon generally to take any other matter into consideration. All over India the troops are now suffering from being permanently fixed in places where they ought not to be, simply because the costly palaces that have been built for troops cannot be thrown away.

CHAPTER VI.

An Expedition under the Author's command into the Momund Hills.—The State of the Weather and the Country, with a description of the Border Tribes, supposed to be the lost Tribe of Israel.—The Death of the Author's Bombay Servant, "Munnoo."

WITH a loaded revolver ever in his belt, and with a couple of mounted troopers in his rear, the author, when he fell into the command of Peshawur, was constantly to be seen in the district. The people of the country, always with matchlocks across their shoulders, pursued their agricultural avocations. It speaks volumes for the state of a country, when men at the plough are armed to the teeth and ready for a fight. One of the first things that happened to the author, after his first arrival in the Peshawur cantonments, was to have a shot fired at him (when leaving a friend) in going home from dinner. This was a "solemn warning." The shot was fired certainly not thirty yards from the place where he had been dining. It was pitch dark, and the man who fired it, no doubt a Khyberee, was not to be found. At this period of our history, it was not safe to dine by candle light in camp, as the lights attracted the fire of the enemy. The Hill robbers sneaked about the ravines which intersect the country, and took a pot shot at any object, apparently for the sake of mischief. On one occasion a shot was fired at the author in riding along the road, and a bullet whizzed past his ear, an unmistakable sound, that no one can doubt about, who has heard it. The two native troopers, however, (riding behind the author) were called upon to ride off the track with him in pursuit of the enemy, who at once dropped into a ravine, beyond the reach of horsemen. One of the troopers said, "Oh, they were only firing at a bird." "You scoundrel!" said the author, "I can see no bird; the bird they fired at was certainly not a blackbird." The fact was that the troopers did not much like the look of the sort of gentlemen that had fired upon the party, and as the better part of valour is discretion, and as nothing was to be gained by shooting a nigger, even if we had succeeded in doing so, it was the worst of policy, they thought, to incur an additional risk by going in pursuit. A few anecdotes, such as these, are necessary to show the state of the country.

One morning, in the month of August, in exceedingly hot weather, inconceivably hot, the Assistant Adjutant General of the Division called upon the author with a paper in his hand, on behalf of the Major General commanding, offering him the command of a force which was about to be organized for field service. The author's thermometer rose at once to blood heat, and of course he accepted the generous offer. The paper contained a return of troops proposed for the expedition. With a thorough knowledge of all local circumstances, this staff officer informed the author that no time was to be lost, "Instant Action" being the motto. On perusal of the state document, the author observed that no European troops were included. The weather was so excessively hot, that it was not deemed prudent to take them. Bearing in recollection the advantage of Europeans in covering the retreat of the Force from the Bori Valley, as before related, the author begged that an addition of two hundred European infantry might be made to the general programme. The soldiers of the author's regiment were mad for a fight, and the "sheet of brown paper" which at that moment stood between them and those regions which shall be nameless, was by no means to be considered a bar to their inclinations. Two hundred of the two two's (by which designation the 22nd Regiment is known) were therefore included in the return, and on going to barracks, a deputation of non-commissioned officers implored of the author to make no distinction, and take the whole corps, adding, "We long to have a hand in all that is going on;" and the author, who was for ever anxious to have his splendid regiment under fire, bitterly lamented that nothing more could be done.

Now a passing word for the gallant Cheshire, the 22nd of the line. There never was a finer regiment, nor one in which the *esprit de corps*, so necessary to military success, in a greater degree prevailed.

The Momund expedition was not likely to be a battle of Waterloo, Alma, or Inkerman, and moreover, in a hole or corner of the world, such as the regiment was about to act in, (removed so far from observation), the authorities in Whitehall were not likely to give them much credit for their services. However, such as the service was, or might be, they must take it, their anxiety for a fight being quite refreshing.

With the thermometer at 110° in the shade, what must be the heat in the lower ranges of hills, and on the bank of the Cabul River? Never mind what the heat is, the companies selected for the service were on the tiptoe of expectation, whilst those who were not selected were, in proportion, dejected.

The plan of operations had been somewhat arranged by the Major General commanding, and his Staff, ere the author received his order, and as far as he could judge of the localities (parts of which he had seen in his travels before) the proposed arrangements were good.

No one undertakes such an enterprise (if he be moderately sane) who has not a *carte blanche* to do as he thinks fit when the time comes. The force proceeded by different routes to the "meet" at Mitchnee, which has been described before as one of our frontier outposts, a small fort, well built, with a rampart, ditch, and keep, sufficient to contain a few hundred infantry, and an out-work to contain a couple of hundred cavalry, more or less. This place is on the left bank of the Cabul river, and not very many miles from the intended ground of our operations at Shah Moosah Khail, where a chief resided and commanded the entrance to the plains from Affghanistan, at the point where the Cabul river first makes its appearance. The force being collected, and the author having reconnoitred (as far as possible with reference to local obstructions) the enemy's position, he proceeded at once to inspect the troops placed under his command, with whom he had no previous acquaintance, excepting with his own men. The force was well chosen ; the staff of the Peshawur division, who accompanied the author, were well known, and in their frontier duties were unerring. The author had no fault to find, and was as cheerful as a bird. It will be necessary now to explain and describe, as far as possible, the nature and strength of the enemy's position, and the arrangements that had been made. To cover the advance of the column of attack, which was to move from Mitchnee, up the left bank of the Cabul river, another force of horse, foot, and artillery, had been placed in a camp on the right, or opposite bank. The officer placed on that side of the river (of course under the author's orders), Colonel Chamberlain, was directed to throw out to his front a battery of artillery (nine-pounders and twenty-four pounder howitzers) with a cavalry escort, and take up a position at some old towers which commanded the entrance to the plains, by the Cabul river, on an elevated plateau in the British territory, apparently made for the same purpose in olden times. The towers had long been deserted, although the plateau remained. From the plateau looking across the river, the town of Shah Moosah Khail could be seen distinctly. Nothing could be more picturesque or beautiful than this sequestered spot, as most of these places are. The river, rushing down like all mountain torrents, with considerable strength, brings down from Cabul with it, rafts of timber, and articles for sale in the plains. A considerable revenue is derived from the river traffic by the Momund Chief, where it at first appears. With the *casus belli*, the author had no concern, his duty being simply to hammer the heads of those tribes on the Momund border who had misbehaved generally, and had presumed to trespass on the Crown and dignity of England. It was stated that the Chief, who had presented himself at the Commissioner's Durbar, in Peshawur, had insolently remarked, when called upon to pay up some money that was due to our Government, "All you have got to do is to come and take it," never dreaming, that during that season of the year in particular, for a few rupees, it could be worth while for us to accept his invitation.

During the time that the force was in camp, under the walls of the little fort of Mitchnee, one of the most awful storms of thunder, lightning, rain, hail, and wind took place, that the author, who had seen some of the worst by land and by sea, had ever witnessed. It came on in the evening, when all the officers of the force had assembled in one large tent for dinner. The tents of the whole camp, except one officer's tent, were instantly knocked to the ground, and the officers had to struggle for their lives to save themselves from being smothered in the canvas. One officer of artillery was much injured by a tent pole, and the author escaped with the utmost difficulty. All were huddled up in the one standing tent, awaiting the return of daylight with anxiety. On such occasions as this, the spirits of men rise with the difficulties of their position; the whole ground on which the camp had stood was one sheet of water several feet deep. The men of the 22nd, who had not joined the camp, were on an island all night in the river, and were nearly drowned, and expended ere the operations commenced. A day or two was wasted by this. On the day previous to the engagement, the author summoned all the officers, to allot to regiments and batteries their respective duties, to explain how the ball was to be opened, and to give some salutary cautions which were necessary to the success of such an enterprise. The author was not at this moment quite a greenhorn. It is true this was his first command of a force in the mountains, but he had gained a good bit of experience before in his first adventure. The hill men, with their matchlocks, are admirable shots after their own fashion. Their matchlocks are rifled, and were so long before we used rifles; usually they are good for six hundred yards or more. We had only old Brown Bess, good in those days for eighty on a pinch, clumsy, cumbersome, and quite worthless for hill warfare. These hill operations give little or no chance for the bayonet, and we could scarcely expect to get a chance of administering cold steel. The hill tribes are certainly the best light infantry in the world. They bound from precipice to precipice, and conceal themselves behind rocks, and, moreover, they are always in high training for their movements in the mountains. The odds, therefore, are all against the European soldiers in particular; indeed, against all soldiers of all colour of the plains. The ordinary arts of war, of which we boast, are valueless in such a country, and John Bull soon gets disheartened when he finds the superiority of a nigger force, and the uneven terms on which he is engaged. The gallant fellows of the 22nd were seen during these fights to throw down their muskets in despair, saying "this thing is of no use"—puffs of smoke, reports of matchlocks, and shots striking constantly, are all that can be seen or heard. The mountaineers are nowhere, so well do they conceal themselves, and so quickly and ably do they cover themselves from injury. But now for the work. Before dawn of day, a short time, but not very long, the force moved from its encampment towards the mountains; at first there was flat alluvial ground on the river side, and low ranges of hills on the right. The Sikh Regiment seized and took from the enemy these low hills without much difficulty, and swept along them in skirmishing order, so as to cover the flank of the column on its right, which slowly moved along the open, on the river side. The artillery, infantry, (European and native) and the mountain battery, formed the column, with a regiment of cavalry in rear of the whole for such services as might be required. This is no country for cavalry, but the author found a job or two for them during the operations. The force, in this order, progressed, protected, or rather assisted, by the fire of the artillery from the opposite side of the river (as before described). The spectacle was very beautiful, and very instructing. The shell thrown from the howitzers on the right bank of the river and across it, passing over the heads of the columns, cleared the front in our advance, and swept away these reckless mountaineers into the hills which command their capital. Very few shots were fired from the walls of Shah Moosah Khail, or indeed from the village of Sardine, or Dubb, by which the column had to pass. With our glasses, we could see at first the matchlock men, in great numbers, on their towers and the tops of houses, and we suspected the bayonets would be required, but the mountaineers knew a trick worth two of that, and so fled to the almost inaccessible hills, which on three sides command their capital. It is scarcely possible to conceive anything more exciting and interesting than these mountain affairs. At first it appears to be like a scene in a play, and no one can conjecture how matters are ever to terminate.

After a time the enemy had fallen back from our artillery and musketry fire, and they had mostly deserted the town, with the loss on our side of only two or three men; but then they were seen in vast numbers on the hill sides, in all directions, in a most imposing attitude. At first the author thought that he had found a good plateau in the town which would enable him to bring some of the twenty-four pounder howitzers into position, and he had hoped to shell out the enemy from one side at least of the hills, whilst the town was being burnt and destroyed. One European artilleryman, however, whilst the battery was getting into position, being hit, this arrangement necessarily failed, and some other scheme had to be used; in fact, as it was manifest that the gunners would soon be annihilated where they were, so there was nothing left for it but to take the hills from the enemy. Troops in skirmishing order, with supports, were thrown out on all sides for this purpose. The scene of these operations can well be imagined; hours were expended in an unequal contest between the forces of the hills and plains. The enemy were fighting on their own dunghill, whilst our troops were puffing and blowing, and struggling to get a footing, if nothing more. The heat of the weather was excessive, but the British troops struggled and went on, and finally succeeded in sweeping the mountains, of which for hours they were in possession, (tops and sides).

The object of the expedition was gained by the

destruction of the towns; and most of the beautiful trees on the side of the river were greatly destroyed by the elephants, so soon as they could safely be brought to work. During all these operations rafts were rapidly coming down the river, whilst mussick men, that is men floating on leather bags, inflated like foot-balls, with wind, were passing to and fro, conveying orders between the forces on either side of the river. There were several European officers wounded, but none killed, strange to say, in this struggle. Numbers of men were killed and wounded; but the severe trial was with the extreme heat of the weather. When everything had been accomplished that was either required or intended, the most difficult part of the operations (the retreat) had to come off, and never, in the author's recollection, was a retreat more difficult. The mountain battery covered the retreating force by firing and retiring half batteries; with European Light Infantry extended, and by shells from the twenty-four pounder howitzers, kept back the mountaineers from pressing down the hill, on the rear of our troops, as they were drawn off. At one time, as if for a general attack, the mountaineers were seen descending in great force, with a rush, apparently in desperation, and squares of infantry were formed for the protection of the guns. It turned out that the rush was caused by the mountaineers coming down for water, and they were seen rushing headlong into the river. They had been hours shut out from water, and were in a state bordering on madness, from the want of it.

The force, after a heavy day's work, and with considerable loss, now retired, and got back, late at night, into camp, jaded and worn out by heat and fatigue. On the following day the services of a portion only of the troops were again called for, to seize and destroy another town. On this occasion, the enemy retreated hastily; and, with a charge of cavalry, on a plain between the hills, the operations were brought to a conclusion. The Momund Chief escaped by flight; he and his son got across the river on mussicks.

The Momunds had thus received a lesson which they did not easily forget, and were more respectful in future. Hill operations are most exciting; but the troops of the plains fight with great odds against them. During the first day, in conversation with an old grey bearded Native officer who had been in the old Sikh army of Runjeet Sing, he told the author that the Sikhs never could venture into the hills, and our advent amongst them, as herein described, had caused them unmitigated astonishment. Our intercourse with these demi-savages might be vastly improved if we encouraged them to cultivate lands in our territory; to come down from their hills, in fact, and earn an honest livelihood. They suffer greatly from want, and rob and plunder from necessity. The author is of opinion that we have been slow to do what is right in these matters, although much has been done of later years, and a marked improvement has taken place in the character of the people, and still more will take place. The Hill tribes cannot live without intercourse with the plains, and we have only to shut them out from our markets when they misbehave, and it is the opinion of the author that their passes even would be thrown open for our reception on amicable terms, if we rigidly enforced such rules as would shut them out from our plains whenever they shut us out from their passes.

Great improvements were made in the time of Sir Herbert Edwards and Major James in these respects; but let it be remembered that no favour must be shown to demi-savages without an equal amount of stern and resolute measures, as otherwise they will attribute our good nature to fear.

The force shortly afterwards returned to quarters, the sick and wounded being lodged and taken care of in the little fort of Mitchnee, and the author and his force received unbounded applause from the Government. It was acknowledged everywhere that no mountain expedition had been conducted in a more satisfactory manner, and certainly the spectacle, from first to last, was most imposing. The troops had been well selected, and the staff was of the best quality, so that the Commander had an easy and agreeable duty to perform.

Before concluding this chapter the author cannot refrain from alluding to the loss he sustained during those operations, in his faithful servant, "Munnoo," who was ever in attendance on his master, wherever he went, and had been so for years. On the Momund expedition he was killed by the mountaineers, and literally hacked to pieces, probably out of revenge for his master's proceedings. "Munnoo" was well known by his personal appearance, being a native of Bombay, and as unlike an Afghan as his master.

Poor "Munnoo" was ordered to accompany his master with an escort of cavalry, but he chose to neglect the order, and travelled to Mitchnee with only a native groom. He was mounted and well armed, and vainly imagined that he was a match for any one. He was attacked by three mountaineers, who soon discovered that poor Munnoo could not defend himself, he had overrated his own courage, and surrendered without offering resistance. The native groom, who was on foot, played a very cunning trick. It was nearly dusk in the evening, and he threw down his white turban on the ground, and then left it, crawling into some high grass hard by, and there he lay concealed, watching the destruction of Munnoo. As soon as the mountaineers had finished him up, they rushed towards the white turban, and of course expected to find under it the groom's head, but he had escaped, and lived to relate these particulars.

Elephants, in mountain warfare, must now be described.

Of all the animals of the creation there are none so intelligent and so useful in military operations as the elephants, and sufficient value and importance is not attached to them in the British service. It might be an immense saving to European troops if elephants were employed in transporting them, when long distances are required. Each elephant can carry six men, with arms, ammunition, and bedding, besides rations. The author resorted to this expedient with great advantage to the service, although he never heard of its being done before, or since.

Besides this, the great powers of elephants, under the tuition and management of the mahouts or keepers, are brought to bear upon heavy ordnance, in places and at times, where no other power can be applied.

They raise heavy guns by simultaneous movements, and the power can thereby be increased to any extent, and this is certainly one of the most extraordinary parts of the elephant's value. In throwing down trees of great size, their services are most valuable. The pioneers having cut the roots, the elephants undertake the remainder of the work. Their heads are armed with bullock hides, and to work they go. By simultaneous movements, they push the tree from them, very gradually at first, and so on more and more, (to and fro,) and having got the tree on the swing, at one desperate push, down it goes.

Nothing but the combination of power could effect the object, and there are always two elephants to each tree. It is quite manifest that they are brought to understand that their only chance of success in what they are about, is by unity of action.

There are no beasts of burthen that traverse a mountain's side so successfully as elephants. They can climb on hills where even mules cannot go; and during the operations at Shah Moosah Khail, the author continually employed them in supplying the Light Infantry in extended order, with ball-ammunition, when no other animals could have been found to do it, even to the every tops, as well as to the precipitous sides of the mountains.

The author does not pretend to know anything of the subject, on which he is now about to offer a few observations, and he is not even aware that there are any good grounds for the supposition, that the hill tribes, who surround the Valley of Peshawur, take their origin from the lost tribe of Israel. There is, however, a prevailing opinion to that effect, and certain it is, that many of the hill men have a Jewish cast of countenance, and very remarkably so.

Persons more deeply versed in ancient or sacred history than the author presumes to be, may unravel the mystery, if there really be one.

Not only have the people a Jewish appearance, but their towns and districts have names, as well as themselves, which bear a close resemblance to those used in sacred history; "Euzofzaie," for instance, "Zaie," is a town or district, and "Euzof," very much resembles Joseph, Euzofzaie or Joseph's Town.

In travelling through the sequestered places in the hills, the names of men, villages, and districts, often attracted the author's notice in like manner.

Freemasonry is also found in these mountains.

There can be no doubt, but that we have been sent by Divine Providence, to these out-of-the-way corners of the globe, for some much more important purpose than to satisfy ourselves; and there can be no doubt, either, but that the civilization and restoration of these demi-savages and fanatics, must be mainly the great object of the mission which has been allotted to us.

CHAPTER VII.

The Author being appointed to the Command of a Force of Ten Thousand Men of the Three Arms assembled for Field Exercise in the Cis-Sutlej Districts, leaves the North-West Frontier for a time.—Suggestions as to the value and importance of assembling large bodies of troops in India, as a "Demonstration of Power," with comments on the Non-Military Systems prevailing in that Country.

THE author's temporary removal from the North-West Frontier was attended with much anxiety to himself, as even a temporary absence was not pleasing; but he consoled himself on considering the circumstances in which he was about to be placed. The nomination to the command at Umballah evinced a feeling in his favour on the part of the high authorities of the country, which was most satisfactory.

The author, commencing in the Bombay Presidency, when in command of the Field Brigade at Deesa, had constantly devoted himself to the manœuvring of troops of the three arms in the field, and the new appointment he now received was strictly in accordance with his own views and wishes in that respect; but to the frontier he looked confidently as the scene of his future career.

So far back as the time when the late Field

Marshal Viscount Combermere was Commander-in-Chief in India, an effort was made by that gallant officer (to whom the author was then Aide-de-Camp) to obtain the sanction of Government for the assembly of a large force of thirty thousand men annually for exercise, in the north-west provinces of India; and well, indeed, it would have been for the country, as was discovered by after events, if such "demonstrations of power" had been sanctioned and enforced.

In India the Government has ever been the very reverse of military, and to this, in all honesty and truth, the author emphatically declares, may be attributed all the disasters of the empire.

It will occur to those who know somewhat of the history of India, that the Sikh army invaded the British territory, (which cannot be too frequently referred to,) and found it so unprepared for defence, that the empire shook to its very foundations. Troops, footsore and harassed, with munitions of war, were hastily brought up from distant parts of the country, to meet a great and impending danger; and it is by no means unreasonable to come to the conclusion, that the Sikhs would never have attempted the enterprise, had they not seen that our frontiers were exposed. In fact, the want of preparation was nothing more nor less than an invitation to them to embark in the cause, which well nigh succeeded in subverting our empire; and after all, this is only one of the many instances of the evils attending the civil administration of India.

On the author's arrival at Umballah, within the limits of which cantonment the force for exercise was to be assembled, he (considering the insufficiency of the ground to be allotted to the purpose) earnestly implored of the high authorities, to permit him to take the force into camp. He desired to proceed to the left bank of the Sutlej, in the first instance, with a view to manœuvring on real military principles in the field; and to work out evolutions of a practical nature, such as the passages of great rivers, with the difficulties incidental to campaigns, which the natural features of all countries must present. The author, contemplating, in fact, the invasion, by our enemies, of our old frontier of the Sutlej, and desiring that the troops under his command might see active service; if not in earnest, something as near to it as could be contemplated, resolved on fighting over again the battle of Aliwal (*certainly not Budiwal*), Ferazeshah, &c., &c.; and it might then have been seen, that if the British Government had originally been prepared with an army of thirty thousand men or more on its frontier, *as it ought certainly to have been*, under what very different circumstances the gallant soldiers of that time, Hardinge and Gough, might have met the Sikh invasion (had it ever taken place).

The ground which the author proposed for the campaign, was familiar to him, and he would have finished it (if he had been allowed) at Lahore, the capital of the Punjaub, where, it may be remembered, Lord Gough's brilliant achievement terminated.

It may be well to explain here, that the country, through which the author would have manœuvred his troops, was, and is, mainly lying waste, not cultivated, nor enclosed like England; and no crops were on the ground at the time of the intended operations.

Taking a mercantile view of the question, the agents of a trading government declined the author's suggestions, as had been done before, in Lord Combermere's time, considering that such an expenditure on an unnecessary military campaign (as it was looked upon) was not called for. Moreover, it was stated, that such movements of troops tended to excite the independent states. The author maintains, that neither the one plea nor the other, could in reason be accepted. Money laid out in preparing a noble army for the duties that might at any moment be required of it, and without which, neither the army itself, nor the commanders, nor the staff, nor yet the commissariat, could possibly be in readiness, most assuredly would not have been thrown away; and as to the neighbouring states, the author does not hesitate to say that, for ever watching the turn of events, and calculating the powers of the British Government, they only want the opportunity to rid themselves of our company as neighbours, and the stronger and more powerful we appear in their eyes, the greater hold most assuredly we must have upon their respect and affection. *Sat est.*

The force of ten thousand men being now assembled, commenced its operations on a space of ground wholly unsuited to the purpose, and it is not possible to conceive a more efficient body of troops. It was composed of three troops of Horse Artillery, and a light Field Battery; five of her Majesty's best European regiments, horse and foot; many corps of Native Infantry, the very *élite* of the Bengal army; and a regiment of Irregular Native Cavalry, Lancers. Well, indeed, might the author feel proud in finding himself at the head of such a *corps d'armée.*

General Sir William Gomm, then Commander-in-Chief in India, with strong military feelings, had urged on the Government in vain (as stated above), to meet the author's desires for camp service, and so it ended, that all that could be accomplished was the turning and twisting of the force in an unusally small piece of ground in different directions, under such ordinary rules and regulations, as were to be found in the Drill Book:—an imaginary attack here, and an imaginary defence there, over and over again repeated; with charges of cavalry supported by artillery and infantry on a well rolled and level parade ground; *the Commander with his brilliant staff,* staggering under cocked hats and feathers. Everything was, however, done, that could be done, under such circumstances.

The author, in after times, at Peshawur, instilled into the minds of those under his command, that Parade Grounds were simply the fields of exercise of riding masters and drill instructors; and that, as soon as the rudiments of army services had been passed over, the troops must leave their nursery, and encounter the difficulties of movement which natural obstructions afford. It is well known to professional men, that the machinery of war, like all other machinery, must be kept continually oiled, and in order, or else it becomes worthless. Heavy ordnance getting into swamps and difficult country, brings horses, unaccustomed to such difficulties, to the jib. The drag ropes are called for, and fifty or sixty infantry soldiers are hastily put upon them for an effort, the ropes, so long untried, in all likelihood snap, followed by the exclamation, "who'd have thought it!" and all this sort of thing prevailing.

The author had in his force the 9th Lancers, the 32nd, 52nd, 53rd, and 1st Battalion 60th Rifles of the line. He had noble officers and splendid troops, and all that was really wanted, was the sphere for action which had been denied to them.

The author is almost ashamed to acknowledge that there are men in the service, more especially in India, who, preferring ease and comfort and an idle life to soldiering, spurn all attempts to work out such military demonstrations—they pooh-pooh the whole affair as unnecessary, and satisfy themselves with a good dinner, a ball now and then, and the whist table. With such the author's suggestions were of course unpopular; but all this arises from the non-military feelings of the country which the prevailing systems have ever sanctioned and encouraged.

In countless instances, the author has had to meet with discouragement of that nature in his frontier command, when calling together troops for exercise on a more than ordinary scale; but he can safely assert that there are those even of high rank who will admit (on reading these remarks) that all with one accord have *in the sequel* acknowledged that the first lessons they had received in that part of their duty as soldiers, was in the trans-Jhelum territories.

The author does not pretend to make a boast of his own proceedings in thus offering his remark; but he does so in justice to others, being thoroughly convinced that no army in the world is composed of better materials, and none in which its members have stronger military feelings, if the circumstances under which they are placed tended to call them forth.

The results of the author's efforts in this line, had been on the whole satisfactory, and he feels deeply grateful to the officers about him for the support he experienced in his humble efforts for the good of his profession.

General Sir William Gomm, at the termination of the service for which this *corps d'armée* had been called together, visited the Umballah cantonment. He carefully inspected the troops and witnessed their evolutions, and in a very handsome general order, His Excellency made known to the army that a very useful work had been accomplished, giving to the author and to his troops the most unqualified praise.

Thus terminated an Indian Chobham, one of the

first, and perhaps one of the last—although the author, as will be found herein, afterwards did persuade the Government to allow him to take a force actually into the field in the Euzofzaie country for exercise and instruction.

CHAPTER VIII.

The Author returns to the Frontier, having been appointed to the command of the Peshawur district permanently, as referred to in the letter of the Marquis of Dalhousie, copy of which has already appeared in the introduction to this work.

DURING the temporary absence of the author on duty at Umballah, the 22nd Regiment, which he had so long commanded, had passed away, and was *en route* for England, necessitating him to obtain an exchange of regiments, with a view to remaining in India, and continuing on the North-West Frontier. The author is removed accordingly into the 10th Foot. This is the second time, since the author became a Lieutenant-Colonel regimentally, that he had to expend a large sum of money in effecting an exchange. With all due respect to the high authorities, it is a pretty well understood fact in the army, that when an officer has once adopted any particular line of his own, the more he clings to it the better for his own interest. India had ever been the author's sphere of action, and to India he must cling; the die having been cast, he had no other course to pursue. In the present instance he was a very willing instrument in his own banishment from his native country. In the early part of his career (a career of half a century) he certainly had no ties in India, and nothing could be more unsatisfactory than grillings in the torrid zone. The prospects of attaining rank, in which any advantages could be gained, were distant and dreary. It is a long lane, however, in which there is no turning, and at last the prospects brightened, and something good for the author seemed to be looming in the distance.

The health of the troops under his command in a sickly country, was one of the author's first considerations; in furtherance of which he commenced a correspondence with the higher powers on the subject of a soldier's garden at Peshawur. During the winter in particular, the soil and climate of Peshawur had been found to be peculiarly good for the cultivation of every description of European vegetables, whilst in the summer season, the vegetables of the country are produced of the best quality, and in abundance. The European soldiers (two or three thousand in strength) were sadly deficient in that part of the necessaries of life in which the health is most materially concerned. After a lengthened correspondence, a sum of money was sanctioned by the court of directors of the late India Company, at the urgent request of the author, for the purpose of establishing a garden at Peshawur on an extensive scale. There could be little doubt but that this outlay would prove to be very usefully incurred. At all events, by the introduction of European vegetables into a country where they had not been previously known or heard of, a step in the cause of humanity had been taken which must prove to be beneficial in the end.

Fifty acres of ground, within the limits of the cantonment, were selected, with a stream of water for irrigation running through it, and the ground, being tested, was found to be of the best quality. The place selected had been barren and waste. It was an eyesore to the station, and, notwithstanding all precautions, it was the receptacle of filth. In a very few months, so rapid is vegetation in hot climates, this garden became a very beautiful feature of the cantonment, and exceedingly productive. A European superintendent was appointed, and a house for himself and family was built in the grounds. One of the principal objects that the author had in view, was the employment and healthful occupation of the European soldiers in this garden. It was open to any man of good character to work in it, and his services were paid for amply out of the garden fund. The author never gave more encouragement than he could help to soldiers' gardens round the barrack-rooms. The irrigation of gardens under the noses of men is unhealthy, and there is always uncertainty in a soldier's life, particularly at a frontier post, which renders his working in his own garden most unsatisfactory and disappointing, "here to-day and gone to-morrow," and then what becomes of his garden? Besides, soldiers seldom stick to work, even if they can, and the supply afforded by such partial and uncertain means, can be of no great benefit. The men of a regiment, in a body, at one time came to the author and asked him to intercede with the government to re-imburse them for the money and labour they had expended on gardens at some military post, *on the express promise* of one of the highest authorities, that the regiment they belonged to should not be disturbed for one year. Where is the man on the face of the earth who, in an enemy's country, such as India really is, and ought always to be considered, could make such a promise? The regiment, six months afterwards, was on the frontier, and the men were not within four hundred miles of their gardens.

The scheme of the author in regard to soldier's gardens, was totally of a different character. He had established a garden where an abundance of vegetables could be produced for three thousand Europeans or more, and it was open to the soldiers to work in it, and earn money for themselves and families; and whilst these advantages were to be gained, the removal of a corps from one station to another was of no sort of importance; indeed, during the total absence of the troops, in the field, the garden continued to flourish under native agency.

Without intending to reflect more than is absolutely necessary upon the schemes of others, the author strongly advised the adoption of such gardens as his, instead of the so-called "soldiers' gardens," but the author claims to himself a peculiar feeling in all matters connected with the employment and amusements of the soldiers in India in their leisure hours. As it has ever been his desire, exhibited officially and otherwise, in countless instances, that the Government of India should be, for its own security, conducted on strictly military principles, and that the troops should be for ever in a state and condition for "instant action," he arrives at the conclusion that the establishment of soldiers' gardens (that is, gardens of individual soldiers) and workshops, in such a country as India, inducing to sedentary habits, is absolutely at variance with the interests of the state, and injurious to the soldiers. The recruit, on first joining his regiment, or its depôt, undergoes a total change in his habits of life, and if an artizan or a manufacturer, as very many are, his sedentary habits must be got rid of as soon as possible, and the powers of his limbs must be developed, or he will be good for nothing when the duties of a campaign, or the works in the trenches, come upon him. Then, again, into the minds of the officers and soldiers of a service army (such as the army of India ought to be, although it is not) must be instilled the feeling that they are for ever on the move, or liable to be on the move, and they must be at all times encouraged in the belief that no one place is more than another their place of residence. To keep this strongly on their minds, constant movement of the troops is essentially necessary. To encourage men in working at trades for the use of the public, which must fix their mind on particular localities, is to induce them to consider that they are not liable to "instant action."

There is very nearly sufficient occupation for soldiers in India in the ordinary duties of their profession, if those duties are properly conducted and cared for. Unhappily, in hot climates, owing to the prevailing sickness, the duties become extremely heavy, and it is quite impossible, therefore, to look to any certainty in the working of soldiers, at their trades, for the public; and without certainty, it had better not be attempted. The soldiers, too, are not easily satisfied with fair and reasonable prices for their work, which must be reasonable when they have to compete with the natives. Moreover, their work is frequently very indifferent. At Peshawur there was a native gunsmith in the Bazaar, to whom the armourer sergeants of regiments, even, appealed when they required any very delicate work to be performed, and the man laughed heartily when he heard of the absurdly extravagant charges, which the sergeants made for what they called their own work; besides this, no dependence can be placed in the promises of soldiers for the completion of their work, owing to their calls of duty. In all corps in which the author has been concerned, the number of good tradesmen are found sufficient to make everything that is required for the use of the regiment. A good carpenter's shop, tailor's shop, shoemaker's shop, a few painters, a shoeing-smith or two, with a good printing press, are essentials in all regiments, and should be insisted upon; but beyond the supply of its own wants, nothing is gained in a regiment by sedentary pursuits.

The author strongly advocates (what he has ever known to exist in all well regulated regiments) the establishment of places of amusement and comfort for the men, such as reading-rooms, coffee-rooms, and theatres, whenever the public service admits; and these can be attained in the rough, in temporary buildings, or even in a standing camp.

The author has always advocated the employment of the troops in the use of the spade and pickaxe by making roads and levelling grounds for military purposes, when working money is granted. These are really works essential to the efficiency of the soldiers, and are greatly neglected.

A regiment of Highlanders, at the author's earnest suggestion, after the usual lengthened and stormy correspondence, was permitted to make a road of political importance at the elevation of eight or ten thousand feet above the level of the sea, in the Hazarah country. They commenced their work with all the sickly appearance of manufacturers, and finished as hearty and ruddy as English ploughmen, and then were seen, not a regiment of cripples, but a body of men in vigorous health, capable of any exertion, and enabled by their training to work up the sides of precipitous mountains with the agility of mountaineers.

Regardless of all fear of contradiction, which is quite sure to be given, in the spirit of the times, to the author's observation, he unhesitatingly declares that the efficiency of the British army in the East Indies had been greatly impaired by the sedentary pursuits of the troops, by their idle habits, and by indoor occupations. In the hottest climates (and the author has had his share and experience in them) our soldiers are altogether too much spoiled and coddled. The healthiest men of an infantry regiment were always the long bullet men, who, with their forage caps to mark the goal, and bare heads, play for hours in the sun, if the non-commissioned officers do not happen to catch them at it, whilst the soldiers of the cavalry and artillery forces, whose avocations are necessarily more out of doors, evince the advantages they possess over infantry, by their ruddy and healthy appearance. It is of late years only that officers in authority have exacted such confinement for the troops as is at present ordered and encouraged. The author declares that he served in the very hottest place in India, in a regiment of Light Dragoons, when turbans and cap covers were unknown in the ranks of the British army, and when an iron helmet, or a small forage cap, covered a man's head. Seated on their horses, in watering order, with nothing on but their forage caps and long drawers, at the hours of 9 a.m. and 3 p.m., the men of a regiment were marched in the sun, to water. Were the heads of men harder in those days, and were their bodies stronger than they are at present? Certainly not. The troops were hearty and strong, and the only difference is they were not addicted to idle habits and sedentary occupations. The author always encouraged his men at cricket and other out-door amusements, and he believes the only improvement in such matters that has taken place since those days is the gymnasium, which is doing a world of good.

The evils arising from such measures as have been referred to, are by no means confined to the men themselves. The system strikes at the root of all military efficiency, and with it, of course, the security of our great empire of India. In cases of emergency, all tender feelings towards the European soldiers must of necessity be cast aside, and then, being unaccustomed to the rays of the sun, and being nurtured in idleness, their efforts are made under the greatest disadvantages. The pluck and hardihood of the Briton carries him forward; he may succeed, and indeed generally does, but unnecessary casualties have to be recorded, whilst almost impossibilities have been demanded of troops, unprepared and unsuited to such services as are required of them in the terrible climate of India.

At the outbreak of the great mutiny, in 1857, there were two or three powerful regiments of European infantry in the hills, near Simla, and a powerful European force of the three arms, at Meerut. The mutineers rushed from Meerut to Delhi, of course by preconcerted arrangements with the descendant of the head of the Mogul Empire, and nothing at that moment was wanted but "instant action," and the rebellion might have been as quickly crushed. By want of carriage for the camp equipage of the regiments in the hills, and by want of energy of the Commanders at Meerut and at Simla, the golden opportunity was lost, and the rebels, getting firmly secured within the walls of Delhi, the British Empire was in a blaze. Are such "solemn warnings" as these to be disregarded, and will the Civil Government never take heed? The want of carriage for the regiments was certainly the fault of the government of the country, and to the same may be attributed also the want of energy in the military commanders. *Our old seniority system*, which had very strictly prevailed in the service of the late East India Company, was the sole and only cause of the failure at Meerut, whilst the social position and ministerial influence system, always at that time prevailing with the Home Government, was the cause of failure in the hills. Sad, indeed, is it to reflect on such matters as these, and on the direful consequences of such misrule, but we gain nothing by experience, and although disasters have been from time to time overcome with the utmost difficulty, again and again we risk our position in India, and replace ourselves under the same difficulties.

Working strictly under one system for the public

good, as far as lay in his power, the author never ceased to exhibit the forces under his command, as a military *demonstration of power.* As he had failed in the Cis-Sutlej district to obtain the sanction of government to a camp of exercise under canvas in the field, he resolved to try again under his own more immediate authority on the frontier. The people on the Euzofzaie border, with the Swattie and Hindostanee Fanatics, in communication with each other, were troublesome and insolent; and the author recommended that a force should take the field, for active service if necessary, and if not, for the practice of these essential field duties, which at any moment might be required of them. The Government sanctioned this measure, and a force of about three thousand men took the field under the author's personal command.

During the very hottest seasons of the year, these predatory tribes on the frontier ride the border with more than ordinary insolence. But the heat was never sufficient to check the author; and his approaching campaign was to be carried out in the very hottest weather. The troops being prepared for field service, crossed the Cabul River, and proceeded into the Euzofzaie Country. The usual slovenly habits of the country were strictly prohibited, and the force moved on principles as if in the immediate presence of an enemy. It was difficult at first to break through the ancient and confirmed habits of the line of march of an Indian army, and the officers called for their usual indulgences. But the object of the march was of that nature, which could not be interfered with, and nothing being permitted to go forward on the march, officers and men were made to wait in patience for their breakfasts. It is a singular fact, and one deserving of consideration, that in a very few days, with the camp equipage and baggage of the force moving on its reverse flanks, *and not a single thing in advance*, according to Indian custom, affairs progressed as usual, and grumbling speedily disappeared. The heat in the camp was excessive, and some were of opinion that such services were an unnecessary exposure for the troops, but it turned out just the reverse. The season was most unhealthy, and the troops in quarters were cast down by fever, whilst those of the field were in the highest health and spirits. This was, in point of fact, a necessary *demonstration of power*, and it bore its fruits, without any collision with the enemy, who stuck to their hills, and received a "solemn warning" for the future. The author, about this time, received a letter from an experienced officer in Hindostan, warmly congratulating him on his success in squeezing out of the Government, money for an expedition in the field on this occasion, and he added, "I verily believe the sun and moon will turn from their course, now that the Indian Government have taken a step so useful and essential to the interests of the military services." Nothing could be more satisfactory than the result of this expedition, the eyes of officers and soldiers having been opened to the fact that the advantages of *strictly camp life* could not be over estimated.

A bloodless campaign, but a most useful one.

A force of the three arms, consisting of three brigades of infantry, a strong brigade of cavalry, two or three troops of horse artillery, with two light field batteries, were continually to be seen on the plains between the Peshawur cantonment and the mouth of the Khyber Pass. These *demonstrations of power* were again most essential to the interest of government, and became exceedingly interesting to the officers and soldiers of the force. The author making the cantonment of Peshawur the base of his operations, and the passes the objective, carried out a series of combinations under the supposed invasion, by the Affghans, of the British territory.

Intelligence (it was supposed) had reached the author, to the effect, that his position was about to be attacked by the enemy in force, and the troops of the Peshawur cantonment took the field. The author confesses with pride and satisfaction, that every officer and soldier supported him in the proceedings. The soldiers even anxiously enquired when these field days were to be renewed, and they greatly enjoyed the operations.

Working up to the mouths of the passes, with heavy firing of cannon and musketry, and brilliant charges of cavalry, the mountaineers turned out and manned their hills, in anticipation of an attack, whilst the news writers of Cabul informed the public that thirty thousand British troops were *en route* to Central Asia. These demonstrations did more to preserve tranquillity and overawe the restless tribes of the border, than any other means that could possibly have been adopted. They had seen that at last the British Government was on the alert, and prepared for "instant action." Their nightly intrusions and robberies of horses in cantonments, from this and other causes, ceased altogether. But be it remembered, that, although bearing the best fruits, these demonstrations were simply the acts of one individual. They were not the acts of the Government, but apparently just the reverse. Certainly no orders were ever given to the author to discontinue them, but the Viceroy of India, when visiting Peshawur, desired that no such movements of troops should take place in his presence. It may well be imagined how it happened, with European notions and feelings, that his Lordship disapproved of warlike preparations; and certainly it must be necessary in civilized countries, bordering on each other, to beware, lest the peace of the world should be disturbed, but in such countries as we have been thrown into, it is by prestige alone we can maintain our position.

On the Affghan border in particular, where the

demi-savages are always armed to the teeth, and would ravage and plunder their neighbours if they could, such *demonstrations of power*, as have been above described, simply lead to the preservation of order, and to the maintainance of tranquillity.

CHAPTER IX.

The Extraordinary Administration of Civil and Military Government on the Frontier.—The Confusion and Disaster arising from the same.—The Author proposes the Establishment of a Sanitary Station on the Kuttuck Hills at Cheratt.

IN recording the principal events of the time, it is scarcely possible for the author to do justice to all the matters with which he was concerned during the nine years he served on the North-West Frontier of India. To render even intelligible the anomalous and confused condition of the arrangements for the management of a line of frontier which could alone succeed, by the most simple and well understood administration, is next door to impossible, without spinning out a work which was intended to record events only of an important character. The author had resolved when entering upon this work, as with every other work he has taken in hand, to be as concise as possible, and not to tire the patience of those who may honour him by perusing his narrative. As he works on, notwithstanding his resolutions to be concise and to exclude such matters of hourly occurrence as may not be considered worthy of notice, he feels his difficulty increasing. This chapter, notwithstanding his wish to the contrary, must be lengthy.

It contains a few recorded facts which must not be overlooked, because their omission would leave unexplained, in a great measure, the erroneous systems prevailing.

It is in opposition to the measures at that time pursued by the governments of India in Europe and Calcutta, and not against the local authorities, either civil or military, that the author offers his observations, because those to whom such duties have been entrusted must work their own way in the spirit of their instructions, without yielding to circumstances, which would almost appear to overrule all other considerations. It has been already shown, in the introduction to this work, that the Marquis of Dalhousie had been quite wide awake to the errors of the frontier system, so far as concerned the military responsibility, and that he had resolved to bring under one head the military authority; but it has never been shown that he was desirous of curtailing the civil power with a view to leaving the military commander of the frontier in a position to act on his own responsibility, so as to enable him to meet impending difficulties, and counteract them by "instant action," although that was in fact the first and great desideratum.

How it happened that Lord Dalhousie, the Governor-General of India, had failed to take the steps in the right direction which he had proposed to himself, and which was so palpably necessary, does not appear; but there can be no doubt that the conflicting interests of the Commander-in-Chief of the army, and the Civil Government of the Punjaub, stood in the way of a settlement of the question in this respect, as in all other matters connected with the Punjaub and Trans-Indus territories; but up to this very hour the same confused systems prevail. To record a few facts as tending to show the evils that have arisen from palpable mismanagement, is now the object, and of course the sole object of the author, who has been far removed from the very interesting scenes of his former labours, and cannot possibly return to them. He can have no interested motives in thus urging on the world's consideration circumstances which have occurred, and may at any moment occur again, "solemn warnings" which never as yet have been heeded.

The principal feature in the author's narrative of his own proceedings on the North-Western Frontier of India, will be found in the record of events of the Indian mutiny. No parallel case will be found in the world's history; and it is imperatively necessary that he should prepare the reader's mind by explanatory statements, tending to show the gigantic dangers which presented themselves, "when to the chronic difficulties of a rugged border was suddenly added the defection of the native garrison which had so large a share in holding it." It has already been briefly explained that two military commands exist in this frontier, the head quarters of which are within four-and-thirty miles of each other. It has already been shown that the civil government prevails in all directions round these military posts up to the very confines of the stations, and it has been shown that unconnected chains of small military posts lay along the border, some of which were under the author's command because of necessity garrisoned by the troops of the Peshawur cantonment, and some were not ; all isolated, as regards their positions, having civil government close up and all around them.

It must now be explained that the officer commanding the Khohat force, which is entirely removed from the authority of the Commander-in-Chief of the army, is solely under the orders of the civil government of the Punjaub. He has under him a splendid native force of the three arms in the highest state of efficiency, a frontier force as well commanded and officered by Europeans as any such force could possibly be ; but having no European ingredient of its own, he was compelled to borrow of the officer in command of the Peshawur force such troops of that sort as could not be dispensed with. Part of the Peshawur European force was therefore, and is still, under the command of the rival Chief of Khohat, whilst in the very midst of the author's command, and in the *chain of posts*, was Hoti Murdan on the Euzofzaie border, in the valley of Peshawur, entirely removed from his authority, being part of the Khohat force ; and it must be here described that the author, a general officer, ruling over a force of ten or twelve thousand men in Peshawur, and having right and left of him divers small outposts along the border, had troops also right and left of him under a different military authority. Such a melange of troops and positions as can hardly be imagined or conceived, and all arising out of the admixture of civil and military government, which even the Governor-General himself could not disturb, and which is the root of all evil—and why ? because the civil government of the country is paramount, and if, as at present constituted, it be disturbed at all, the whole fabric of the empire must tumble to pieces.

Between the cantonments of Peshawur and Khohat, many circumstances occurred tending to show the absurdity and even danger of this confusion of interests. Five different authorities prevail within that space (only thirty-five miles), viz., the General commanding at Peshawur, and the Commissioner of the Peshawur district, between Peshawur and the mouth of the Khohat Pass ; the native tribes who occupy and hold the Khohat Pass ; the officer in command of the Khohat force, and a Civil Commissioner there also. At Buddebeer, about seven miles from Peshawur, the enemy appeared in force, and a body of three hundred hill men attacked a European officer in his tent, who was making a road under the Civil Government with an armed force. A severe conflict ensued. The officer was badly wounded, and lost the Government treasure chest, having defended himself with the greatest gallantry and determination. The Tanadar, or chief of police at Buddebeer, in a small defensive tower, with a strong police force, was within a few yards of this occurrence, and was dismissed from his post for not rendering the necessary aid to the European officer. The author was informed that he (the Tanadar) was concerned in the adventure, of which there could be little or no doubt. And how could anything else be expected of him?

The author was taking a ride the morning after this occurrence, when a native told him of what had happened during the previous night, and this is all he ever heard of it, to the best of his recollection, excepting from the gossip of the place. Would it be believed that such a state of things could exist; that the general officer commanding a frontier post of so much importance had heard accidentally only of an attack being made of that nature, and in almost within his hearing of musketry, by the very tribes which he (the general officer) had been placed to control and overawe? On another occasion, on the very same road, and close to his post, the author accidentally heard that a European traveller had been killed by hill men, having been mistaken for the Deputy Commissioner, to whom, on account of his long beard, he bore a personal resemblance; and numerous affairs of this nature which have occurred might be recorded. These sad affairs passed off without retribution at the very door of the author's position; and even when he accidentally heard of them, he was not only not in a situation to take measures to prevent their recurrence, but was absolutely by the orders of Government prohibited from doing so. It must be very clear that the military Commander, and there ought to be but one, should be empowered in such cases to take "instant action," without waiting for orders from authorities at a distance, who really cannot realise in their minds the evils prevailing. The author thinks it must be conceded, that civil government in such a disturbed country is entirely out of place. In the very midst of enemies, armed to the teeth, ever ready to fight, and ever fighting, is it not the legitimate duty of the troops to act, and act with vigour? It must also be conceded, that the conflicting interests of so many and such divided authorities, heaped together in a mass of confusion, must infallibly be fatal to the interests of the State. Thus the road connecting the two principal frontier posts (as before described) of Peshawur and Khohat (about thirty-four miles in extent) has been the scene of such desperate outrages, although the country was full of troops capable of crushing in an instant such matters, but from jealousy of interference with the Civil Government they were never brought out to preserve the peace of the country. Would any other nation but England dream of sanctioning such a state of things? Certainly not. At all events, when such serious evils had occurred, measures would have been taken to change a system which had been proved to be so defective. At one time, owing to the great sickness prevailing in Peshawur, it was necessary to borrow troops from Hoti Murdan (part of the Khohat force); and the officer in command of them having waited on the author to report his arrival at Peshawur, a conversation took place between the two, which led to important results.

The chain of loaded sentinels at forty yards intervals, which had for years surrounded an enormous station of three miles in length, could not be supplied without still further increasing the returns of sick, as the troops had scarcely one night out of two in bed; and the author enquired of the guide officer if he could suggest any means by which the night robberies of the Khyberees could be averted. The civil authorities had evinced no power or ability to check such marauding, although the whole of the intermediate ground between the Khyber Pass and the cantonment was in their hands, and now the force in cantonment was unable, from sickness, to protect itself. The officer considered for a moment, and then said, "I will try what my men (guides) can do; some of them are hill men, themselves, and are intimately connected and acquainted with all their proceedings." A man was found, who had been turned out of the Guide Corps for some misconduct, and was constantly entreating his officer to overlook his offence, and reinstate him. The officer told him to give him intelligence of some intended raid or attack by the enemy, on the Peshawur cantonment, and if he succeeded in giving timely notice, he should be reinstated.

The man went into the hills, and either concocted

an attack, or got intelligence of an intended one, which he made known to the officer. Certain it is, an attack came off, accordingly, and numbers were killed, the troops being placed in ambush ready to receive them.

Several things of this nature occurred, and robberies for a long time ceased altogether. The cordon of sentries was now removed, and was never replaced. The fact was, the enemy could see the sentries, and could, in the dark of the night, evade them, but now they could not attack the cantonment without imminent risk, because, by this new scheme, they met with a warm reception from an unexpected quarter. The treachery, towards each other, of these scoundrels is inconceivable; their very fathers and brothers they would sell, in like manner. A grand object had, however, been attained, and the garrison was relieved of long continued and harassing duties. The author's project, which he still hopes to hear of being carried out, has always been to cut down this frontier force of Peshawur from twelve to two thousand men, and to entrench their position with a mud wall and ditch, never to keep troops in so unhealthy a post more than six months at a time, and to keep the main body of the frontier force within the Indus, the healthiest country in the world. The Hindustani troops suffer in Peshawur equally in health with the European garrison. For ever recommending very useful measures for the benefit of the troops, the author expended quires of paper in his endeavours to obtain for them such advantages as he well knew they required, and whilst continually, as it were, at war with the higher powers in that manner, he, after all, had asked no more than what in justice to the troops, and indeed to the Government itself, he ought to have been empowered to order, on his own responsibility.

Amongst other things, he had implored of the Government for years, that he might be permitted to send European soldiers to Cheratt, in the Kuttuck Hills. Cheratt is about three thousand feet above the sea level. It is about twenty-four miles from Peshawur, and twelve miles from Nowshera, being near enough for any purpose. Sick men, almost in the last stage of disease, can bear the fatigue of being sent there, because their removal can be accomplished in a single night, that is, between the heat of one day and another. The mountain has a level top, with soil fit for gardens, and it is a cheerful place. The European soldiers are charmed with it. To no other sanitarium could the invalids, in a very bad way, be removed from either Peshawur or Nowshera, without injury, owing to the distance of all other places being too great.

Cheratt has its disadvantages, but none which are insuperable.

First of all it was proposed by the author to send two European regiments of the line to Cheratt, viz., the 27th Inniskillens, from Nowshera, and the 70th Foot, from Peshawur. It was not the author's intention to expend much Government money upon an experimental measure. The extravagance of all the Government arrangements for troops without any beneficial result is proverbial. Millions of money are expended in India in military affairs, which never ought to be expended, whilst a few rupees are refused for the most useful purposes. This is one of the crying evils of civil government; the intention may be good, but certain it is, the result is very lamentable.

It had been suggested that the Europeans should hut themselves at Cheratt; with the double object of improving their health by residing in a moderate climate, and by adding to their efficiency, which certainly would result from working with tools in the open air, in a cool temperature; employment which must benefit men much more as soldiers, than the in-door schemes of workshops and such sedentary occupations. Ample means might be found in India to give wholesome employment to the European soldiers, if we could shake off the old stations of the army, which, by habit, men have got wedded to. The schemes for in-door occupations would never be thought of if the troops were not, as it were, bedridden in excessively hot places. The 27th Inniskillens had recently gone out to India, from the Cape of Good Hope, under Colonel Kyle, who, after having inspected the Kuttuck hills, and having found the best materials for "Wattle and Dab" buildings, resolved to show us, at Peshawur, how well the men could cover themselves. The Cheratt scheme was of course disapproved of, *cum multis aliis,* by the local civil government. It was not a project emanating from it, and it was pooh-poohed for a time, altogether. However, at last the Commander-in-Chief of the army, and the Inspector General of Hospitals espoused the cause, but to no purpose. *Nolens volens,* however, the troops occasionally used this very desirable locality, and always received especial benefit.

Here, again, it may truly be said, was an exhibition of misgovernment as far as the civil power was concerned. The author was privately informed that the real objection to Cheratt was that it might prove to be a rival station to Murree, on which the Punjaub Government had expended oceans of money. This, if it be true, was as absurd as every other matter turned out to be; the object of Cheratt being quite different from that of Murree. It was clear that at Cheratt the troops were so close to the frontier that there could be no danger to the state in placing them there; whilst at Murree, which is one hundred and forty miles from the frontier, they would be out of the way altogether. Cheratt is within signal distance of Nowshera and Peshawur, and, by having the elephants at hand, six hundred European soldiers might be brought down during the night.

So long as Peshawur is kept up as at present, Cheratt is, and ought to be, a most valuable post.

It almost tires the patience of the author to write any more on the subject of Cheratt, so thoroughly has he exhausted the subject in times gone by, in his fruitless endeavours to obtain a benefit of so much value to the troops and to the State.

CHAPTER X.

The Chief Commissioner of the Punjaub arrives at Peshawur, and encamps with a Force of three or four thousand men, near Jumrood, anticipating a Visit from Dost Mahommed, the well-known ruler of Afghanistan.—Interviews of the Dost with the British Commissioner, A.D. 1857.—Central Asian Policy.

The Chief Commissioner arrived in the cantonment of Peshawur in the winter, between 1856 and 1857, to meet Dost Mahommed, the ruler of Afghanistan.

The Dost, as the author was at the time informed, had a double object in presenting himself on the border of the British territory; and to the author his visit was particularly satisfactory, as it enabled him to make his acquaintance, and also to become better informed on the mysteries of Central Asian affairs. The Dost, it was said, desired to obtain assistance from his British allies, by troops or by money, or by both, in prosecuting a war which he was then carrying on with the Shah of Persia; and he desired also to reclaim that lost portion of the Afghan territory which is now occupied by his ally, the Queen of England, on the right bank of the river Indus, called the valley of Peshawur.

He urged, and not unreasonably, that being no

longer enemies, but friends, we were not justified in keeping from him the most valuable and most fertile portion of his territory. It was said also that he wished the British Government to establish a subsidiary force of British troops at his own capital, as an unmistakable proof that we sincerely desired to uphold his power and authority against all foreign intrusions, such as Russian, Persian, etc. etc.

The author, being military, was of course rarely or never in the State Councils, and he learnt most of this from the Afghans themselves. One of the Dost's sons frequently visited the author, and at last induced him to sell one of his carriages for the use of the Afghan family, being unmindful of the fact that there was not a carriage road in all Cabul or its vicinity.

There never was a doubt in the mind of the author, but that the proper policy of England is to occupy Cabul, more especially if we can do so with the concurrence of its ruler, and once established there, in cases of succession, the rightful heir to the throne would of course be upheld, and all the internal commotions of that country, which must be more or less an annoyance to our Government at present would cease. Restless neighbours, such as we have, certainly cannot be satisfactory to us ; besides, our occupation of Cabul would be a sure and certain check upon the progress of foreign powers in Central Asia, and must become a very necessary measure of security to our Indian Empire.

We have heard quite enough, from time to time, of the feelings towards us of our own subjects, in the provinces of India, to doubt the course that would be pursued by them on the appearance of any foreign power of importance, in the vicinity of our own frontiers.

Ever ready to shake off the British yoke, advantage would most assuredly be taken of any serious embarrassments that we might be involved in, and heedless of other consequences, that one object, and that alone, would be aimed at, by the people of Hindoostan and Central India. The natives of those countries would care but little to whom they might look, as future masters, so long as they got rid of their present encumbrances; and, probably, would entertain the faint hope, that in a general struggle, they would be enabled to reassert their own independence.

Russia has something more in view than an extension of her trade; and is, at this moment, gradually working on towards the Golden Prize. She may have, perhaps, no easy matter to accomplish her object, if left to herself, but she well knows the frailty of our institutions, and must be well aware that an empire of such magnitude, composed of such restless and disaffected materials, cannot easily be held together amidst foreign and domestic difficulties, more especially with our existing systems of civil government.

Is it the old policy of pooh-poohing all indications

of impending evils, that causes us to be inactive? or is it that the policy of the time may be found in the old proverb, "sufficient unto the day is the evil thereof"?

The British authorities, if really invited to Cabul, would entertain but one feeling, and that is, the dread of another disaster in those regions.

The sad affair of McNaghten and Elphinstone is for ever staring our Government in the face, and a fixed and everlasting dread of grappling with Afghans hangs unworthily over the heads of British rulers, simply because a "disaster" once occurred there, shaking to the very foundation, (as every "disaster" does,) the very existence of British rule in India. But that "disaster," like many other "disasters" that have been recorded of India, ought never to have occurred. It was simply a disgrace to our arms; and God forbid, that by our non-military institutions and arrangements, and by the incapacity of our civil and military rulers, India may ever again be thrown into a similar predicament.

There is really nothing whatever to dread in Afghanistan. It is a mere bugbear. A few resolute men, it is well known, might have saved our troops and our credit at that unfortunate period of our Indian history.

England has plenty of men, and so has India, of the best quality; then how is it to be accounted for, that our empire is frequently thrown into jeopardy by such unaccountable arrangements in the selection of officers for command?

The meeting of the Ruler of Afghanistan, with the British Ruler of the Punjaub, must now be described.

Under the orders of Government, a considerable force of Europeans and natives, three or four thousand men of the three arms, were removed out of the Peshawur cantonment, and encamped about four miles from that place, and the same distance from the old fort of Jumrood (which is at the mouth of the Khyber Pass), on a fine plain of considerable extent with water in a small stream adjacent to it.

The Commissioner encamped with the force, and there awaited the intelligence of the Dost's movements. Information at last arrived, that the great Ruler of Afghanistan had encamped within the Khyber Pass, and as a measure of precaution, he desired the British Commissioner, in proof of his fidelity and sincerity, to have their first interview outside the border of the British territory. Afghan treachery is so proverbial, that no one ever believes a word that an Afghan says, and their rulers estimate others by themselves. The Dost, therefore, had taken this precautionary step.

When the morning arrived for this first interview, one or two of the Dost's sons came down from the Pass into the British camp, accompanied by a large body of wild-looking and well-armed horsemen, who were destined to escort the British Commissioner through the Khyber Pass to the Afghan camp. It was particularly the object of the author to avail himself of this opportunity of seeing the Khyber Pass: he knew not at what moment his services, and those of the troops under his command, might be called for in Cabul; and it was of very great importance that he should make himself acquainted with such localities. Strange as it may appear, the author, who had been several years on the border, had never before had a chance of looking into the Pass more than a mile or so. The Khyberees murder all Europeans that they can lay their hands on; besides which, by order of the British Government, no officer is permitted to go near them; an erroneous policy (in the author's opinion), tending to much mischief, not only as regards the British Government itself, but as regards the hill tribes, because they consider themselves so secure in their mountain fastnesses, that they can come down into our plain, steal horses and other property, and even commit murder, and then in perfect security, take refuge in their hills again; and this is certainly not to their ultimate advantage, any more than it is to ours. The author is thoroughly convinced, that no such state of things as this need exist. Stern measures and determination might long ago have relieved the British Government of this disgraceful state of things. The Khyber Pass should never have been held up *in terrorem,* as it has been, since we came in sight of it. It has been bad policy, highly injurious to our military reputation, and we have continually smarted under it, by the incursions of the Khyberees.

However objectionable it might have been considered to have made a movement, from time to time, in that direction, the author maintains that we ought to have done so, rather than be placed in a position so humiliating, as to be standing in awe of such demi-savages as the Khyberees. These Khyberees are far less civilised than many of the other tribes of the border.

We ought to have penetrated that Pass at times in force, if the object could not be otherwise attained; but it is the author's firm belief, that if the British Government had resolutely blockaded these passes, and had peremptorily forbid all trade being carried on through them, until we could, in like manner, carry on the trade without interruption, and without risk of life, we should have had access long ago, without danger to Cabul itself. It will be readily imagined how much the aspect of affairs must change in that quarter, as the restless beings of Central Asia become habituated to our civilizing policy, and honest dealing in matters of trade.

The advantages, both to Europeans and Afghans, would have been so great, that by general consent, all obstructions to trade would have been freely or forcibly removed.

Over and over again, the author has heard the Afghan traders say the same thing, and this is, indeed, one of the numerous instances in which, from mistaken notions and non-military feelings, we have failed in the great and important mission that has been allotted to us.

The civilisation of demi-savages is certainly one of the most important of the great objects of Divine Providence in placing us where we are ; and, generally speaking, mistaken motives of humanity are perpetuating the horrors of those blood-thirsty wretches, which, in countless instances, might have been put down by resolute and determined measures on our part.

It may be said in answer to all this, that even the Afghans cannot coerce the Khyberees, as Dost Mahommed, under whose rule they nominally are, has to pay them in money for his passage through their passes. This is done more by custom than otherwise, and certain it is, if the trade was stopped, the injury to Cabul would be so great, that the Afghans must take measures to coerce the hill people, and conjointly with us, they would very speedily find it necessary to yield to our wishes. They are miserably poor, almost starving at times. The author has known their chiefs willingly accept from him four annas, or sixpence, to buy rice. They burrow in the earth like foxes, where they live, and by-the-way, their earths are well worth seeing as indicative of their primitive condition. To be kept at bay by such people in the manner we are, and ever have been, is monstrously absurd.

The Dost's sons on horseback early in the day, with the Chief Commissioner of the Punjaub, the

Commissioner of Peshawur, the author, and one or two others, with a mob of horsemen surrounding them, entered the Pass. The hills on either side were densely covered by matchlock men, and the cavalcade had been so arranged as to prevent the Khyberees singling out and firing down upon the Europeans, which they most assuredly would have done had these precautionary measures not been taken.

Before leaving the British camp in the plains, the Chief Commissioner requested the author to give orders to the officer in command of the troops to move the force quickly into the Pass *if any firing was heard within it.*

Such is the treachery of the Afghans, that it was by no means certain that the Europeans would ever come back again. It was manifest also that the Chief Commissioner, who knew them well, had his doubts about it. The cavalcade proceeded at a native shuffling pace well into the Pass, which is in most parts on both sides as steep as a wall ; in fact, the entrance to the Pass by which the party was conducted (there are two) was nothing more or less than the dry bed of a mountain stream, coming down, no doubt, from the melting of the snows with considerable violence at the commencement of the summer season.

After proceeding several miles into the pass, the camp of Dost Mahommed appeared. It was indeed a very beautiful object, as native camps usually are, particularly those of crowned heads, whose magnificence is displayed throughout all Asia by flags of divers colours, and other well-known indications of pomp. A battery of guns was formed up in front of the Dost's own tent, whilst his Sepoys, dressed in red (armed and accoutred like our own) manned, in countless numbers, the lower ranges of hills; the hill tribes in vast numbers covering the upper ranges. This was truly a magnificent scene, and is here but faintly described. No sooner had the British Commissioner made his appearance in the Afghan camp, than an ordnance salute was commenced in his honour, and with it a discharge of musketry from the upper and lower ranges of hills in all directions, and in extent beyond all description, the whole hills being as it were in a blaze.

At the sound of the first gun, it instantly occurred to the author that all the Europeans might be in jeopardy, and such would have been the case had the small arm fire been heard in the plains below. The embassy had been accompanied by a squadron of cavalry and a troop of European horse artillery as far as the mouth of the Pass, and no further. The artillery officer, aware of the order that had been given for the troops to move up in case of need, listened attentively, and wisely determined, by the regularity of fire, that the guns he heard were no other than a salute. He did not hear the musketry, so all remained quiet, and no alarm was given in the British camp.

Now it is as certain as any thing well can be, that had the British troops at that moment rapidly entered the Pass, their appearance would have been the signal for the immediate destruction of the Europeans. The Afghans would at once have come to the conclusion that our visit was of a hostile character, and that treachery was at work. With the advantage they had in holding the surrounding hills, which would have completely commanded the troops in the Pass, few would have escaped to tell the story. The author often thinks of this narrow escape from a "disaster," and always congratulated himself on the lessons he was taught, and the knowledge he had acquired by all these local circumstances.

There was a grand Durbar in the Afghan camp, at which the author was introduced to all the Afghan chiefs and leaders of note; a set of designing scoundrels, looking the very essence of treachery and deceit, who only wanted the opportunity to cut our throats. Amongst others, was to be seen "Saardat Khan," the notorious chief of the Momunds, our everlasting and determined enemy, whose removal from the Durbar tents was insisted upon. The Dost ordered him off accordingly, but there were many others there as bad as him. The Dost, after this interview in the Pass, descended to the plains, and came, with his retinue, upon British soil, where it was finally settled, as the author was informed, that he was to receive a lac of rupees *per mensem* for a limited period; that he was to receive no assistance in troops; and that no part of the valley of Peshawur would be restored to him. The Dost remained only a few days in the British territory, and appeared to enjoy himself. The Commissioner gave him a return Durbar, which was attended by all the British officers of the force in full uniform. The author was very glad to make the acquaintance of the Dost; he had all the appearance of an English country gentleman, was fair in complexion, and with a healthy and ruddy appearance. Of course his camp could not get away without a "disaster" or two, and a young British officer, who had strayed away from curiosity to see what was going on, was assassinated simply for the sake of mischief. This young officer had disobeyed the orders by going where he did, and he fell a sacrifice to his own temerity.

The Dost was a wily, cunning fellow, and he knew well how to deal with his European neighbours. He screwed a lac of rupees *per mensem* out of John Bull; and John in India, with money in both pockets, gladly forks out to avoid the *circulating medium of swords and bayonets.* It is a mistaken policy, nevertheless, although frequently resorted to, and does more mischief in the long run than could possibly result from the use of saltpetre.

Be this as it may, the author is of opinion that when the Dost did the Commissioner out of his rupees, something more than his good will might have been exacted from him: for instance, a free passage through the passes might perhaps have been effected, and that being accomplished, the murders, horse robberies, and such like, by the Khyberees, in our territories, must have come to an end. Simultaneously with that, these mountaineers might have been taught that bread, by cultivating the soil, could be obtained, and in furtherance of which, waste lands, (as suggested before) in our territory, might have been allotted to them. This cannot be too frequently repeated.

The Sikhs, when they held Peshawur, ruled with a rod of iron. They never waged war in the hills as we have done, but they had an "Avitabilé," armed with the most despotic powers, who threw the delinquents (when caught marauding) from the tops of towers in the city of Peshawur, and so, terror-stricken, these savages were overawed, and kept in subjection. The author would not advocate such measures as those, neither would he abstain from punishing the tribes generally for sins committed in the plains, by a dash into the hills occasionally. Severity of punishment is always attended with less absolute mischief to all parties than lenient measures, and under the reign of "Avitabilé," it is said that tranquillity universally prevailed.

There can be no doubt that great improvements have been effected by our Government in the affairs of the border, by excluding the tribes who have committed depredations from our markets; but incalculably greater improvements might have been effected in countless instances, if more prompt, determined and resolute measures had been resorted to.

In one respect the Sikhs' system was immeasurably

superior to our own. The authority of the Frontier was vested in one individual, who had no conflicting interest to embarrass him, no commissioner, no deputy commissioner, no assistant commissioner, and no rival commanders; he reigned supreme, and had power to act without reference, even, to Runjeet Singh, his master.

To follow in the wake of such a government as that of old Runleet was of course disadvantageous in many respects to the mild systems of the English; still, in contrasting the two governments, there can be no doubt that our political conscience must be more clear than that of our predecessors (if they ever had any); but our conscience might have been still more clear, had we ruled from the beginning with a more stern and resolute system, because many of the petty wars of the border (as they are termed) might have been altogether avoided if we had assumed throughout a military instead of a civil attitude. "Instant action" should have been the ruling principle of Government, as the author here asserts, and has over and over again asserted.

After the many "solemn warnings" that the civil government of India had received by disasters which had arisen from placing "implicit confidence" in the natives, it would scarcely be believed that on the occasion of Dost Mahomed's visit to Peshawur it was urged upon him by the Government to receive at his court, at Cabul, British officers as envoys, unprotected by British troops; but such was the case.

The Dost, who was at that time engaged in a war with Persia, and was promised by the British Government the subsidy of a lac of rupees *per mensem*, strongly objected to the offer of an English envoy, knowing full well that the lives of unprotected officers would be in jeopardy, and that in the event of their being assassinated, his subsidy must cease. He, however, reluctantly agreed to an embassy being sent to Khandahar, and with those who really felt and understood the nature of that mission, and the peril of those officers who had accepted it, it was not expected that they would ever return to the British territory. They miraculously escaped, notwithstanding the extreme danger of their position.

Surely amongst the many "solemn warnings" they had received, the Punjaub Government should not have lost sight of the case of Agnew and Anderson, who were deputed to Moolraj, at Mooltan, without sufficient escort, an act of temerity on the part of the Lahore Board of Administration, which cannot be forgotten. In most cases of that nature, such is the good fortune which attends us in India, good comes out of evil, as, in consequence of that sad affair, our Government was necessitated to annex the Punjaub (as the only alternative), a measure of paramount importance to our interest in the East, which the Civil Government had most positively determined, previously, should not take place.

To have sent British officers as envoys to Cabul, early in 1857, with a subsidiary force of reliable

British troops of sufficient strength, to maintain them in security, was indeed the proper policy of that time; and, had such a measure been resorted to, the British Empire would not have been exposed, as it was, to the extreme peril or impending evil of having thirty thousand Afghan horsemen assembled for the purpose of invading the British Territory, when mutiny was raging in the provinces of Hindostan, and our empire was staggering to its very foundation.

On the death of Dost Mahommed, it may be safely affirmed, had British troops been at the Afghan capital, the appointed successor to his throne would never have been molested. This may be said to be a matter of opinion, and the author gives it as his, whatever may be said or thought to the contrary.

Whether the Dost applied to the British Government for an auxiliary British force at his capital, or whether he did not, the author maintains that he would most readily have accepted, at that time, such countenance or support; and if we had consulted our best interests, we should have taken advantage of the opportunity, and have given it to him.

As regards meddling with Afghanistan and with Afghanistan affairs, it must be remembered that we are already in possession of a highly valued portion of the Afghan territory; besides, it is one thing to go forth in aid of, or to support one party against another, and another thing to uphold legitimate authority ere discord prevails. This may be well understood.

To interfere with Afghan quarrels while the different parties are struggling for power in Afghanistan, is certainly most undesirable: but to prevent discord by our presence, and so to maintain legitimate authority there, is manifestly the principle on which the British Government, *for its own security, throughout the whole empire of India,* should act. For it must be remembered that the evil effects of this continued discord in Afghanistan is not confined to the country primarily concerned. The author, in these opinions, is supported by the Afghans themselves—men of consequence and importance, with whom he has, from time to time, been associated.

Although the treachery of the Afghan is proverbial, yet many of the most respectable of them entertain the highest respect for our sincerity, and have learned to place confidence in our good intentions.

A man, once seated on the throne at Cabul, with the controlling influence of British power at his elbow, would speedily discover that the most prudent course he could pursue, would be to act with justice and moderation: he would soon discover that acts of tyranny and oppression, to which (when left to themselves) all Asiatics are addicted, must be given up, and are not needed; being mostly resorted to for the purpose of striking terror into the minds of those who are ambitious for their own sakes, of disturbing legitimate authority.

Hence our presence at the seat of the Afghan Government would be beneficial in all ways, and anarchy would cease to prevail. This certainly might fairly be calculated on.

It will have been observed of late, that civilians, when writing on the subject of our policy on the North-West Frontier of India, calculate largely on the aid that would be afforded to us by our Asiatic subjects, in the event of Russian or other threatened aggression in that quarter, and also on the advantage we should possess in having railways throughout the country. With all due respect to those gentlemen who entertain such notions as these, the author emphatically declares that no dependence whatever can be placed on either.

The natives of India, who at present uphold our rule, and outwardly appear to respect it, inwardly detest us. They are much too wise and too crafty to avow their dislike to us, whilst we are in the plenitude of our power; they anxiously watch the turn of events, as we have seen over and over again, and the very best of them would shake off our yoke to-morrow, if they could. It will take ages to win over the affections of those whose territories and independence we have encroached upon; it will take ages to induce the fanatical races of India to bow down in sincerity, or to court, the Government of the Dog or Infidel, as we are at present considered. Universal prosperity, derived from our rule, will not accomplish what we desire in that respect; we must raise up future generations in a widely different spirit ere we can trust our power in their hands, and even in after times, when we may have firmly attached the majority of natives to our Government, there will ever remain a sufficiency of discordant spirits capable of cutting off our lines of communications by rail, and thereby, in times of foreign complications, shaking the stability of our empire to its very foundation.

Trust not then in native agency, not yet in rails as conducive to our military defences. Thousands of miles of rails can never be effectually guarded.

The conflicting interest of divided power, civil and military, in which the former is the superior, is and always has been, the source of evil in India, as it has been elsewhere; and as the civil authority cannot possibly work without the aid of the military, it is manifest that military authority in such countries as have been referred to, must altogether prevail.

It is the author's firm belief also, that with a British force at Cabul, the incessant and continued struggles at Heratt and elsewhere in that part of Central Asia, being within the reach of our influence, would be averted, and as certainly would the tranquillity, not only of Afghanistan, but of Central Asia, be secured, when the power of the British Government was seen and thoroughly understood.

Moreover, the expenditure of British money at Cabul, and the introduction of carriage roads and such like, which would emanate from the British camp, would give an impetus to trade, by which alone these people live, and would greatly strengthen our position. The people of the country too, would soon discover that we are not robbers like themselves.

Above all things, let the high authorities of India never lose sight of the fact, that impending dangers on any of our frontiers cause a general feeling of disquietude and restlessness throughout the empire, from one end of it to the other, tending to the repetition of struggles for our very existence.

Even the Abyssinian affair, now in progress, is, with the people of India, an encouragement to disaffection. The extent and nature of that expedition is misunderstood by them, as such matters usually are, and they exaggerate of course, everything they hear.

At this moment there is a general opinion prevailing in India, that we have entered upon a war of great difficulty and importance, *the object of which cannot be accomplished without their assistance.* They have seen troops, European and native, hurrying down through the provinces to all the principal sea-ports of the country, to embark for Africa, where a great Emperor (as they imagine) has contemptuously defied our authority, and who knows but that, as our struggles in the Crimea really and truly produced the Indian Mutiny, so the petty affair in Abyssinia may produce a similar result. At all events, we must not lose sight of the "solemn warnings" we receive, nor forget the inflammable nature of the inhabitants of our vast empire in the East, which are so little understood or thought of in England.

CHAPTER XI.

The Character and Condition of the Native Armies of India, under the Government of the late East India Company.—"Solemn Warnings" for ever disregarded.—Implicit Confidence in the Troops tending to produce the final Catastrophe which took place in the year 1857.

THE author, in the year 1810, landed at Madras for the purpose of joining his regiment, as a Cornet of Dragoons. Previous to his leaving England, the sad news had been received of the defection of the European officers of the Madras army, who had openly rebelled against the Government, and had even marched with their troops against the European forces. General Bell, an East Indian officer, was one of the principal leaders, and he marched against Seringapatam, whilst others took the field in different directions. The history of this business is too lengthy for insertion here, but it tends to shew that mutiny in India is not of recent date, nor yet confined to any particular part of the country, but has appeared from time to time all over the empire. At Travoncore before that, a battalion of Sepoys marched down with loaded arms upon the European officers of the force, who had assembled in a mess house on the King's birthday, in honour of the occasion, and all would have been massacred, had it not been for some man giving notice of their approach just in time for the officers to fly. The affair at Vellore, where the 69th Regiment of Foot were nearly all cut to pieces in their beds by the native garrison, was another great display of the feelings of the native troops towards the British Government. The gallant Robert Rollo Gillespie, quartered at Arcot with the 19th Light Dragoons (about fourteen miles distant), crushed this rebellion ; and both at Travancore and Vellore, as was well known, there was a secret understanding with the army at large, in all parts of the country, for a general rising, which would have assuredly taken place, had success attended their first movements.

When the author arrived at Madras, in 1810, matters were settling down ; and Sir George Barlow, by bold and resolute measures, restored order.

In the Bengal Presidency, at various periods of our history, the Sepoys had rebelled. In the year 1835 or thereabout, Sir Edward Paget, at the seat of government, crushed a mutiny by resolute and determined measures ; he sacrificed a battalion of Sepoys who were in open mutiny, and so crushed a rebellion which would have spread throughout the empire, had not such a man as Paget been at hand to put his foot on the serpent's head.

There were various instances of this nature, and indications of mutiny at Sukkur in Scinde, at Govingheur in the Punjaub, and various other places in later years, all tending to prove the little confidence that ought to have been placed in such a mercenary force, the very *élite* of the population of those territories which the East India Company had either seized and appropriated, or were (although nominally independent) with the British sword and bayonet hanging over them, such as Oude and other provinces.

That any one in his senses could have supposed for a moment, that such troops could be depended on, is most marvellous. Priest-ridden and fanatical, the ears of the soldiery were ever open to the evil machinations of designing men, their object being, as naturally might be expected, to rid the nations of India of their common enemies the infidels (as they are termed), the European intruders.

These troops so trained, were probably one of the most perfect machines in the world for good or evil, and, with a power vested in them by that training, which they never before possessed, were ever restless in heart, and prepared for the grand struggle which at last came off; beautiful regiments in drill, and steadiness under arms, almost unequalled; battalions of men with the average height of five feet ten inches, really giants in appearance. The European officers of these corps, led astray by the sycophancy and deceit of their native officers, placed the most *implicit confidence* in them; and even when in the great mutiny, murder was prevailing in all quarters, scarcely could they bring themselves to believe, that their Sepoys could deceive them, and in countless instances, officers, their wives, and families, whilst labouring under this delusion, were massacred.

Now it is quite necessary to explain many other circumstances connected with this army, as tending to shew the almost entire impossibility of holding it together; by which it will be seen, that it is only marvellous that it had been held together so long. Whether from fear of so dangerous a machinery, or from the mistaken idea that it was best to conciliate, and keep on good terms with them, certain it is, that the troops were petted to such a degree, that it may even be said that a premium was held out to them on insubordination.

During the time of Lord William Bentinck, flogging in the Native army was abolished, or nearly so, whilst in every part of the country the Sepoys were cantoned with European troops, and witnessed the degrading punishment inflicted upon them, whilst they (the natives) were exempt.

In every shape and form that the mind of man could contemplate were these Sepoys indulged in the most extravagant manner.

A few instances, and a few only, need be adduced, in proof of that assertion. A Sepoy, cooking his dinner within a circular space of ground well cleared and prepared for his cooking-pots, with the fire within the circle, held sacred the spot which he had allotted to himself for this purposc; and if a European officer, under whom he was serving, accidentally passed by, and came within a distance of it which was considered offensive, in the presence of his officer, and in a rage, the cooking pots were thrown down by the Sepoy on the ground, to shew that his *repast had been polluted.* Now this insulting behaviour (for the Sepoy's food could not in reality have been affected) was fully upheld and justified, and grossly insulting as it was, the officer had no power vested in him to punish; it was to be considered simply a *caste affair*, which seemed to place a power at the Sepoy's disposal, to offer insult to his officer.

The author had frequently matters of this sort under his own observation. Riding up to the tent door of the Commanding Officer of a Sepoy regiment, and jumping off his horse, he was about to give him in charge, for a few minutes, to a Sepoy orderly standing by, when the Regimental Commander came forth, urgently requesting that his Sepoy might be spared from acting in a menial capacity. The General, of course, forced it on the Sepoy, but held himself open to severe censure, if such a dereliction of duty had been reported.

On one occasion the soldiers of a European regiment, hastily loading their camels in camp, for service, were much pushed for time, when a Sepoy regiment, lying in camp, close by, was called upon to assist. The Commander of the Sepoy regiment resolutely opposed the measure, as being derogatory to the dignity of the Sepoys. Of course the Sepoys were, nevertheless, made to do what their own Commander had objected to, and it may confidently be stated that they (the Sepoys) most willingly obeyed the summons. The petting system was, however, carried out to such an extent by the European officers, under the established orders, that they knew no bounds to their unsoldierlike proceedings.

The troops on escort duties, scattered all over the country, were in hourly intercourse with the Priesthood at the villages, who, of course, lost no opportunity of sowing the seeds of disloyalty amongst them, and no measures were taken to prevent it.

The troops were well clothed, and well paid, indeed beyond all reason, and their families were highly pensioned ; and really nothing was wanting but the discipline necessary in all armies. They were spoiled, and, at last, ruined, under these sad circumstances, whilst those that remained after the struggle were left to deplore the mischief that had been inflicted on them by a system at variance with reason, most unjustifiable and most unaccountable. But such was the true state of the case, antecedent to the rebellion. Many other circumstances of a like nature, tending to account for the great rebellion, might be adduced.

Officers, in command of Sepoys, have informed the author that they had even received confidentially, *at times*, orders to abstain from carrying out certain measures of discipline "at present." The Sepoys must have understood this, and the unfortunate men were actually led into the great and dreadful evils that occurred. It is even said and believed that, two years before the mutiny, the Government had been warned of its danger, and some time before the mutiny actually broke out, rumours were continually afloat as to the impending event. That the Government of the country should have been unprepared for it, is indeed most marvellous.

One day, many months before the outbreak, the author was called upon by his own domestics, about one hundred in number, to be permitted to leave him. Somewhat astonished at this, he enquired on what account they, one and all, had resolved on quitting his service? They were all natives of Hindostan, and most of them had been many years in the author's employment. He could not consent to so wholesale and general a break-up of his establishment; but they informed him that there was about to be a general rising in the country, in which the Sepoy army was to take the lead, that Peshawur could never save itself, and they desired to get away quietly to their homes, ere the struggle commenced. The author quieted the minds of these men by saying that he knew of nothing of the kind, and that as the Government of the country was at ease, neither they nor he had any cause for alarm.

The greased cartridges, if they had any weight at all, which is very doubtful, must have served only as the fuse, by which the great mine of rebellion was ignited. Something was necessary, of course, when it broke out simultaneously in all parts of the country, to cause the general conflagration, and the priests had industriously circulated amongst the troops a rumour which was sure to excite them, fanatical and weak-minded as they are; and the Hindoos, in particular, yielded to the pressure.

The author has thus endeavoured to prepare the minds of his readers for the great mutiny, by showing the real state of affairs antecedent to it. He has shown the extreme difficulties of his own position. He has shown that our natural enemies and only pretended friends and allies, the Afghans, had been seeking to recover their lost possessions (now within our frontier) and which the British Government had seized, and held in defiance of them. He has shown also the state of the Hindostanee portion of the Frontier force, which, in common with their comrades, all over the country, were imbued with the same feelings, and were ripe and ready for the struggle. Intercepted correspondence, indeed, had disclosed all of this, if common sense had been wanting to discover it.

At the time of the first indication of actual rebellion, which occurred at Barrackpore, close to the seat of the British Government, and at the time of the actual outbreak at Meerut in May, in 1857, there were under the author's command nine thousand seven hundred Hindostanee troops placed on the frontier to defend the empire against restless and turbulent spirits, which are for ever with arms in their hands, and are wedded to murder, rapine, and devastation.

It is true that during the last few years the influence of a regular Government (such as never before approached these border tribes) had slowly made its effects felt both in the valley and in the surrounding hills; but an Afghan border must ever remain rude, fanatical, and uncertain, so long as it retains its independence; and the cantonment of Peshawur stands within twelve miles of mountain tribes, who own allegiance to no government whatever.

Much certainly has been done, although vastly more might have been done, as the author has before stated. Still steps had been taken of late in the right direction, and although no war or trial of strength at the moment was going on between the law and the lawless, it would justly have been said by any observer of affairs, that a more dangerous juncture for a revolt could not have been chosen by the wisest of the mutineers.

The first indication of mutiny at Barrackpore, which was not long before the actual outbreak took place, was on the identical spot where, in the year 1835, Sir Edward Paget, Commander-in-Chief in India under Lord Amherst, had summarily crushed a rebellion of the native army of Bengal by resolute and determined measures, and with that in recollection, it surprised the world that the Government of India should not have seen the necessity for at once carrying out in like manner strong and decided measures. An amiable nobleman, surrounded by men full of *implicit confidence* in the Sepoys, advised a widely different course, and the Government satisfied itself by reading a lecture to the mutineers, or little more, who returned to their duty to ruminate on approaching events, of which they could not at that time have been otherwise than aware.

To the military men who knew and well understood the danger of *trifling with mutiny* at its first indication amongst the troops of all armies, it must certainly have occurred that such mild measures would not only lead to "disaster," but must eventually tend to the destruction of discipline. All over India there were officers in authority knowing well the prevailing disposition of the Sepoys, who received the intelligence from Barrackpore with consternation.

That the mutiny of the native army, if not altogether crushed, might have been checked by the execution of the ringleaders, there cannot be the slightest doubt. Mistaken motives of humanity are perhaps, of all others, the most dangerous, not only in military, but in civil life. The army of India, it may be truly said, was ripe and ready for mutiny, and possibly sooner or later the dire calamity would have arrived; still, to have averted even for a time so terrible a catastrophe, would have been an advantage, indeed measures of discipline might have been adopted on the solemn warning that had been given.

Notwithstanding these remarks, it is not just and reasonable to condemn (as some do) the Governor-General of India, on whose responsibility the terrible tragedy had rested for pursuing a line of conduct of so very dangerous a nature. He was no soldier, and could not have understood the troops as others more intimately connected with them must do. Some of his advisers were only nominally soldiers, as is unhappily frequently the case in India ; but still it cannot fail to occur to the reader, that if proper measures had at the first moment been resorted to, in all likelihood the terrible disaster which ensued might have been then averted.

CHAPTER XII.

The Great Mutiny of the Native Armies of Bengal, with its immediate effects on the North-West Frontier.

On the night of the 11th May, 1857, the following telegraphic message was received at Peshawur from Delhi: "We must leave office; all the Bungalows are being burned by the Sepoys from Meerutt; they came in this morning; we hear that nine Europeans are killed." Shortly afterwards another telegram was received from Umballah: "Many native troops are in open mutiny; cantonment south of Mall burned; European troops under arms defending barracks; several European officers killed; electric telegraph wires cut."

On receipt of the foregoing intelligence, a council of war was held at Peshawur on the 13th of May, 1857, for the purpose of considering measures for the safety of the frontier and the Punjaub.

At the council, measures were at once resorted to to meet the great and impending difficulties, and by the arrangements then made, the author fell into the undivided command of the Peshawur frontier. The chief civil and military authorities at Peshawur (Colonel Herbert Edwardes and the author) at once proceeded, in concert, to adopt every precautionary measure that was in their power with a view to the security of the valley. By the letters of the native troops, which were intercepted, it was found that mutinous and incendiary communications were arriving. A summary stop was of course put on their communications, whilst all important secrets were revealed as to the nature of the mutiny in the provinces, and the intentions of the Sepoys.

The ladies of the officers of the force were concentrated at the residency, a large building nearly in the centre of the cantonment, and a European guard of forty men of the 87th Fuseliers placed to protect them. The troops at the fort of Attock were put in possession of the passage of the Indus (hitherto under the native police), and the civil authorities placed the police in charge of the other ferries of the Indus.

In order to be in readiness to meet any outbreak of mutiny that might occur in the district, a movable column of European and supposed reliable troops was organised to patrol the country, whilst the wing of a European regiment was thrown into the fort of Attock, a measure of imperative necessity at all times, and more especially so at such a moment.

The passage of the Indus, at Attock, was throughout the mutiny under charge of European troops, and never should be otherwise. A body of Europeans are at present in the fort—they are locked up at night, and have no control whatever over the bridge of boats and ferry line of the river, which are entirely in the hands of the natives, who might at any moment cut off the communication with the frontier posts. A passport system, and a strict system of espionage, were adopted at all the passages of the Indus leading into the Peshawur Valley, because as soon as it was discovered that post communications had been intercepted, emissaries were despatched from Hindostan to keep up the communication between the Sepoys in the provinces and those at the frontier. This is a fact worthy of special notice, because it tends to show that the author's position at Peshawur was entirely surrounded by combinations; in front, on both flanks, and in rear, indeed, in every direction, requiring the strictest surveillance. Unhappily for the interests of the State, the Chief Commissioner of the Punjaub would not allow such military interference to be continued after the mutiny, and he addressed a letter to the author, in which he expressed his sentiments on the passport system, describing it as *anti-English*, and desired that it should be forthwith discontinued. The consequence of this was disaster, as will be explained hereafter.

But to proceed: During the middle of the night, immediately preceding a most eventful day, the author was awakened, and found by his bed-side, the two Commissioners, Edwardes and Nicholson, who informed him that they had received intelligence from Nowshera, which would render necessary the adoption of very stringent and immediate measures of security, and proposed disarming native troops. The

55th Native Infantry, and 10th Irregular Cavalry were quartered at Nowshera, and the former regiment had evinced a spirit of disloyalty, and even the 10th could not be depended on. They were removed to Hoti Murdan.

Previous to sending European troops from Peshawur to coerce the 55th, it was imperatively necessary to disarm a large portion of the native garrison, and not a European soldier could be spared until that disarming had taken place. No time was to be lost. *It was certainly a desperate measure when considered in all its bearings, and could not be accomplished except by stratagem and well concerted plans.*

On the proposal to disarm being made to him by the two Commissioners, the author had well and deeply to consider the step he was called upon to take.

The troops and the frontier posts being under his command, the responsibility of such a measure (if it were carried out) must rest with him. It was proposed, in fact, to disarm for its own internal security a large portion of a garrison which had been placed there by Government to maintain order on the border, and to defend the British Frontier from intrusion by the wild and unsettled inhabitants of Central Asia.

The Afghans, upon whom no reliance ever can at any time be placed, were within a few marches of British territory. They had recently, as has been shewn, demanded of the Chief Commissioner, the restoration of the much valued valley of Peshawur, which is part of Afghanistan, and which had been wrested from them by the Sikhs, and annexed to the British territory after the last Sikh war. The armed population of the hills in front and on flank, are known to be hostile, and ready for any mischief; and now (as had been discovered by intercepted correspondence) the native garrison of Peshawur were ready for revolt, and only waited for a favourable opportunity. It must be acknowledged that the position of the author was one of extreme peril, difficulty, and responsibility.

However, duly weighing all circumstances, he resolved on the measure of disarming, and arrangements were made for carrying the same into effect; for which purpose the Staff officers, the Brigadier of Peshawur, and all the Commanding officers of regiments were immediately summoned to the author's quarters, in order that directions might be given as to the duty of each individual. The hour fixed upon for the disarming was seven a.m.; and when the clocks struck that hour, each corps named to be disarmed was to be removed from its arms, so as to ensure simultaneous action. The officers in command of European regiments and artillery, had their several positions allotted to them, to act in case of resistance, whilst the author and the Commissioner on the one side of the cantonment, and the Brigadier of the station and the Deputy Commissioner on the other, were to be at the posts arranged for them to act in case of need. The cantonment of Peshawur is three miles in length.

One of the greatest of all difficulties, which the author had to encounter, was the determined opposition to the measure of disarming which had been evinced by the commanding officers of the doomed corps. They were turbulent, and expressed their conviction that the Sepoys were loyal, and that the measure was altogether uncalled for, and one of them who commanded by much the most efficient native regiment in garrison, declared that his men would not submit to such a degradation, and would be sure to attack the guns. The author stood almost alone in this proceeding; the Commissioner (Edwardes) supporting him manfully. However, the measure had been resolved on, and the stern opposition of so many of the officers of the highest rank in the force, only served to increase the author's responsibility. Two of these commanders became insubordinate, and more serious consequences towards them would have been adopted, had it been prudent to exhibit such a division in the European element in the eyes of the native troops and the people of the country.

The author desires here to express his sentiments on this subject, as regards the conduct of these old and, heretofore, deserving commanding officers, who were of high rank and long standing; and in after times he could not help thinking that every reasonable allowance ought to be made for their indiscretion. Suddenly and unexpectedly called upon to take from their regiments, the arms with which they could no longer be trusted, with all their hopes for the future cut off; with the long established pride that they had taken in their men; and not understanding too, at the time, the dangers which surrounded them; no one could well be surprised at the resistance they offered.

On this subject, the Commissioner of Peshawur wrote to the author at a subsequent period as follows:—

EXTRACT.

"Peshawur, 13th January, 1858.

"The memorandum you have kindly sent for my perusal, seems to me a strictly accurate outline of the measure of disarming the Sepoys here on the 22nd of May last. Two details occur to me which might or might not be worth adding.

"One (as indicative of the previous state of the troops), that you had found it necessary to tell them off into two wings under the commanding officers of the two European Regiments, with six guns attached to each ready for immediate action.

"The other (as indicative of the serious nature of the undertaking), that one of the commanding officers of the native infantry, during the discussion, expressed his opinion that his regiment (the most efficient in the force) would never submit to such a disgrace, and would be certain to attack the guns.

"I also think that the difficulty of the measure was very seriously added to by the (at the time) violent partisan feeling of the majority of the European officers of the corps designated for disarmament. I have always thought, as I looked back to that stormy council, that you were placed in a most arduous and difficult position, and that it required no common resolution to resist the protests of all the commandants.

"If you would favour me with a copy of your memorandum at your leisure, I should be greatly obliged."

The disarming on that morning of nearly four thousand men, took place as ordered, and happily without struggle or bloodshed. The affair was everywhere executed in the most dexterous manner. The infantry were marched away from their firelocks, which had been piled as if for some drill purpose, and when clear of them, the European troops with loaded arms (who were concealed behind barracks and ready for action) rushed forth, seized the arms, and conveyed them under a sufficient escort to the arsenal. At all points was this carried out simultaneously and in like manner. The Sepoys, motionless with surprise, were utterly powerless.

The people of the country seeing and hearing of the advantage that had been gained, came in and offered their assistance, instead of taking advantage of our position; but who could have formed an opinion at that moment as to the course which would be pursued by the neighbouring states, and, indeed, by our own subjects in and about cantonments, when a large portion of the troops had suddenly been deprived of the means of defending themselves.

It must here be observed that the people of the district were evidently awaiting the issue of an expected struggle in our garrison, for although the neighbouring chiefs had been repeatedly invited to come forward and bring men for the service of the British Government, the call in not one single instance was responded to until the measure of disarming had been carried out. Even the Affredies and other hill tribes, our enemies continually in times of peace, against whose depredations, up to that very moment, measures were being taken, came forward and tendered their services, and thus the first fruits of the great measure of disarming were happily realized.

The difficulties of our position on the Peshawur Frontier were perhaps never greater than at this critical period. The inhabitants of the Peshawur district, even those holding lands under Government, it is thus shewn, withheld their aid at the time when we were most in need of it, and the only reliable troops at that moment (the Europeans) including sick, all ranks and branches of the service, *in all parts of the district,* amounted to two thousand and fifty-two men only.

It must be, however, recollected, that the Affredies and others had an object in view very different from that which at first appeared. The object being to go down to the provinces of Hindostan for plunder, and not in reality to assist the British Government in its extremity.

Perhaps in no place in India did the prompt disarming of the native troops produce such beneficial results as on the Peshawur frontier. It struck a blow at the root of the mutiny from which it never recovered, whilst it brought in the aid of the wavering inhabitants of the valley, who had really, from the aspect of the affairs, good reason to doubt our power to maintain authority; and they naturally hesitated ere they espoused a cause, which, to all appearances, would involve them in nothing short of ruin and destruction, in common with ourselves.

It came to the author's knowledge, afterwards, that a general rising of the Hindostanee troops, in Peshawur, had been determined on, and the day appointed was the 22nd of May; but the disarming of the troops, as above described, took place very early on the same day; so a terrible catastrophe, by the timely measure of disarming, had been averted.

A few days previous to the disarming of the Sepoy regiments, a letter was intercepted at the frontier post of Shubkudder, addressed by a Sepoy "Gopâl Misser," of the 51st Regiment, N.I., (on behalf of others of that corps), to the 64th, N.I., (who, like themselves, were highly disaffected), inviting them to come to Peshawur, from the outposts, to assist in a contemplated general movement by the native soldiery, against the Europeans, which was to have taken place on the 22nd of May, as above recorded, the very day when the measure of disarming was carried into effect in the Peshawur cantonment; and it is generally supposed that the outbreak of the 55th, N.I., in the district, on the 21st of May, was resorted to, by that corps, with a view to a simultaneous rising.

No sooner were the arms out of the possession of the Sepoys, than many of them evinced a most restless spirit. Of one regiment, in particular, (the 51st Native Infantry), between two and three hundred men deserted. At their head was the Subador Major, or senior native non-commissioned officer of the regiment. The men fled into the district, mostly making for the surrounding hills. Here was another danger of a most formidable character. The disarming of soldiers in a country like the Peshawur valley, where every soul is armed, could avail but little, unless the utmost vigilance was adopted; the troops had only to go forth, and armed they soon might be in such a country. To put a summary stop, therefore, on "desertion," was, perhaps of all others, the most important consideration. Pursuit was ordered, and the Subador Major and one hundred and twenty of his men were captured.

The author at once resolved on punishing the offenders in the most resolute and determined manner. The Subador Major was tried by General Court Martial, for desertion, and sentenced to be hanged. The whole force in cantonment, consisting of seven or eight thousand men, of all castes and colour, armed and disarmed, horse and foot, and artillery, were formed up on parade, to witness the execution.

A gallows was erected on the parade ground, and notice was given in the surrounding country of the approaching event. This was intended to be, at so critical a moment, and proved to be, the most important step that could have been taken. An old commissioned officer, with great influence amongst the Sepoys, was probably, of all others, the best man that could have fallen into the hands of the author, for an example. The troops were unsteady and unsettled on parade. A large body of Hindostanee cavalry were present, over whom there could be no restraint whatever, if they had broken into mutiny, as there was not in the Peshawur valley, at that moment, one European cavalry soldier.

This first execution of a deserter, was, under all circumstances, a measure of desperate uncertainty. Many thousand people of the district had flocked in, to witness it; and it was quite impossible to say how such a matter would terminate. The European force, of course ready for action, was comparatively small in number, (including artillery, not more than twelve hundred men), whilst the Hindostanee troops on parade, amounted to nearly six thousand.

The European troops, from excessive duties thrown on them, the heat of the weather, and constant night watchings, speedily decreased in number of effective men, and soon became so weak in numbers and condition, that they could not be exhibited on parade without giving encouragement to the disaffected.

During this exciting scene of the execution, the author, with his Staff, passing the several columns which were formed up on three sides of a square, addressed every native regiment in this manner—

"Soldiers! The Native Army is everywhere in a state of revolt. This Subador Major, who is about to suffer, had deserted his regiment and his colours, and was apprehended in the district, near a large body of men of his own corps, endeavouring to escape into the mountains, *which are full of our most bitter enemies.*

"There are two great crimes prevailing, just now, in the Bengal Army—Mutiny and Desertion. One, under the circumstances, equal to, and the same as the other. Stern examples must be made, and I solemnly assure you, that so surely as Sepoys are caught in the commission of such offences, so surely will they be tried, and, if found guilty, executed."

As affairs progressed, many instances of this kind occurred, and so long as the Europeans were equal to the duty, a general parade was held every Tuesday morning, at which the troops were compelled to witness rewards and punishments given and inflicted; rewards for acts of loyalty, and punishments for the great and prevailing crimes of the army.

The news of these executions, and the mode adopted in carrying them into effect, spread far and wide, and even in the city of Cabul, itself, were the subjects of discussion and of astonishment. It was clear to all that discipline was upheld and maintained (notwithstanding the rumours to the contrary) amongst the troops, on the British frontier; and the Afghans, keenly watching the turn of events, on finding that the supremacy of the British Government had prevailed, were deterred from an aggressive movement.

Thus it may be truly said that the discipline of the British force was the discipline of the Border. Order prevailed, and the foot of legitimate authority was placed on the serpent's head.

The subsidy, given by the British Commissioner to the Sirdar Dost Mahommed, which has already been referred to, no doubt had some effect in the mind of that sordid monarch; and to him, personally, a rupture, at that moment, with England, would have been attended with the loss of the lac of rupees *per mensem*, which he was receiving—a pecuniary benefit which (as the author was informed) he had appropriated solely to his own use, instead of to his troops, for the prosecution of the Persian war, and for which latter purpose it had been ceded to him; but the Afghans themselves, ever restless and unsettled, were throughout meditating an attack on the British frontier, and a rich harvest in Hindostan; and were alone deterred from the movement by the imposing attitude which had been assumed at Peshawur; and it came to the author's knowledge, afterwards, that thirty thousand Afghans had shod their horses at one time, ready to invade our territory.

In after times the native gentlemen and traders of

Central Asia repeatedly informed the author that his security on the frontier had entirely depended on the determined measures he had resorted to.

In confirmation of this, the author here inserts a letter addressed to himself, at a subsequent period, by the viceroy of India. That esteemed nobleman, although so highly estimating the services of the author, was not really and truly sufficiently aware of the gigantic difficulties which had been overcome on the North-West Frontier of India, and when alluding to his "sedative" occupation, had little idea of the extraordinary efforts of body and mind which the author underwent during this eventful period.

Extract of a letter from the late Lord Canning, K.G., late Governor-General of India, to Major-General Sir Sydney Cotton, K.C.B., dated Camp Karragola, November 22nd, 1860 :—

"For yourself, I can truly say that I expected, and for a long time hoped, that it would be possible to use your great experience and proved ability in some more active service during 1857 and 1858, than in the *sedative* task committed to you on the North-West Frontier. But there is not a doubt that the interests of the State were best consulted by keeping that frontier in your hands, *for it would have been much less secure in the charge of any other Divisional Commander* in India; and if any outbreak upon it, or inroad across it had occurred, and had not been met promptly, and with a knowledge of all local difficulties, or of the way to overcome them, (*which no officer possessed in any degree to compare with your-*

self), neither you nor I should now be in India, according to all human probabilities.

"So far as the Government of India is concerned, and the opinions expressed by it—upon the transactions referred to—be assured that full justice is done to your promptitude and sound decision, and to those high soldierly qualities, which have led me to look upon your presence in command upon the frontier as a mainstay of safety.

"Believe me, dear Sir Sydney,

"Very faithfully yours,

(Signed) "CANNING."

And the author here takes the liberty of introducing two extracts from letters which were addressed to him during the mutiny by the present Viceroy of India, Sir John Lawrence, Baronet, Grand Cross of the Bath, and Grand Cross of the Star of India, who was at that time at the head of the Government of the Punjaub.

The first on the 26th of September, 1857 :—

"In the number of good men round me in the Punjaub, I have been most fortunate. *Whatever credit is due to the Punjaub administration, should be fairly shared amongst us all.* No officer has had a more difficult part to play, or played it more ably than yourself.

"The postal communication between this and Moultan, is still interrupted. We have not had a dawk from Bombay for twelve days. How fortunate this did not occur before Delhi fell."

And again on the 5th of May, 1858 :—

"No officer in India deserves better of his country during the late crisis than yourself."

The originals of all documents referred to in this work are in the possession of the author.

The following is a copy of a general order by the Commander-in-Chief, issued on the author finally quitting India, and also the copy of an address to the author by the Parsee merchants and traders of Peshawur, tending to show (in common with other documents) the universal feeling prevailing in regard to the author's services :—

"General Order by His Excellency Sir Hugh Rose, Commander-in-Chief in India. Head-quarters, Camp Morar, Gwalior, 1st December, 1862.

"The Commander-in-Chief in India has great pleasure in recording in this General Order his high sense of the valuable services performed by Major-General Sir Sydney Cotton, K.C.B., who now, at the termination of his period of service, vacates the command of the Peshawur Division.

"This distinguished general officer's service is of more than half a century, a great part of which (some forty years) has been passed in India.

"His Excellency, and the army under his command, can never forget the excellent service which Sir S. Cotton performed during the eventful period of the mutinies.

"There can be no doubt that the calm decision with which Sir S. Cotton met disaffection and controlled disorder within his command, and his just appreciation of the state of affairs at that period, enabled, in a great measure, the Punjaub to furnish the reinforcements which marched to Delhi, and contributed so essentially to the fall of that most important stronghold.

"The best wishes of Sir Hugh Rose for his welfare attend Sir Sydney Cotton on his return to England.

"By order of the Commander-in-Chief.
(Signed) "E. B. JOHNSTONE,
"Officiating Adjutant-General of the Army."

"To Major-General Sir S. J. Cotton, Knight Commander of the Order of the Bath, Commanding Division, Peshawur.

"HONOURED SIR,—We, the undersigned, Parsee merchants and residents of the Camp of Peshawur, cannot allow you, Sir Sydney Cotton, K.C.B., to depart without first testifying to you our sincere regret.

"It is now nearly (9) nine years since you came among us to command the troops at this—the gate of India; and surrounded as we are by turbulent and warlike tribes, our homes and property have never once been molested, which state of peace we are fully sensible has been entirely due to your watchful care.

"We have always met with your kindest support and patronage, for which we most heartily return you our humble thanks.

"We shall never forget either when the mutiny, in the year 1857, of the army devastated other provinces, how secure we felt while you, Sir S. Cotton, K.C.B., were amongst us.

"In leaving us for your home, we beg to assure you that our entire community regrets your departure, and wish you a happy and prosperous voyage, with long life in your native land.

"Your sudden and early departure being unknown to us, we are unable to show you our admiration and regret in a more substantial form; and therefore we hope you will accept these expressions of our gratitude to you, though we are fully aware they convey but a poor idea of our feelings.

"We have the honour to remain,

"Honoured sir,

"Your most obedient and humble servants,

"COWESJEE FRAMJEE JEHANGEER,

"And Others.

"Camp Peshawur, 17th October, 1862."

CHAPTER XIII.

The Affairs of the Indian Mutiny continued.

THE record of events, as detailed in the last chapter, will have convinced the reader that the proper mode of grappling with mutiny had been resorted to, and that no circumstances in this world, however desperate, can arise beyond the reach of human effort, if aided by the hand of Divine Providence, without which all our endeavours are vain.

It is impossible to conceive a state of things more desperate than that in which the frontier post of Peshawur was found at the outbreak of the great mutiny. In no other part of the empire were the same dangers impending; in no other part of the country were collected an organised force of ten thousand Hindostanee troops, the very *élite* of the army; and in no other part of the country were rampant enemies staring the authorities in the face, without the possibility of relief being afforded. The late Sir Henry Havelock, in writing to the author from Oude, *just before his death,* stated that in all his own anxieties in that country, none had weighed so heavy on his mind *as the author's position on the Afghan frontier.* Sir Henry Havelock, it may be remembered, was with Colonel Sale at Jellalabad, when the British troops were all but annihilated, and he well understood all circumstances connected with Afghanistan. Jellalabad is only thirty miles from Peshawur.

It is true that great and important steps had been taken, as explained in the last chapter; but the next consideration was, how to maintain the advantages gained, which, at any moment, might have been set aside, had not the same resolute and determined measures been continued.

The "disarming" of a large body of Sepoys, it is true, had been effected, and three other regiments of the same class had subsequently become non-effective.

The 64th Regiment had been disarmed at the outposts, and had been marched into Peshawur to be closely watched. The 55th Regiment N.I., had revolted at Hoti Murdan, thirty miles from Peshawur, and the 10th Irregular Cavalry had been broken up, for disloyalty in not acting, when called upon, against the 55th.

There were, however, an immense amount of armed and disarmed Hindostanee troops in and about Peshawur, requiring the utmost vigilance; and the duty of watching them had devolved on a very limited number of European troops, who, from excessive fatigue in so doing, were reduced to a very insignificant body of effective men. It must be remembered that the armed, as well as the disarmed native regiments, required to be closely watched. The disarmed, it was discovered, were collecting and secreting arms, of course for some ulterior object, and it was found necessary to destroy the barracks, and remove the troops into camp. The European officers of the disarmed regiments were compelled to go under canvas with their men, which was considered by them a sad grievance.

Amongst the many unaccountable arrangements prevailing in the Sepoy army, none could be more dangerous than that by which officers and men are separated ordinarily in quarters in India. Under the existing systems, the European officers see nothing scarcely of their Sepoys, their quarters being so far distant from each other. When, therefore, the officers were compelled to go with their men, there was a general burst of indignation, and in one copy of a local newspaper, no less than seven highly insubordinate letters appeared, abusing the author for having adopted this manifestly necessary precaution. No one but the officers themselves could have written these letters.

This display of bad feeling on the part of the European officers, is referred to in order that the great difficulties of the author's position may be understood. The fact is, that in all directions the most appalling difficulties stared him in the face. Owing to this arrangement, not a move could take place amongst the Sepoys without instant discovery.

It is foreign to the author's purpose to record events of hourly occurrence, beyond the pale of his own responsibility; but he cannot help remarking on such cases as had occurred, in which the most serious evils had arisen from want of such like precautions as were taken at Peshawur. In one instance a Sepoy regiment, or regiments, had been disarmed, and were left so far removed from observation (when disarmed) that they broke away, and made off to join the King of Delhi, after having murdered their commanding officer, and a European sergeant-major. Such was the "implicit confidence" placed in these Sepoys by their European officers, that although they had seen the necessity for disarming, they had been trusted away from European surveillance, and there was a European regiment in garrison all the time. The native regiment alluded to was afterwards cut up by a civilian with his police, whose very laudable exertions alone prevented the men from joining the rebels in Delhi.

Disarmed rebels, on joining the King of Delhi, were speedily rearmed, as, under the incautious arrangements of Government, he had been provided with ample means of carrying on the war.

In winding up the affairs of the great Mutiny, whilst praise was almost indiscriminately bestowed by the highest authorities in England on the ruling powers of India, no notice was ever taken of their terrible mismanagement which had led to the great catastrophe.

To the erroneous systems of Government must be attributed the mutiny of the native army, which would never have occurred under proper discipline;

but it has no where appeared that censure had been passed upon those whose gross neglect and mismanagement had brought about disasters of such enormous magnitude.

In the escape from the horrors of the Mutiny, the good people of England, it appears, must have lost sight of those on whom the responsibility should have rested as before alluded to.

What had the Government of India been about, which permitted the great arsenal of Delhi to be placed at the King of Delhi's disposal? On the shoulders of the Government at that time must be fixed the onus of affairs, which led to the city of Delhi being in a position to throw the Empire at large into such extreme peril.

Very little must have been known or understood in England of the Great Mutiny, where even the Imperial Parliament voted thanks to some who should have been made responsible for the rebellion, while its thanks were withheld from others who had brought the country out of it. The affairs of Hoti Murdan, where the 55th Regiment of Native Infantry broke out into mutiny with arms in their hands, and rushed into the adjacent mountains, must now be chronicled.

The author, whilst in a position of extreme difficulty and embarrassment at Peshawur, was unable, with safety to that important post, to quit it for a moment, and was unable, of course, to detach a European force for the purpose of proceeding to coerce the 55th Native Infantry at Hoti Murdan, then known to be in a state of undisguised mutiny; but as soon as the troops had been disarmed at Peshawur, the author at once set to work to organize a European and reliable force to cross the Cabul river, and proceed into the Euzofzaie district, in which the fort of Hoti Murdan is situated.

During the whole time in which the troops at Hoti Murdan were in the condition above described, the author had directed the officers in command of the 10th Irregular Cavalry and 55th Native Infantry (there quartered) to report daily, by cosid and otherwise secretly, the state of their corps respectively.

From each commander he received the most favourable report of the state of his own corps. The commander of the 55th, whilst reporting his own regiment to be loyal, advised the author to be cautious of the 10th Irregular Cavalry. The commander of the 10th Irregular Cavalry in like manner reported his own regiment to be loyal, but cautioned the author against the 55th Regiment.

In recording this, the author desires to invite his readers' attention to the fact that everywhere throughout the Indian empire, the natives, by their habits of deceit and sycophancy, led astray their European leaders and employers. It is not only so (as we have witnessed throughout the Great Mutiny) in the army, where such deceit is practised, but in the affairs of the Government of the country; and the author, in emphatically declaring this to be the case, adverts to it as a "solemn warning," which must not be lost sight of.

As soon then as a column of reliable troops could be spared for a few days from Peshawur, they were despatched to Hoti Murdan. The heat of the weather was unbearable, and H.M. 70th Regiment, about six hundred strong, more or less, were mounted on elephants, under escort of Mooltanee horse, who were certainly not concerned in the Hindostanee Mutiny. The force was placed under command of an active and intelligent officer (Colonel Chute), and with Colonel Nicholson, then the Deputy Commissioner in company, it proceeded on its mission with a couple of guns.

Of all the military spectacles that could be witnessed, there could be none more interesting and remarkable than this; on each elephant were six European soldiers, fully accoutred, with their arms in their hands, and dressed in white clothing, with such necessaries as were required for a couple of days' service; one man looking to the front, two on each side facing to the flanks, and one looking to the rear; the six men had the appearance of being in a fortified position. The hundred elephants thus armed as it were, were surrounded by the wild horsemen of the Mooltan Frontier, who were seen dashing about in all directions as is their custom; and so the cavalcade moved off in the dusk of the evening, for a night's march. The author had personally superintended the fitting out of the expedition; it was a spectacle picturesque in the extreme, so thoroughly soldier-like and so effective.

Well it would be for the Indian Government to take "warning" by the past, and in order to meet cases of emergency, to be prepared in like manner for the "instant action" of its European forces. When the Sepoys first broke out at Meerat and rushed off to Delhi, what would have been the effect of such a movement as this? six hundred European Infantry with arms in their hands, fresh and ready for "instant action" at so critical a moment thrown during one night into the city of Delhi, when no time for preparation could have been found.

When the Sepoys in the fort of Hoti Murdan saw in the distance this armament approaching, a column of dust being the first intimation, they rushed from the fort with their arms, and made off towards the hills, and the 10th Irregular Cavalry refused to act against them. The gallant Nicholson and Chute made every effort in their power to prevent the escape of these rebels; they vigorously fell upon their rear and overpowered such stragglers as came within their reach, but as the Cavalry would not act, the main body escaped.

The European officers, with about one hundred and twenty Sepoys of the 55th Native Infantry, were found within the walls of the fort. Their commander had destroyed himself, and they were marched into Peshawur. At a future period, the author had to encounter some of the men of the

55th Native Infantry on the Mahabund Mountain, who had joined an Hindostanee Colony of Fanatics, as will be explained subsequently.

It has already been stated, that a moveable column had been organized for the purpose of patrolling the country. It was destined to act at any and all points in the Punjaub, where mutiny was raging, and the command of it was confided at first to that chivalrous and distinguished soldier, Sir Neville Chamberlain. The services of Sir Neville Chamberlain, however, being required elsewhere, the command of the column fell into the hands of as gallant a soldier as ever lived, Nicholson, who was destined to perform the most important service, in the capture of Delhi. This column, as it traversed the Punjaub, was fiercely engaged with rebels, and greatly distinguished itself. It was more or less remodelled after it crossed the river Jhelum, but it finally reached Delhi at a most critical period, and was found at the assault when Nicholson fell mortally wounded. The historian who takes in hand the History of the Siege of Delhi, with the antecedent circumstances, it is to be hoped will honestly and with truth record the events of all that important achievement.

No delicacy towards the living, nor towards the memory of the dead, must lead him away from his path of duty. It is foreign to the author's purpose to record events of that siege and of the circumcumstances connected with it, but he was so intimately connected with the result, by which the neck of the mutiny was broken, that he is called upon to describe the share he and his civil co-adjutors of the North-West Frontier had in it.

It has already been shewn that the most dangerous point of the empire, and on which its destinies most materially depended, was the Peshawur cantonments; and it has now been explained how it happened, that being the weakest point, it became after a time, the strongest. Even the sea-boards of Calcutta and Bombay did not afford such timely aid as was sent from Peshawur to assist in the operations against Delhi. A little army, as will be explained hereafter. was raised and trained in the Peshawur district, and every reliable soldier that could possibly be despatched from thence, made his way to assist in the siege, and it can be safely asserted, that without the aid poured in from Peshawur, Delhi could not at that time have been recaptured. The historian must give a faithful account of the nature and extent of the services of Nicholson and his column at that time; *and he must also record all particulars as to the effects of the demonstration of power at the great crisis of the rebellion, which was exhibited by the author and the troops under his command on the North-West Frontier.*

Of all the important duties which devolved upon the author during the great crisis of the rebellion of 1857, there was none of such deep interest, and on which so much depended, as the consultation and decision of the Peshawur officers in authority, upon the proposal of the Punjaub Government to withdraw from, and to surrender to the Afghans the Peshawur district.

When this proposal first reached Peshawur by electric telegraph, the author commanding the Peshawur division, Lieutenant-Colonel Edwardes, C.B., the Commissioner of the Peshawur district, and Lieutenant-Colonel Nicholson, the Deputy Commissioner, were the officers consulted.

It was urged by the Punjaub Government so early in the siege of Delhi, as the month of June, 1857, that it would be prudent to restore to Dost Mahommed, of Cabul, the Peshawur province, which the British Government held to the great annoyance of the Afghans; and the Government desired (*ere it was too late*) to confer a favour upon the Dost, by the *voluntary* restoration of that valuable portion of the British territory, with a view, in the first instance, to conciliate the Ruler of Afghanistan, his subjects, and the border tribes generally; and by making an apparent merit of what was considered (although not admitted at the time) a real necessity, to concentrate the British forces in the heart of the Punjaub.

The Government also suggested, after surrendering the province, that the troops should at once recross the Indus, and proceed to Lahore, where it appeared they contemplated the assembly of an army of reserve, in support of the forces then under the walls of Delhi, the siege of which, it appeared, might very possibly be of necessity raised.

The affairs of the country were at that moment dark and gloomy in the extreme in all quarters ; still the proposal to withdraw from the frontier was received by these Peshawur officers with astonishment and indignation. Each officer, as called upon, freely gave his individual opinion on the proposed measure, one and all agreeing that nothing but the most disastrous consequences could be anticipated were a *retrograde movement* made at that moment by a single British soldier.

Indeed, even the withdrawal of the ladies from Peshawur, which was contemplated by some, was considered by the Peshawur Council as highly inexpedient, tending to excite in the minds of the people of the country, distrust in the general stability of British power.

It is a fact acknowledged by every one conversant with the subject, that the fate of India depended on the resolution of the Peshawur officers at that moment, and its final security resulted from their firm determination to hold on to the Peshawur Frontier at all hazards.

There was no doubt in the minds of the officers then, and there is no doubt now in the minds of all Europeans and natives, that, had the British troops recrossed the Indus at that critical period, the Sikhs, Punjabees, and other inhabitants of the countries Trans-Sutlej, who afterwards so materially aided in rescuing from destruction the tottering power of Great Britain in India, seeing the dilemma in which its Government was placed, when driven to the necessity (*as all would then have certainly considered it*) of retreating, would have risen with one accord upon the retiring forces; and an army of ten thousand Hindostanee native troops, then composing the Peshawur force, ripe and ready to join their comrades in arms against the British Government, would (after crossing the Indus) have broken away from all restraint, and rushing down with the Sikhs, Punjaubees, and even the Afghans at their backs, like an avalanche upon Delhi, would have swept every station in the Punjaub of its troops and treasure; and increasing in numbers and power as it went along, a force of twenty or thirty thousand of the best Hindostanee troops in India (horse, foot, and Artillery) would have fallen on the rear of the besieging army, then under the walls of Delhi, annihilating every European engaged in the operations.

On this momentous decision, then, of the Peshawur officers (Edwardes, Cotton, James, and Nicholson), *hung the fate of India at that time*, and of every European (man, woman, and child) in the Punjaub and elsewhere.

The under-written demi-official letter was addressed by the author to the Punjaub Government, in which that officer's individual opinions on this all-important subject appear recorded; and the same were afterwards officially reported for the information of His Excellency, the Commander-in-Chief of the army, through the chief of the Staff, Major General Mansfield, and for the information also of the Government of India.

The sentiments and opinions of Lieutenant-Colonel Edwardes, C.B., were entirely in accordance with those of the author, and were transmitted similarly and simultaneously to the British ruler, who, by the blessing of Divine Providence, was induced at length to abandon altogether the project, *and Peshawur was retained.*

On this subject the author addressed the Punjaub Government in a demi-official form, as follows :—

"Peshawur, 26th June, 1857.

"Last evening the all-important subject of the 'Evacuation of the Peshawur District,' by the British troops, was again brought under the consideration of Colonel Edwardes, Captain James, and myself, consequent on the receipt of an electric telegraphic message which had just then reached the former officer, and that measure was again very fully discussed in all its bearings.

"There cannot be a doubt but that the prestige or great name attached to British power in India, is and always has been, the chief and primary cause of our continued supremacy.

"The justice of our laws, and the respect we have ever shown for the rights of our subjects, and for their religious prejudices, although in countless instances so ill understood by them, and so injurious to our interests, have tended, in a measure, towards upholding our government in India; but the government is one of opinion, and our great name, at all events, is the first and great cause of our supremacy.

"We have extended our territory, from time to time, by means of the sword, and as we have gone along, we have armed and disciplined the conquered, requiring of them almost, and, in many instances, altogether to hold the country for us.

"Placing *implicit confidence* on this very uncertain state of things, we have been lulled into the belief that our position was secure, when suddenly the bubble bursts, and our true condition is exposed.

"To redeem, then, our supremacy, which is unhappily tottering, is now our object; and it may be asked, can any one thing be more likely than another to effect this object, than the maintenance of our great name, as far as possible, amongst the various nations of India, with which and over which we are now ruling? Certainly not, because an exhibition of weakness on our part in any quarter must shake the confidence of waverers, and would determine such, perhaps, at once to espouse the cause of the strongest power.

"We have pushed our conquests up to the very mouths of the Afghan Passes, and, at this very moment, by God's blessing, our strongest position in India is at the mouth of the Khyber.

"By our present proceedings we have, for a time, at least, engaged the services (I may say) to a considerable extent of the border tribes, and in the hour of need, they, (who, not many days since, were our most bitter enemies,) relying on our great name and power, have come to help us against the disaffection of the very troops by which the same Sikhs, Punjaubees, and others had been conquered, and held in subjection.

"A retrograde movement from Peshawur, believe me, would turn all these parties (now apparently our friends) against us. The Kohat force and Pathans, with the Sikhs, Punjaubees, and such like, no longer respecting our power, would, in all likelihood, turn against us, and their most valuable services would be lost to the State for ever.

"Our removal from Peshawur cannot fail to be disastrous, and cannot be effected without immediate confusion throughout the whole of this part of the country, and throughout the length and breadth of British India.

"Hence the measure will seriously injure the interests of our forces in all quarters, whilst the additional strength to be gained by our presence, if we can get there, would be small, and indeed we could afford no timely aid.

"In handing over to the Dost the Peshawur district, (a measure which we may pretend to be a mere matter of just expediency, and not of necessity), the Afghans will at once see our weakness, and will duly profit by the same, against their common enemy, the Christian conqueror.

"To this frontier, and to the present strength of our position on it, as well as to Calcutta, at the opposite ends of our territory, we must look for the recovery of our power throughout the intermediate kingdoms of the Bengal Presidency. Our great name is now upheld on our frontier, whilst Calcutta and the sea-board, in the plenitude of power, with European reinforcements continually arriving, will afford, eventually, and more surely, the necessary succour.

"At this very moment, six or eight regiments of Europeans must be between Calcutta and Delhi, *en route* to the seat of war, and treble that amount will eventually be thrown in from home, and elsewhere; and by such means must our supremacy be recovered.

"When could our troops reach the seat of war? and in what numbers?

"These questions must be duly considered, and by them the loss or gain of our removal from hence must, with other matters, be balanced and determined.

"I implore of the Government, to hold on to the frontier. When the reinforcements from above and below, at present in progress towards Delhi, have reached their destination, every confidence may be felt that that city will fall again into our hands, and disaffection will, in all likelihood, cease in all quarters."

The date of the above letter, viz., the 27th June, 1857, tends to show how early in the rebellion the Government of the Punjaub had desired to withdraw the British troops from the Frontier Post of Peshawur, and from the valley generally.

The author finds it necessary, here, to record transactions at Rawul Pindee and Jhelum, of an important nature, which cannot be overlooked, as both those stations were in the Peshawur division, and within the limits of the author's command, during the mutiny, although so far removed from his immediate observation, as to be beyond the reach of his personal control. The following is extracted from an official despatch of the author's, under date 19th June, 1858:—

"In the beginning of July, the Commissioner, who was residing at Rawul Pindee, reported to the author certain arrangements which he proposed to make, for the purpose of simultaneously disarming the 14th Regiment N.I., at Jhelum, and the 58th N.I., at Rawul Pindee. In the former corps, especially, a most mutinous spirit had existed for some time previously, and the measure was therefore urgently called for.

"A force, consisting of three guns of the 1st troop, 3rd Brigade Horse Artillery; three companies of H.M. 24th regiment, with a body of Mooltanee Horse and Foot, was despatched from Rawul Pindee, with orders to reach Jhelum at day-break on the 7th July. On the approach of the force, the officer commanding the 14th N.I. having, under preconcerted arrangements, paraded his regiment at 4 a.m., attempted to explain to his men the necessity that existed for depriving them of their arms, and he exhorted them to give them up with a good will. Instead of responding to the call of their commanding officer, the men began deliberately to load, and then to fire on their officers, who hastily rushed towards the advancing column, which by that time was not far distant. The Sepoys at the same time broke off, and ran tumultuously towards their lines, which, together with the quarter guard room, a building of solid masonry in front of the lines, they held with great determination, although exposed to a heavy fire from the guns of the approaching column.

"The mutineers were, however, dislodged by a party of H.M. 24th regiment, very gallantly led in person by Colonel Ellice, who fell severely wounded. The command of the force then devolved on Colonel Gerrard, who proceeded to clear the lines. After a continued resistance, the latter retired to a walled village named Laulah, not far distant from the lines. It was by this time two o'clock in the day. The troops from Rawul Pindee had been marching since twelve o'clock the previous night, and with the efforts they had made under a burning sun were perfectly exhausted.

"Colonel Gerrard now halted the force for the purpose of refreshment, and after some delay proceeded to storm the village which the mutineers had occupied. Unfortunately the ammunition of the artillery, of which a large amount had been expended during the day, now ran short, and one gun fell temporarily into the hands of the mutineers.

"A most gallant attempt was made by the European artillerymen to recover this gun, but failed, the horses brought up for the rescue being shot down. Colonel Gerrard now considered it expedient to draw off the infantry, which was unsupported, and to form up the force on the plain, so disposed as to prevent the mutineers re-occupying their lines. The mutineers during the ensuing night evacuated the village, and fled in great numbers towards the Cashmere territory. The following casualties took place in this force on this occasion amongst the European troops :—

"H.M. 24TH REGIMENT.

"Colonel Ellice—severely wounded.
"Captain Spring—mortally do.
"Lieut. Streatford—severely do.
"Lieut. Scott—severely do.
"2 Sergeants, 1 Corporal, and 21 Privates killed.
"1 Corporal and 42 Privates wounded.

"HORSE ARTILLERY.

"1 Gunner killed.
"1 Gunner, 1 Farrier, and 1 Lascar wounded.
"19 Horses killed, and 8 Horses wounded.

"Besides these were several other casualties amongst the Mooltanee horse and foot under Lieutenant Lind."

In forwarding the proceedings of a Court of Enquiry, with the reports connected with the mutiny of the 14th regiment of N.I. to the Adjutant-General of the Army, the author recorded the following opinion :—

"1st. That the troops from Rawul Pindee arrived much too late in the day on the parade ground at Jhelum, as the 14th N. I. must have been on the ground some time before the troops under Colonel Ellice came up. The 14th regiment might, it is true, have resolved previously to fight, but, with proper management their resistance could not have been so effective. An evident want of judgment was displayed in parading the regiment in such close proximity to its lines, that a short run enabled the men to shelter themselves in their huts.

"2nd. The horse artillery guns, too, were wrongly placed near the village of Saulah, where they must have been within point blank range of musketry fire. Hence the number of horses killed and wounded, and the consequent loss of a gun for the time being. The commander of the 14th N.I. also committed a fatal error in addressing the Sepoys on the subject of disarming before the column from Rawul Pindee was on the ground to coerce them if necessary.

"On the same day, viz., the 7th of July, 1857, at Rawul Pindee, the disarming of the seven companies of the 58th N.I. and two companies of the 14th N.I. was carried out under the orders of the Brigadier commanding the Sind Saugor district.

"The serious error was also here committed of parading the native troops to be disarmed so near to their lines, that when they became alarmed and excited at the threatening position taken up by the guns, the Sepoys rushed tumultuously to their lines, and forthwith commenced loading their muskets.

"Providentially, the European officers of the corps, who acted with great spirit and resolution, were enabled to induce the Sepoys to give up their arms, the Brigadier, with his staff, having, with the regimental officers, quickly followed the Sepoys into their lines.

"The Brigadier, no doubt by his personal efforts, together with those of the other European officers, brought the Sepoys to a sense of their duty; otherwise, the disarming at Rawul Pindee would probably have proved as disastrous as that of the 14th N.I. at Jhelum. Thirty Sepoys on this occasion fled into the district, but were apprehended, and were brought in by the police, and were tried and executed. The commander of the police, Captain Miller, of the 1st Bombay Fusileers, received, in the very gallant discharge of his duty, a severe and dangerous wound."

CHAPTER XIV.

The Affairs of the Mutiny Continued.

THE disarming of troops in an armed country like Peshawur could have been of little avail, had not the most careful measures of surveillance been carried out afterwards.

The breaking up of native lines was a measure, as it turned out, of absolute necessity; as, on searching for arms, the roofs of the buildings and elsewhere (in all the lines) were found to contain weapons of all sorts, with ammunition, secreted. This has been alluded to before, but it must be repeated here. The 51st N.I., a disarmed corps, during the searching of their lines, broke out into open mutiny, and endeavoured to seize the arms of a newly-raised Punjaubee corps, which were piled on parade whilst the regiment was at dinner.

A fanatical Mahommedan priest, the "Syad Ameer," had about that time hoisted the green, or Mussulman flag, in the Khyber Pass, beyond the reach and power of the British authorities, and, by his intercepted letters to the Sepoys, it was discovered that his object in doing so was to raise a force of Hindostanee mutineers for a religious crusade, and an attack on the British frontier. There were five thousand of these disarmed troops in Peshawur, and had the "Syad" succeeded in his plot, the most fatal consequences must have ensued.

The intention of the 51st N.I. on breaking out, was to join the "Syad," and they made an effort to induce the other disarmed corps to join them. No corps, however, broke out with the 51st regiment, and it is probable that the others awaited the result of this movement, ere they plunged themselves into the adventure.

The author was aroused one day about noon, on hearing heavy firing of musketry at the distance of about a mile or more from his quarters. He jumped on his horse, with his Aide-de-Camp, and taking with him a troop of horse artillery, which were always ready for "instant action," galloped off in the direction indicated. He found the troops engaged with the 51st Regiment. The European troops, the 18th Punjaub Infantry, and others, were speedily under arms, and the author found on the parade ground a considerable number of dead and wounded.

The 51st having failed in obtaining arms to any extent, made off towards the Khyber Pass. They were hotly pursued by the 18th Punjaub Infantry, by bodies of Mootanee Horse, Mounted Police, the 18th Irregular Cavalry, Peshawur Light Horse, 27th Foot, 70th Foot, 16th Punjaub Infantry, and others, and few only escaped and joined the "Syad." Many were destroyed by the troops; some were taken prisoners and executed by sentence of drum-head court martial; whilst some remained in confinement. And thus a very dangerous scheme for the invasion of the British territory, by resolute, prompt, and determined measures, was frustrated. No more ingenious expedient, at that juncture, could possibly have been devised, and no effort of the sort was made again; but the "Syad" at a subsequent period twice presented himself at the frontier post of Mitchnee, and Abazaie, having so inconsiderable a force of mutineers, that he excited no uneasiness. These Sepoys of the 51st N.I. were afterwards heard of in great destitution at various places in the mountains.

The author issued a division order of the following nature on this occasion :—

"DIVISION ORDER.

"*Peshawur, 2nd September*, 1857.

"The recent outbreak, *en masse*, of the soldiers of the 51st N.I., in the cantonment of Peshawur, brings another corps on the list of those, who after years of gallantry and meritorious services, have basely revolted; and on no occasion have the resolute measures of the loyal forces of the Government been more conspicuous.

"Prompt and sure have been, and ever will be, the measures resorted to in the Peshawur district: mutineers and deserters will never escape the just penalties of their crimes; and let the occurrences of this day be 'solemn warnings' for the future."

At the mutiny of the 51st N.I., the conduct of the troops was most exemplary; the heat was excessive, and many valuable men died in the discharge of their duty:

The author, in tendering his thanks to the officers (civil and military) and the troops, expressed himself as follows, in Division Orders :—

"The best thanks of the Brigadier-General are especially due, and they are warmly given, to Brigadier Galloway, commanding the Peshawur district; Colonel Chute, of Her Majesty's 70th Regiment; and Lieutenant-Colonel Kyle, of Her Majesty's 27th Inniskillings, commanding wings of the Peshawur Brigade, as well as to the whole of the staff and regimental officers employed in a service of very considerable difficulty.

"The Brigadier-General readily, and with sincere pleasure, avails himself of the present opportunity to record in public orders the valuable services rendered to the State, and to himself, by Lieutenant-Colonel Edwardes, C.B., Commissioner of Peshawur. On the occasion of the outbreak of the 51st Regiment N.I., as on every previous occasion, during the great and lamentable mutiny of the native troops of the Bengal army, when energetic measures have been required and resorted to, this gallant and excellent officer has not only come forward with his personal assistance in the field, but has freely given the Brigadier-General his invaluable advice on most important subjects, when advice and assistance were so much needed. To be associated at such times as these with such an officer, is the Brigadier-General's good fortune.

"To that energetic officer, Captain James, Deputy Commissioner of Peshawur, the Brigadier-General offers his best thanks for his resolute and determined conduct in pursuit of the mutineers of the 51st Regiment N.I. On very many previous occasions has the

Brigadier-General experienced the benefit of Captain James's assistance. By that officer, frequently on the Peshawur frontier have the duties of the gallant soldier been ably combined with those of the civil officer."

It will be remembered that a letter conveyed by Seetul Misser, a Brahmin priest, from the 51st N.I., to the 64th N.I., in which the men of the latter corps were urged to join in a general rising of the native troops against the Europeans, was intercepted in May, 1857, at the outpost of Shubkudder, and that the seizure of this treasonable correspondence was followed by a general excitement and desertion of men of the 51st N.I. Seetul Misser, the author on that occasion, managed to abscond; but a few days previous to the mutiny of the corps, on the 28th August, he had been apprehended by the civil authorities in the streets of the city of Peshawur, was tried, and executed. This will therefore explain the cause of the 51st N.I. being a second time thrown into a state of excitement, and of its ultimate outbreak.

Perhaps it may be considered worthy of remark, that one of the principal objects which the author had in view (even when affairs were in the most gloomy condition) was to assume an appearance of perfect composure.

The bands of music played as usual on the parade grounds. The Mall was thronged with carriages, and the expected invasion by the Afghans with a rising of the hostile tribes of the border, were pooh-

poohed as impracticable. Whilst the chances of the mutineers attempting a general massacre of the Europeans (although prevailing in so very many other stations of the army) *was at Peshawur to be considered totally out of the question.*

Thus the minds of desponding persons were tranquillised, and even the mutinous Sepoys fell into the belief that the authorities must have good reasons for their self-confidence, or they would not display it.

The author attached great importance to this apparently innocent, although feigned demonstration; and certain it is, it had its beneficial effects; and here the author is proud in stating, that under the blessing of Divine Providence, throughout his severe struggles in the mutiny, not one European man, woman, or child, fell by the hands of the mutineers, excepting those who died in the discharge of their duties as soldiers.

Sir Colin Campbell, in writing of the author to the Duke of Cambridge, alluded to this, and so did Sir Hugh Rose.

The former states: "I assure your Royal Highness that Major-General Cotton has been placed in a most arduous position, and during the darkest period, he showed a *cheerfulness* and a *resource*, which had the most happy results for the service, and that it is impossible to reward him too highly." Whilst the latter, in a general order issued to the Bengal army, alluded to the *calm decision* with which Sir S. Cotton met disaffection, &c., &c., &c.

Statement showing the corps raised and organised in the Peshawur Division.

CORPS.	REMARKS.	BY WHOM RAISED OR ORGANISED.
4th Troop, 2nd Brigade, Horse Artillery	Re-organised with European Volunteers, from H.M. 24th, 27th, 70th, and 87th Regiments.	Major Vivian Cox, Bengal Artillery.
Peshawur Light Field Battery	Organised with European Gunners, and Drivers from Reserve Companies Foot Artillery.	Captain Stallard, Bengal Artillery.
Peshawur Light Horse	Organised with Volunteers from H.M. 27th, 70th, and 87th Regiments.	Captain Francis Fane, 87th Royal Irish Fusileers.
Peshawur Eurasian Corps	Organised with Christian Drummers from Native Infantry Regiments.	Captain Wood, 81st Regiment.
8th, 9th, 14th, 16th, 18th, and 19th Punjaub Infantry	By direction of the Chief Commissioner of the Punjaub, under the orders of Major General Sydney Cotton.	8th, Lieut. Brownlow, Bengal N.I.; 9th, Capt. Thelwell, 24th Foot; 14th, Maj. Shakespear, Beng. N.I.; 16th, Capt. Cave, Bengal N.I.; 18th, Capt. Bartlett, Bengal N.I.; 19th, Capt. Doran, Bengal N.I.

During the great struggle for the existence of the empire, it not only fell to the lot of the author successfully to guard against internal and external disasters, but to raise a small army of horse, foot, and artillery, under the exigencies of the State, to assist in the great work of restoring order throughout the country; and troops were raised, organised, and trained under the author's superintendence, as shown in the preceding statement; and here the author acknowledges with feelings of the greatest respect the able and generous assistance afforded to him in that matter by the Punjaub Government.

The author in the discharge of this very essential part of his duty was most ably assisted by the abovementioned officers, to whom the country is so much indebted.

The whole of these troops remain embodied to this day, with the exception of the Peshawur Light Horse, a corps of the greatest value for frontier service. Unhappily for the interests of the State, this corps was, at the expiration of the mutiny, ordered to be disbanded. The author strived all in his power to avert this sad and irretrievable loss. The corps consisted of two hundred European soldiers, obtained from the ranks of the three regiments of Infantry, serving in the Peshawur Division, and one hundred native cavalry, which were enrolled as part and parcel of the same corps. There can be no doubt now (because it has been proved in many instances) that an organisation of this nature is the very best that can be devised for the State security, because, whilst the climate of the Frontier is of that nature that Europeans cannot at all seasons of the year cover the foraging and grazing parties, the natives are ready for such duties, whilst there can be no possible risk in trusting with arms, of the very best quality, a body of natives, associated with Europeans as one to two.

It was urged at the time that the habits of Europeans were of that nature that they would lower themselves in the eyes of the natives, if brought so closely together. This is an entire mistake, the natives become exceedingly proud of the association, and the Europeans are pleased to have such valuable coadjutors. They work together in the most admirable manner. On parade the natives were placed as skirmishers, on the flanks of squadrons; and in quarters, although quite separate, they came together voluntarily in sports and amusements.

The author ascertained, during the mutiny, that natives of all castes, tendering their services to the British Government, would engage under *any* stipulations, and he arrived at the conclusion that caste prejudices, which had led to the destruction of the whole army of the country, were capable of being set aside altogether, had proper measures been resorted to, by allowing them to have separate rooms for sleeping and cooking in, and allowing them also to feed themselves.

In no instance would the author enlist a native,

who was not prepared to conform to all the necessary matters of military discipline ; and in consulting the most experienced officers of the native army, who had been for years engaged in raising and training recruits, he received the most complete and thorough confirmation of his views on the subject.

A total change in army enlistment ought to have followed on the breaking up of the old army, and perhaps such may have been the case, although many of the disarmed corps of the old army that had been disarmed for infidelity, were most injudiciously re-armed and continued in the service, an imprudent act, sufficient to sow the seeds of rebellion in the newly organised corps, and ruin the whole of them.

The author, to the utmost of his power and ability, opposed that measure, and he was supported in his views by Lord Clyde, the Commander-in-Chief of the army ; but the civil government, always working, no doubt, with the best intentions, failed in this, as it did generally in all military matters of importance.

In regard to the mode of worship of the natives, the author would no more interfere with them than he would with Roman Catholics, Jews, Turks, Infidels, and Heretics, amongst the European soldiery of the British army, if such were enrolled in it.

During the time that the British Frontier was in jeopardy the author anxiously applied himself to every matter connected with its security, by which the position could be strengthened.

For a time military authority was somewhat in the ascendant; and although not supreme, matters could be taken in hand by the author, which ordinarily could never even have been dreamt of; and whatever was done or could be done under military orders, the changes were only temporary, as no sooner were the terrors removed, than the little temporary power, enjoyed by the military authorities, was removed with them.

The author established two posts of considerable importance in and about cantonments, viz., Hurree Sing's Boorj, and the Mackeson post. He established a Land Transport Train, for the movement of troops; and of all the numerous changes and measures brought into play on the Peshawur frontier, during the great rebellion, the Land Transport Train has been in its operation the most successful, and will prove (it is to be hoped) the forerunner of an improved system of transporting troops throughout the country.

Runjeet Sing once said, speaking of English soldiers, "If I had troops of so much value and importance, they should never undergo fatigue; they should be brought to the field of action, and there let loose like bull-dogs, on their enemies, in all their vigour." A passport system (as before stated) was established, with a strict system of espionage. A frontier cavalry regiment had been raised, without which in time of trouble, the safety of the State could not have been secured. Public offices were established in a centrical position, in cantonments, for the ready and prompt discharge of public business; and other changes had been made too numerous to mention. Of all these essential works scarcely a vestige now remains. The public offices were in existence up to a recent date, but they are unsuited to Indian habits. Military life in quarters in the East is much too luxurious, Commanders and Staff transacting their business in their drawing-rooms, unmindful of the fatigue and exposure that others are put to by having to attend there.

A military force at Hurree Sing's Boorj would have been most essentially necessary at all times, as covering the front of Peshawur cantonment, although it certainly could avail but little whilst the civil power rules in all directions around it; but as soon as the mutiny was over, the post was occupied by a Thannadar, and twenty native police. The Land-Transport Train was worked by commissariat bullocks, and might have occasionally interfered with commissariat arrangements, so it was broken up. All matters of this sort, which are suggested or carried out by military officers *under the exigencies of the service* are sure to be defeated in India, either by the civil authorities or demi-military departments.

The author for years in vain urged on the consideration of Government the necessity for establishing a farm under military surveillance on the right bank of the "Jhelum" for rearing and breeding horses for military purposes, and for breeding horned cattle for draught and slaughter. The Government stud department had to be consulted, although the Viceroy of India (Lord Canning), seeing the imperative necessity for the measure, most warmly supported it. It was, however, an interference with a department; and so the interests of the State were lost sight of, and the object was never accomplished. The description of horse required for carrying dragoons and horse artillery was scarcely ever to be had, although the Punjaub might, by proper management, produce the finest cattle in the world; and, owing to the great expenditure of animal food by the European soldiery, beef and mutton were becoming very scarce. The author, therefore, persuaded Lord Canning that if left to himself he would supply his men's wants in both particulars. The old departments in India are the ruin of everything.

A company is now about to establish a breeding stud for horses and cattle on the right bank of the Jhelum, where, years ago, the author advised the Government to do precisely the same thing.

The "Mackeson" post commands several gates of the city of Peshawur, a city full of the most turbulent and restless characters. Two guns, nine pounders, were placed on an elevated plateau. The post is midway between the cantonment and the Balla Hissar, or Fort, and connects the two, which is essential. It also covers the Government elephants, camels, and bullocks of the force, which are always liable to injury by wicked and designing persons.

The carriage of the army in India being the cream and essence of everything. The Mackeson post was abolished after the mutiny was at an end.

And now a few words (in concluding the record of affairs connected with the mutiny of the native armies) as to the risk of life, and liability to assassination, as experienced by British officers who serve the Indian Government in the Trans-Indus territories. During the perilous times of the mutiny, the author several times had detected, or had been warned of, the contemplated assassination of himself. Three particular instances, which come home at this moment to his recollection, may be recorded.

On one occasion, during the night, an Afghan presented himself at his bedside, and in haste informed him, that he had just heard that a scheme had been concocted for murdering him on a road, where he was in the habit of riding about dawn of day in the discharge of his most anxious duties. The informant strongly advised him to change his plans for some days, and he took the hint. After events proved the accuracy of this warning. A captain of the 98th Regiment had some time previously been warned in like manner, but disregarded the caution, and was murdered when riding in company with a lady.

On another occasion, when inspecting some artillery horses in the middle of the day, an Afghan of suspicious appearance was observed with his arms folded across his breast approaching the author at his back;

and the author, having received a caution from a bystander, turned sharp round, when the Afghan hastily made off, and was pursued. He escaped, dropping a dagger as he fled.

On another occasion, a native officer of the mutinous 64th Regiment, then in the garrison disarmed, had offered the sum of 300 rupees for the author's head, which was overheard at night in the bazaar by a man, who warned him of what was going on. The native officer was quickly arrested, and did not deny the charge, but prayed for mercy. The author had him put in irons, but spared his life, not wishing that publicity should be given to such matters ; but he told the culprit that he was a fool for offering so large a sum for so worthless a commodity as his head, and added that it might be had for one quarter of that amount.

By day and by night at Peshawur, the risk of life is imminent, and it may well be believed that narrow escapes of a like nature must be frequent, although a few only come to light.

In winding up the affairs of the Great Indian Mutiny, many general officers, employed like the author in its suppression, were promoted over his head under an "army system," because it was stated they had been in "action" in the Hindostanee Provinces. Lord Clyde told the author, that he much regretted his absence from the campaigns in Central India, which had caused his supercession.

Would it be believed by those who have not

studied our "army systems" that, after all his risk and responsibility with the all-important services he had rendered to the Government in saving the Empire, *as acknowledged by Lord Canning,* the "army systems" can be of such a nature as to *necessitate* the sacrifice of the author in so extraordinary a manner.

CHAPTER XV.

Operations of the Peshawur Force on the Euzofzaie Border.—Remarks on the Satanah Expedition of 1858 under Major-General Sir Sydney Cotton, by the Author.

THE outbreak and mutiny of the 55th Native Infantry at Hoti Murdan has already been described, when, by the defection of the 10th Irregular Cavalry, the Sepoys of that corps, with arms in their hands, were permitted to escape into adjacent mountains on the Euzofzaie Border.

The mutineers made off towards the Swat country, and made a lodgment at Naringee, a place in the hills near the Swat Frontier, also to Satanah, a Hindostanee colony of Fanatics, in the hills near the Indus, and elsewhere. They were well received at all these places, the inhabitants being open and avowed enemies of the British Government, on which account only they were harboured.

Measures were taken as soon as convenient to follow up the runaways, and a force, in the first instance, was despatched by the author, under Major Vaughan, of the Kohât force, with the Deputy-Commissioner James in company, to destroy the rebels, and to punish the inhabitants of Naringee for having harboured them. Two attacks were made on Naringee. The first was only partially successful, and re-enforcements were sent by the author, of Riflemen of the 27th, 70th, and 87th Regiment of Foot, with two nine-pounder guns, and other light troops. A second attack was made, and the village of Naringee was finally carried. The enemy suffered severely, and amongst them were killed many of the Sepoys of the 55th Native Infantry.

It is well to dwell for a moment on such matters as these, because they tend to prove, amongst other things, the extreme difficulty of the author's position at Peshawur at the time of the great mutiny. In every direction, within a few miles around him, were rallying points for the mutinous Sepoys, strong-holds ready for their purpose, from which they might look down and defy our authority. But the summary punishments inflicted by the author on deserters, when they were endeavouring to escape into the mountains (together with the constant watchings) prevented them from passing away from the Peshawur district in masses to effect such very dangerous objects. It must be always remembered that there were ten thousand Hindostanee Sepoys at the outbreak of the mutiny in and about Peshawur.

The operations under Major Vaughan were completely successful, and the force was withdrawn.

The author issued the following Division Order on the occasion :—

"Division Order.

"*Peshawur*, 5th August, 1857.

"Brigadier-General Cotton, Commanding Peshawur Division, has received with much gratification, despatches from Major J. L. Vaughan, reporting the successful termination of the operations of the column placed under his orders on the Euzofzaie Border.

"2. The defeats of the enemy on the 21st of July, and again on the 3rd of August, have been most signal and complete.

"3. The village of Naringee has been totally destroyed, and its inhabitants have received a lesson which will be long remembered by the turbulent and restless tribes on the borders of the British Frontiers.

"4. Upwards of eighty of the enemy have fallen, amongst them some of the mutineers of the 55th Native Infantry, whilst the loss on the British side was one Naik and five Sepoys killed of the 4th, 5th, and 6th Punjaub Infantry.

"5. The Brigadier-General has much pleasure in tendering to Major Vaughan, the officers, non-commissioned officers, and soldiers, his best thanks for their services on these occasions, a favourable report of which will be forwarded to his Excellency the Commander-in-Chief; and he takes leave at the same time to offer to Captain James, Deputy-Commissioner, his best thanks for his valuable services and co-operation, the benefit of which he has so repeatedly felt in operations of a like nature in the Peshawur District."

Some months after the return of Major Vaughan's force, and when troops suited to the purpose were available, an expedition was again fitted out, and proceeded to the Euzofzaie border under the author's personal command. The mutineers of the 55th Native Infantry still remained in many parts of the hills, and were known to be with the Hindostanee Fanatics at Satana. The under-written despatches regarding these operations will be read with interest, and are transcribed in full, in order to be explicit, having been published at the time by the Government of India for general information.

Despatches regarding the Operations of the Force employed in the Euzofzaie border under the Command of Major General Sir Sydney Cotton, K.C.B.

"No. 184 of 1858—The Right Honourable the Governor General is pleased to direct the publication of the following despatch from the Deputy Adjutant General of the Army, No. 353 A, dated 27th May 1858, forwarding one from Major General Sir S. Cotton, K.C.B., Commanding the Peshawur Division, detailing the operations of the Force under his immediate command, recently employed on the Euzofzaie border.

"The Governor General fully appreciates the ability and judgment of Sir S. Cotton, in the conduct of the expedition, and it will afford his Lordship great satisfaction to bring to the favourable notice of the Home Authorities, the eminent merits of the Major-General, and the excellent services of the Officers and troops under his command.*

"R. J. H. Birch, Colonel,
"Secy. to the Govt. of India, Mily. Dept. with the Governor General.

"To Major H. W. Norman,
"Depy. Adjt. Genl. of the Army, Army Head Quarters."

* Of which the author never, to this moment, heard another word.

No. 353 A.

From the Depy. Adjt. General of the Army, to the Secy. to the Govt. of India.

"Military Department with the Governor General.

"SIR,—I am directed by the Commander-in-Chief, to transmit a Despatch dated the 6th instant, (received this day) from Major-General Sir Sydney Cotton, K.C.B., Commanding the Peshawur Division, detailing the operations of a Force under the Major-General's immediate command, recently employed on the Euzoffzaie border; and in submitting it to the Right Honourable the Governor General, I am to request you will draw the attention of His Lordship to the skill and judgment displayed by the Major-General in conducting the service, and in attaining the objects of the expedition.

"2. Sir Colin Campbell recommends the Officers and troops employed to the favourable notice of His Lordship.

"I have the honour to be, Sir, your most obedient servant,

"H. W. NORMAN, Major,

"Depy. Adjt. General of the Army."

Divisional Head Quarters.

"Camp Kubbul, 6th May, 1858.

"SIR,—In continuation of the report made by me to the Quarter-Master General of the Army, (copy of which is enclosed) announcing the assembly of a field force under my personal command, for service on the Euzoffzaie frontier; I have the honour to state for the information of his Excellency the Commander-in-Chief, that having been joined by the Commissioner, Lieutenant-Colonel Edwardes, C.B., the force marched from Nowshera on the 23rd ultimo.

"2. On the morning of the 25th ultimo, the force reached the Euzoffzaie frontier, village of Selim Khan (distant from Punjtar about five miles) and at the mouth of a Pass by which the Punjtar valley is entered.

"3. Reconnoitring parties, one under Captain Wright, Chief Staff Officer of the Force, and the other under Lieutenant-Colonel Edwardes, C.B., Commissioner, were at once sent forward, when it was found that the fortified town of Punjtar was only occupied by Mookurrab Khan, the Chief of the Khoodookheil tribe, with about sixty Sowars, the inhabitants having previously wholly evacuated the place.

"4. Mookurrab Khan, apparently under the impression that the reconnoitring parties were closely followed up by our Column, fled, leaving the town entirely unoccupied.

"5. It was now determined to enter the Punjtar District, on the following morning, the Force being told off for that purpose into three Columns, as shown in the margin, and making Selim Khan the "base" of operations, where our Camp remained standing, I proceeded in company with Lieutenant-Colonel Edwardes, with No. 1

No. 1 *Column.*

Arty.	2	9-pr. Guns.	of Capt. Stallards' Light Field Batry.
	2	24-pr. Howrs.	
	1	3-pr. Gun.	of the Peshawur Mt. Train Batry.
	1	12-pr. Howr.	
Cavy.	100	Sabres 7th Irregular Cavalry.	
	200	Do. Guide Cavalry.	
	30	Do. Peshawur Light Horse.	
Infantry.	100	Sappers under Captain Hyde.	
	260	Rank and File H.M. 98th under Major Peyton.	
	200	Do. 21st Rt. N. I. under Major Milne.	
	400	Do. 9th Punjaub Infantry under Captain Thelwall.	
	400	Do. 18th Punjaub Infantry under Lieutenant Williamson.	
	300	Do. Guide Infantry under Lieutenant Kennedy.	

Column, furnished with two days' provisions so as to enter the Punjtar District by the Durrund Pass; whilst Colonel Renny, H.M. 81st Regiment, proceeded in command of No. 2 Column, direct to Punjtar with orders to destroy that place; No. 3 Column, under Major Allan, H.M. 81st Regiment, remaining in charge of our standing Camp at Selim Khan.

No. 2 Column.

Cavalry. — 100 Sabres 18th Irregular Cavalry under Major Ryves.

INFANTRY.	47 Sappers under Lieutenant Tovey.
	200 Rank and File H.M. 81st under Captain Brown.
	200 Do. Kelat-i-Gilzie Regiment under Lieutenant Rowcroft.
	450 Do. 8th Punjaub Infantry under Lieutenant Brownlow.

No. 3 Column.

CAVY.	25 Sabres 7th Irregular Cavalry.
	25 Do. 18th "
	60 Do. Guide Cavalry.
INFANTRY.	105 H.M. 81st Regiment.
	10 Do. 98th "
	155 of 21st Regiment Native Infantry.
	254 Kelat-i-Gilzie Regiment.
	54 of 8th Punjaub Infantry.
	137 of 9th "
	185 of 18th "
	76 Guide Infantry.

"6. At one o'clock on the morning of 26th April, No. 1 Column under my command left Camp for Chinglee, and at daylight entered the Durrund Pass, which is a remarkably narrow defile of about two miles, between two hills. It is not formidable to disciplined troops, because the heights on either side have only to be crowned to cover the safe passage of the Force, and the length of the Pass is so limited, that if stoutly contested, it could not resist for more than a couple of hours. The enemy did well, therefore, to abandon it, and allow us to ascend unmolested into the elevated valley of Chinglee, or Upper Punjtar.

"7. It may be as well to record here, that there is a well of spring water in the Pass at the foot of the last steep.

"8. As soon as the column had reached the top of the Durrund Pass, it proceeded at once by the most direct route, towards the village of Chinglee, which is the chief place in the Punjtar country. Chinglee contains about one thousand houses very substantially built, and is an emporium for the wood trade with the plains of Eusuffzai. Here resided Moobarus Khan, uncle of Mookurrub Khan, of Punjtar, who had a substantial little fort of wood and stone. But no resistance was attempted. During the day it was observed that some of the village people, with their property, had endeavoured to secrete themselves in ravines in the mountain side, overlooking the town of Chinglee, and the 9th Punjaub Infantry, under Captain Thelwall, was ordered by a circuitous route to ascend the mountain, with a view to cutting off their retreat into the Chumla territory, whilst a party of the 98th Foot, under Captain Cotton, my Aide-de-Camp, proceeded straight up the hill to dislodge them from their position. A few shots only were however exchanged, and the enemy hastily escaped, leaving a few killed by the 9th Punjaub Infantry.

"During the day the troops were employed under the direction of Captain Hyde, Engineers, in destroying the fort, town, and crops, and at night were bivouacked on a ridge near Chinglee.

"9. On the 27th April, the force having completed its work at Chinglee, returned to Selim Khan, not by the Durrund Pass through which it came, but through the heart of the country by Swawai and Punjtar; for the importance of adding, on this expedition, to our knowledge of the independent hills, was not lost sight of. On the formation of the force, I attached Lieutenant Taylor, of the Engineers, a very able officer, to the staff of the field force, for the express purpose of making a survey of the country through which we passed. A copy of whose map I beg to forward with this report.

"10. The direct road by which we returned from Chinglee to Selim Khan, proved to be of about equal length with the road *viâ* the Durrund Pass, but there can be no question that the Durrund line is the easiest for an army. From Selim Khan to Chinglee *vid* Durrund, is an open plain, with one difficulty in it, *viz.*, the Pass itself, which can be soon surmounted. From Selim Khan to Chinglee, *vid* Punjtar, is chiefly through a broken country, winding among ups and downs of jungle and ravine, very embarrassing to a column, and at one point passing through a rocky defile called Turrulee (the bed of the stream which flows under Punjtar) which would be infinitely more formidable than the Durrund Pass, if disputed by the enemy.

"11. Mookurrub Khan's horsemen and footmen were seen lurking about our line of march this day, but apparently only in the hopes of preying on stragglers from the force. On our return to Punjtar, we found scarcely a vestige left of the five villages from which it took its name, so thoroughly had its demolition been completed by the troops of the 2nd column, employed under the direction of Lieut. Tovey, Assistant Field Engineer.

"12. We had now destroyed both Punjtar and Chinglee, and might have moved on to Suttana, but there was a stronghold in Mookurrub Khan's country, which he had made over to the Syuds and Hindostanees, and only resorted to it himself in the last extremity. The name of this place is Mungal Thanna. It stands on one of the chief spurs of the Mahuban mountain, and it was the Head Quarters of that Moulvie Enayut Allee, who so perseveringly endeavoured at Narinjee and other places, to raise Euzoffzaie in rebellion during 1857. This Moolvie died about the beginning of April 1858, and his followers were said to have gone off from Mungul Thanna to Suttana, to place themselves under another Hindostanee Moulvie there. But Mookurrub Khan's family and property were reported to have been removed for safety to the vacant fort of Moolvie Enayut Allee at

Mungul Thanna. It would therefore render the chastisement of the Khan more complete and memorable, if we could also destroy this last remaining fastness. By all accounts the road from Punjtar to Mungul Thanna was practicable, though difficult. The Totallye people were our allies, and would show us the road. The troops we had were well suited to such an expedition. I therefore fully concurred with Colonel Edwardes, C.B., in the expediency of attacking Mungul Thanna.

"13. On the 28th ultimo, the Force was again divided into three columns as noted below.* The 1st column to act against Mungul Thanna; the 2nd column to proceed and halt at Punjtar, as a support to the 1st column; and the 3rd column to remain in reserve at Selim Khan, and to protect the camp which was left standing.

"14. At eleven P.M. on 20th April, the 1st column, under my own personal command, left the camp at Selim Khan, and pushed on by moonlight towards Mungul Thanna. The ascent of the hills was very arduous and toilsome, and half the column was ultimately left as an intermediate support at Dhukara, which is midway between Punjtar and Mungul Thanna. The advance reached the height about eleven A.M.; not a shot had been fired at us, as we labored up the steep and wooded road, and on enter-

---

* ARTY.—*1st Column.*—2 Guns Mountain Train Battery; 2 24-pounder Howitzers of Captain Stallard's Light Field Battery.

INFY.—Sappers; 250 men of H. M. 81st Regt.; 8th P. Infantry; 18th do.; Kelat-i-Gilzie Regt.; Guide Infantry.

INFY.—*2nd Column.*—260 men H. M.'s 98th; 450 men 9th Punjaub Infantry; Cavalry, 250 Guide.

ARTY.—*3rd Column.*—2 9-pounder Guns.

CAVY.—125 Sabres 7th Irr. Cavy.; 125 18th do.

INFY.—21st Regiment Native Infantry; Detachments of all Corps over the Regimental Baggage.

ing Mungul Thanna we found the fort abandoned, and every sign of a hasty and recent flight.

"15. Mungul Thanna consists of two villages, upper and lower. The lower contains thirty or forty houses, and is occupied by Syuds, who are peaceable and inoffensive. Upper Mungul Thanna stands on a plateau, in the midst of three crests, which are themselves outworks while held by the Garrison, but as soon as carried by an enemy, command the place. On this plateau stood 1st, the fortified house of Enayut Allee, with enclosures for his Hindostanee followers; 2ndly, the fortified residence of Syud Abbas; and 3rdly, Syud Abbas's citadel, a white masonry tower, the whole having about thirty or forty houses clustered round them. These fortifications had been very laboriously constructed of large stones and fine timber; and the Hindostanee fanatics, and thieves who flocked around Syud Abbas, must have lived here in great enjoyment and security, and it was easy to understand the prestige that surrounded them.

"16. The advanced troops bivouacked at Mungul Thanna for the night; the Sappers being engaged all night under Captain Hyde's instructions in mining the buildings. At daylight of 30th April, the troops being drawn off, the mines were fired, and when the dust and smoke cleared away, Mungul Thanna existed no longer.

"17. Mungul Thanna is probably between five and six thousand feet above the level of the sea. The trees grow thickly about it, and the scenery about it is much like that of Murree.

"18. It would be possible to cross Mahabun from this point and descend upon Sattana in two marches; but all accounts agree that the road is more difficult even than that to Mungul Thanna.

"19. On the 30th April, the whole of the troops

at Mungul Thanna, Dhukara, and Punjtar, returned to their Camp at Selim Khan, and there halted on the 1st May.

"20. It now only remained to deal with the fanatic colony of Suttana, for which purpose the force under my command proceeded towards Kubbul, distant from Sattana about four miles. The Force encamped at Kubbul on the morning of 3rd May.

"21. By previous arrangements, Major Becher, the Deputy Commissioner of Hazara, moved down simultaneously to the left bank of the Indus with the troops as per margin, with a view to crossing the river so as to co-operate with the Force under my command, in making a general attack on the enemy's villages at Sattana and on their Ghurree or defensive enclosure near the village of Mundee.

2 12-pdr Htzs. } Hazara mountain
1 3-pdr. gun. } Train.
300 of 2nd Seikhs.
450 of 6th Punjab Infantry.
300 of 12th do.

"22. Having on the evening of the 3rd of May, reconnoitered the hills and towns of the enemy, and fixed on the following morning to make the general attack, Major Becher with his troops crossed the Indus early in the day, whilst the Force under my command, marched out of its encampment at Kubbul towards the enemy's position, thus coming upon him from the eastward and southward simultaneously; the Chief of the Umb territory, Jehandad Khan, our ally, having occupied the hills northward of Upper Sattana, and by so doing completed the general co-operation.

"23. As we approached the Lower Sattana, the Columns of skirmishers detached as per margin, were directed to crown and hold the heights above the several villages of the enemy. These with other troops, hereafter mentioned, moved up the mountain, at no less than six different points.

150 H.M. 98th.
400 of 9th P. I.
300 of 18th P. I.

"24. During the progress of these troops up the steep and rugged sides of the mountain, I proceeded with Lieutenant-Colonel Edwardes, C.B., towards Upper Sattana, and was there joined by Major Becher, with the 6th Punjab Infantry under Lieutenant Quin, and 2nd Seikhs under Captain Harding, who had just crossed the river.

"These Corps, with the Guide Infantry under Lieutenant Kennedy, proceeded to assist in holding the heights above the town. The Sappers and Miners, under Captain Hyde of the Engineers, were set to work to destroy all the towns. A wing of Her Majesty's 81st Regiment under Colonel Renny was, during these operations, placed in the town of Upper Sattana.

"I could, from this spot, observe the several Columns on the hills, and was enabled from thence to direct the operations generally.

"25. The 18th Punjab Infantry under Lieutenant Williamson having, without opposition, succeeded in reaching the crest of the mountain above Lower Sattana, and having moved northward along the same, and also on a pathway on the side of the mountain in two Divisions, came in contact with the enemy (the fanatics) on the height called Shah Noorke Lurree, where they were strongly posted in a small village, and in a stockade, which position was very desperately defended. Lieutenant Williamson and his gallant corps, the 18th Punjab Infantry, drove the enemy from this height, having killed thirty-six on the hill top, and wounded many more. Lieutenant Vander Gucht of that corps, was wounded in a hand-to-hand encounter, in the thigh ; a Subadar and four Sepoys being killed, and fifteen wounded. The 18th Punjab Infantry for the first time in action with the enemy since being embodied, thus highly distinguished itself under its gallant commander, Lieutenant Williamson, who reports most favourably on the spirited conduct of the European Officers of his corps, *viz.*, Lieutenant Vander Gucht, Lieutenant O'Malley, and Lieutenant Green, H.M. 70th Regiment, temporarily attached to the corps. The 9th Punjab Infantry, under Captain Thelwall, ably supported the attack of the 18th Punjab Infantry, on the enemy's position. The 6th Punjab Infantry under Lieutenant Quin, having ascended the northern spur of the range, took the enemy's position in rear, and thus co-operating with the 18th Punjab Infantry, drove the Hindostanee fanatics towards the latter regiment. The conduct of this regiment under Lieutenant Quin was also admirable. The attack was unhesitating and vigorous, and speedily completed the defection of the enemy. The detachments of H.M. 98th Regiment under Major Peyton; 2nd Seikhs under Captain Harding; also Captain Brougham's Mountain Train Battery, which had several opportunities of making very successful practice in the various positions of the enemy, were all most useful, and efficiently performed the duties allotted to them, respectively, during the operations.

"26. The position of the enemy having been carried at all points, the fanatics were compelled to retreat precipitately in the hills with very severe loss; and the whole of their villages being destroyed, the Commissioner, Colonel Edwardes, C.B., considered that adequate punishment had been inflicted on them, and called upon me to withdraw the troops, *not deeming it expedient* to raise against the British Government, by further pursuit of the enemy into the hills, the Judoon and other independent hill tribes who had naturally become excited by the presence of so large a British Force in and amongst their mountains.

"27. In the general withdrawal of the troops, the detachments of H.M. 98th under Major Peyton, and

Guide Infantry under Lieutenant Kennedy, rendered excellent service in covering the retirement, in presence of the hill tribes, who during the day had assembled in considerable number, and had assumed a threatening attitude on the surrounding heights. And here the practice of the Enfield rifles of the 98th Regiment was most effective, leaving, I am informed, a lasting impression on the minds of the hill people as to the vast superiority of this weapon over their own matchlocks.

"28. The hill tribes with some few of the Hindostanee fanatics, having closely followed up the troops during their descent from the hills, I employed with very great advantage two 5½-inch mortars under Captain Stallard to assist in covering the retirement of the troops. The practice of these mortars was very effective, and thoroughly arrested the further progress of the enemy.

"29. The whole of the Force, it being late in the day, returned to camp, and on the following morning, 5th May, on the requisition of the Commissioner, marched to Kubbul.

"30. These operations having been so completely successful, enabled the civil authorities to come to a most satisfactory settlement with the Judoon tribes, whose Chiefs ratified a treaty, by which they were bound to expel from their territories any of the remaining Hindostanee fanatics who attempted to re-establish themselves among them ; as also to protect the allies of the British Government, *viz.*, the inhabitants of the villages of Kyr and Kubbul, and Jehandad Khan, the chief of Umb, who had rendered us great and valuable assistance during the above operations..

"31. Lieutenant-Colonel Edwardes, C.B., having notified to me that the objects of the campaign having been fully attained, and that the services of the troops were no longer required, I forthwith directed the return of the Force to Nowshera, where on arrival, the troops will be sent to their respective quarters.

"32. It now becomes my pleasing duty to record for the information of His Excellency the Commander-in-Chief, and of Government, my acknowledgment of the valuable services rendered by the various Civil and Military Officers who have accompanied the Force under my command.

"I am deeply indebted to Lieutenant-Colonel Edwardes, C.B., Commissioner of Peshawur, for his very able co-operation and advice which have enabled me to bring the operations of this short campaign to such a satisfactory termination. I beg specially to recommend this officer's most important services to the favourable consideration of His Excellency the Commander-in-Chief, and Government.

"I also desire to bring to notice the excellent service performed by Major Becher, Deputy Commissioner of Hazara, who commanded the Hazara Field Force during the recent action at Sattana. The disposition made by Major Becher of his troops was indeed admirable, and contributed, in no small degree, to the success of the general attack made on the enemy's position. My warmest thanks are due to Major Becher for the very able manner in which he commanded the Hazara Force in the operations against Sattana.

"To Colonel Renny, H.M. 81st, who commanded the 1st Brigade; and to Major Allan, H.M. 81st, who commanded the 2nd Brigade of Infantry; to Lieutenant-Colonel Mulcaster, 7th Irregular Cavalry, who commanded the Cavalry Force in camp: and to Captain Brougham who commanded the Artillery, my cordial thanks are particularly due for the able and energetic support they rendered me in their respective commands.

"To the Regimental Commanders, Major Peyton, commanding Detachment H.M. 98th; Captain Brown, commanding H.M. 81st; Captain Stallard, commanding Light Field Battery; Captain Pulman, in charge of the mortars; Lieutenant Butt, commanding Hazara Mountain Train Battery; Lieutenant Cordner, commanding Detachment Peshawur Mountain Train Battery; Major Ryves, commanding Detachment 18th I. C.; Major Milne, and subsequently, on that officer's illness, Lieutenant Brown, commanding Head Quarter Detachment 21st Regiment N. I.; Lieutenant Rowcroft, commanding Head Quarter Detachment Kelat-i-Gilzie Regiment; Lieutenant Quin, Lieutenant Browlow, Captain Thelwall, Captain Blagrave, and Lieutenant Williamson, commanding respectively 6th, 8th, 12th, and 18th Punjab Infantry; Lieutenant Kennedy, commanding Corps of Guides; Lieutenant Lockwood, commanding Detachment of Peshawur Light Horse; I have to offer my best thanks for the efficient manner in which they commanded their respective Corps: the same are due to the officers and men of the whole Force, whose excellent conduct and discipline in the Field deserve my most unqualified approbation.

"To the Engineer Officers, Captain Hyde, commanding Detachment of Sappers and Miners, Lieutenant Tovey, H.M. 24th Regiment, Assistant Engineer, Peshawur, doing duty with the same; Lieutenant Henderson, and Lieutenant Taylor, whose valuable survey of the country through which the Force proceeded is herewith forwarded, I feel particularly indebted for the ability and zeal which they have displayed in the performance of their professional duties.

"I beg to return my best thanks to the Staff Officers of the Force, Captain Wright, Deputy Assistant Adjutant-General, Chief Staff Officer of the

Force; Lieutenant Greaves, H.M. 70th Regiment, who acted as Deputy Assistant Adjutant-General to the Field Force; Captain Cooper, Deputy Assistant Quarter-Master General; Lieutenant Whigham, Adjutant Peshawur Light Horse, who officiated in the Quarter-Master General's Department; Captain Jones, Deputy Judge Advocate General; Captain L. S. Cotton, my Aide-de-Camp; Captain Fane, Peshawur Light Horse, my Orderly Officer; Captain Tonnochy, H.M. 81st Regiment, and Captain Ellerman, H.M. 98th Regiment, who officiated as Brigade Majors to the 1st and 2nd Infantry Brigades respectively; Lieutenant Tierney, Staff Officer of Artillery; Lieutenant Osborne, 7th Irregular Cavalry, Staff Officer of Cavalry; Lieutenant White, 12th Punjab Infantry, Staff Officer to the Hazara Field Force under Major Becher; all of whom performed the Staff duties of the Force with much zeal and efficiency.

"To Surgeon Mann, 5th Light Cavalry, who accompanied the Force as Field Surgeon, my especial obligations are due for the skilful arrangements made by him for the care and comfort of the sick and wounded.

"I have also to state, that Mr. Sub-conductor Cooper conducted the duties of the Commissariat Department much to my satisfaction.

"33. In conclusion I beg to submit for the information of His Excellency the Commander-in-Chief, and of Government, a map of the country in which the operations above detailed have taken place; and also a return showing the number of casualties in the Field Force in the action of Suttana.

"I have the honour to be,

"Sir, your most obedient Servant,

(Signed) "SYDNEY COTTON, Major General,

"Commanding Peshawur Division.

P. S.—I have the honour to annex, for submission

to his Excellency, the Commander-in-Chief, a copy of an Order which I issued to the Field Force before breaking it up, and which was called for by the excellent conduct of the whole of the troops during the period they were in the Field.

"DETAIL OF THE FIELD FORCE.

"*Artillery.*

"2 24-Pounder Howitzers.
"2 9 " Guns.
"2 12 " Howitzers.
"2 3 " Guns.

"*Cavalry.*

"125 Sabres 7th Irregular Cavalry.
"125 " 18th "

"*Sappers.*

"100 Sappers of 5th and 6th Companies.

"*Infantry.*

"250 Rank and File with Head Quarters and Band H.M. 81st Regiment.
"250 Ditto H.M. 98th Regiment.
"400 Ditto with Band 21st Regiment N.I.
"400 Ditto Kelat-i-Gilzie Regiment.
"450 Ditto 6th Punjaub Infantry.
"450 Ditto 8th ditto.
"450 Ditto 9th ditto.
"450 Ditto 18th ditto.

"*Guide Corps.*

"250 Cavalry.
"350 Infantry.

"T. WRIGHT, *Captain*,
"Deputy Assistant Adjutant-General.

"*Extract from Division Orders issued by Major-General Sir Sydney Cotton, K.C.B. Commanding.*

"DIVISION HEAD QUARTERS:

"Camp Yar Hossain, 13th May, 1858.

"No. 272.—The services of the Force under the command of Major-General Sir Sydney Cotton, K.C.B., being no longer required in the district, the troops will return to their quarters under orders, which will be communicated to corps respectively.

"In bidding adieu to the officers, non-commissioned officers and soldiers, European and Native, of this highly-disciplined Column, the Major-General offers to all his unqualified thanks for the ready and cheerful obedience to his wishes in the discharge of duties frequently under difficult and trying circumstances of fatigue and exposure.

"To the orderly and steady conduct of the soldiers, mainly, must be attributed their efficiency for work, and healthiness in a very considerable heat of climate; the absence of crime in this Force has been most remarkable, and when an enemy had to be encountered, the troops displayed their wonted gallantry.

"The Force now returns to its quarters under the assurance of Lieutenant-Colonel Edwardes, C.B., Commissioner (to whom the Major-General offers his best thanks for his very valuable co-operation at all times), that the objects of Government in assembling it, have been most fully and satisfactorily accomplished. Taking ample guarantees for the future from the border tribes, the Euzoffzaie district has now been placed in an unprecedented state of security; and it is gratifying to think that whilst this all-important object has been gained by the chastisement of the real enemies of the British Government, the well disposed and inoffensive have, by a wise discrimination on the part of the civil authorities, been permitted to remain in the undisturbed enjoyment of their ancient rights and privileges.

"True Extract.

"T. WRIGHT, *Captain*,

"Deputy Assistant Adjutant-General."

It will be observed, by reference to the author's despatch, detailing his operations on the Euzoffzaie Border in 1858, that the Commissioner (under whose political instructions the force carried into effect the object of the Government against the Hindostanee Fanatics) had considered that adequate punishment had been inflicted on them, and had called upon the author to "withdraw the force, *not deeming it expedient* to raise against the British Government, by further pursuit of the enemy into the hills, the Judoon and other independent hill tribes, who had naturally become excited at the presence of so large a British force in and amongst the mountains;" and the author, in his farewell order to the troops, expressed himself as follows:—

"It is gratifying to think, that whilst the all-important object has been gained *by the chastisement of the real enemies of the British Government*, the well-disposed and inoffensive have, by a wise discrimination *on the part of the civil authorities*, been permitted to remain in the undisturbed enjoyment of their ancient rights and privileges."

The main object, then, of the Government, it would appear, was the punishment of the Fanatics, who had committed depredations on the British territory, and at the same time studiously to avoid collision with the hill tribes, amongst which they had settled themselves. In conducting an operation of this nature, almost insuperable difficulties arise. On their hills being invaded, the tribes, of course, become excited, and if time be allowed to them, they congregate in vast numbers, and join together to rid the mountains of what they consider the common enemy. It is most difficult to persuade them, that a European force coming into their hills, can have any other object or intention than the permanent occupation of them. These tribes in most parts positively swarm.

The author, in publishing these memoirs, hopes that some benefit may be derived from his experience. He does not pretend to be infallible. Indeed it may be that his efforts in the mountains ought to be considered "solemn warnings" for the future; or otherwise, wholesome examples to those who come after. Be this as it may, the author strongly advocates in all hill operations "prompt and decisive measures." The assembly of large bodies of troops for the invasion of the hills, which necessarily causes delay, should be as much as possible avoided, and, generally speaking, numbers only create embarrassment. Protracted warfare in the mountains has been proved to be fatal to success, in matters where simple chastisement for sins committed is required.

The proper mode of punishing the hill tribes, and that which is attended with the least risk, is to go in upon them suddenly and unexpectedly, without affording them time to assemble, or otherwise make preparation; for, be it remembered, no preparations in the plains can be accomplished without observation.

There is a sporting phrase which is very applicable to this description of mountain warfare, "In and out clever." Now this "in and out clever" means nothing more or less, than a dash into the hills and out again. Some are of opinion that such a system cannot be sufficiently effective, but no one can fail to observe that the difficulties of all hill operations infallibly increase *by dwelling on them*, and much can be done by sharp practice. Besides which, it would be better to repeat the dose, if really necessary, than to try and work out a series of operations in mountains.

The grand object of all, however, should be, not to allow our grievances to accumulate; but, unhappily, the prevailing system is just the reverse, and we postpone chastisement, owing to the feeling that exists, that these "petty wars" (as they are termed) are not approved of by the *home authorities*, who really do not understand the matter.

A carte blanche given to the Commander of the Frontier force, to act at once, and on his own responsibility, would remove all difficulties; and the tribes, knowing the certain consequences of their transgressions, would cease to transgress. When these depredations can no longer be submitted to, an appeal is made (as the system is at present) to a distant authority, who cannot realise in his mind the nature or the necessities of the occasion, and he hesitates until the proper time of action is lost.

On the expedition under the author's command in 1858, on the Euzofzaie Frontier, a circumstance occurred, which may be considered well worthy of note.

It became an object of political necessity to destroy a small fort on the summit of one of the spurs of the Mahabund Mountain. To Mungletāna, which was the name of the fort, was attached very great importance by the hill tribes; it was, in fact, the pride of the hills, and considered beyond the reach of foreigners; indeed, it is so imbedded in mountain fastnesses as to be almost inaccessible. At all events, such was the prestige attached to the place that no scheme could more effectually have been resorted to, to take the pride out of the tribes, than we had in view, when destroying it.

The troops, by a sudden and unexpected movement, reached Mungletāna (six thousand feet above the sea level) without opposition, and blew the fort to atoms. It was a night march, and the troops entered the hills after dark in the evening, without being observed. A pretended movement in another direction had caused a diversion, and after a march of sixteen hours by narrow mountain tracks, and of very steep acclivity, a small portion only of the force, with the author and his staff, succeeded in getting to Mungletāna, having left, *en route* in support, detachments at various points, to keep open communication with the plains. Everywhere, the hasty retreat of the hill tribes was noticed—pipes alight, and cooking pots on the fires, &c. No British soldier had ever before ascended this spur of the mountain, nor yet European, since the time of Alexander the Great, who is said to have rested his troops on the Mahabund mountains, in a cool climate, after the fatigues of his long campaigns. It was considered too difficult and dangerous for any one to venture there, but in this instance the object was accomplished by the sudden nature of the movement, although every inch of ground might have been disputed had sufficient warning been given.

A glance at the map, and reference to the despatches will have explained to the reader all the circumstances connected with this movement, and it will be seen that having once got to the summit of the mountain, with the enemy's position at Satanah, near its foot (whither the force was bound), the natural course would have been to have made a descent at once, rather than withdraw from the hills, and attack him by an ascent from the plains. The native guides, however, considered it impracticable, being of opinion that the mountaineers, having been thus aroused, and the hills being extremely difficult, they might dispute the ground, inch by inch, when severe losses must have been sustained, and perhaps a disaster; such is the difficulty of warfare in these mountains. To have taken the enemy in his rear, and not in his front (as was done) would have been of the utmost importance, but it could not be accomplished. To attack the enemy in his rear, and so cut off his retreat, *the author supposes, must have been the object of the movement of the British troops up the Umbeylah Pass, in* 1863.

It is by no means the intention of the author to offer any comments on that expedition, unfavourable to the very distinguished commander, who, with a large and powerful army, within the same range of hills, found himself involved in great and almost insuperable difficulties. No officer in the British army could have accomplished more than was done, but the Punjaub government, usually alive to the danger of hill complications, must, in that instance, have sadly miscalculated the nature of the service, or otherwise their troops would never have been placed in a false position of such unprecedented difficulty. And, after all, as regards the Hindostanee Fanatics, perhaps little or no more was done then *towards their final extinction*, than was done in the year 1858; the nucleus of future mischief, no doubt, remains as it did before.

The real cause of the re-establishment of the colony of Hindostanee Fanatics, which necessitated the movement, in 1863, has yet to be explained, and with that, the author is thoroughly acquainted. It was entirely owing to want of precautionary measures in the Punjaub, and at the crossings of the great rivers, more especially of the river Indus. During the rebellion, with the concurrence of the Commissioner of Peshawur, a passport system was introduced by the author, and nothing could cross the Indus without observation. A system of espionage, as before stated, also prevailed. No sooner was the great mutiny disposed of, than these wholesome restrictions were taken off by the Punjaub Government, and the road was thereby thrown open to the Trans-Indus mountains, from Hindostan.

Taking advantage of this, our disaffected subjects in the provinces, sent money, munitions of war, and men, to re-establish this fanatical colony, at Satānah, for the avowed object of disturbing our frontier. No doubt the nucleus of a fanatical colony was already in the hills, but it does not appear that at first they took possession of Satānah. They fixed themselves on a spot further in the hills, where they were less liable to interruption, but, as they increased in strength, they became bolder, and then in defiance of all power, they re-occupied Satānah. The author very early in this re-assembling of the Fanatics, received private intelligence of what was going on; and sent off spies to the Mahabund, to learn all particulars. The information given was apparently most correct, and it was stated that the colony was daily increasing in numbers from Hindostan, and also in power. A native, in whom the author had confidence, assured him that if measures were not speedily adopted, the Hindostanee colony would become a thorn in the side of the British Government, that it could not easily get rid of; and the neighbouring tribes, if the Fanatics gained strength enough, would be sure to espouse their cause.

No time was, therefore, to be lost, and the author implored of the authorities to permit him to take a small force, and (by a surprise, as before,) go in upon them. The Government of the Punjaub, the author believes, was fully as anxious as he was to carry into effect his proposal, but it was necessary to refer the matter to still higher powers, and so the golden opportunity was lost.

The author asserts, that had he been left to himself, he would have undertaken, at that time, with a force of fifteen hundred men (well selected for the purpose) to have put an extinguisher on this Hindostanee colony, and it will not fail to be recollected by those who knew anything of the matter, that it took at least nearly as many thousands, *with great risk even to the empire itself*, and the expenditure of an enormous amount of money.

Now mark the consequences of official references in matters of this nature. This is another proof, if proof be wanting, that the "instant action" of the troops can alone maintain the dignity and security of our empire in India. The expedition, in 1863, cost the country twenty-seven officers, killed and wounded, and seven hundred and thirty-one men, killed and wounded. It is quite necessary to remember, besides, that this Umbeylah Pass business was of much more importance to the empire at large, than would have appeared to the high authorities at a distance.

The Frontier forces of the British Government are so much mixed up by consanguinity, and otherwise, with the hill and border tribes, that, although they fight, and even with desperation, in our cause, against their own relations and friends as long as success attends our movements, they might get dispirited by reverses, and no doubt would ultimately abandon our cause, altogether, if they once discovered it to be a bad one. This was proved at Peshawur, at the outbreak of the great mutiny in 1857, when the border tribes, to a man, kept aloof from us (as before described) until, by disarming the Hindostanee garrison, we had proved ourselves to be master of them. We must ever bear in recollection that it is by upholding our name and our prestige in such countries that we can alone retain our position, and it has already been shown, in various instances, that when we least expect it, we may find ourselves on the very brink of destruction. Nothing can be more dangerous to our empire than that European troops should be seen rushing forward in haste, through our provinces, to a vital point, or even to a point in which danger is apprehended (as was the case in 1863), abandoning their usual garrisons, and causing excitement from one end of the empire to the other.

News of that kind is not slow in travelling, and it is quite on the cards, for the independent states (the Mahommedan Governments in particular) to take advantage of our perplexity, and break out when we are engaged in complications at a distance. There is not a body of men in India, except it may be the Parsees of Bombay and the Eurasians, who would not gladly join against us if there really was a fair prospect of success. This the author asserts, whatever may be said or thought to the contrary.

There is another very important feature in the case, which must not be overlooked, and that is the part that the Afghans would take in our hill complications, if, at any time, they became desperate. It has been clearly shown that we have subjects in Hindostan, who are disposed to wage war, or support a war, against us, in the Afghan mountains, and are quite capable of involving us in most serious difficulties in those quarters. The uncertainty of our Frontier forces, too, has been hinted at, and it has been seen also, that the tribes of the border throughout would assist in a general rising. Nothing would be more satisfactory to the restless tribes of Afghanistan and Central Asia, than to find us involved in serious difficulties *in the hills.* No battle-fields could be better suited to their purpose than the mountains, nor worse suited to Europeans. Europeans could not subsist in those hills nor could supplies be very readily afforded to them. Honestly speaking, Europeans are not a match for these demi-savages on their own ground. There is no fear of their coming down to fight us in the plains.

These difficulties of the Afghan mountains have given some people the idea that we ought to make the Indus our frontier, and so avoid altogether collision with them. Having once taken possession of the Peshawur valley, and having occupied it so long, it would be highly imprudent to make a retrograde movement, which, to the natives of India, would appear as an indication of weakness, a loss of prestige in fact. Besides which, if we abandoned the Peshawur district, it would become the cock-pit *of all the restless and unruly spirits of Central Asia*, and the Indus would be no effectual barrier. We should certainly be in a much more unsettled position than we are at present, with less means of defending ourselves, because, at certain seasons of the year, the river Indus is low enough to be almost or quite fordable in many places, and runs as leisurely as the Thames, at Richmond.

Our only scheme, therefore, is to hold on to what we have got, show a bold front, summarily punish those who presume to trespass upon us, and place the frontier in the hands of an active and an intelligent officer, *with full powers* to act as occasion might require on sudden emergency ; avoid, as much as possible, hill complications ; keep the passages of the Indus strictly guarded ; and the great thoroughfares of the country under military instead of civil control.

If it be worth while, it may be asked what were the police of the Punjaub about at the passages of the Chenab, Jhelum, Sutlej, Ravi, and Indus, when these Hindostanee people were steadily working their way up to the mountains with arms, ammunition, and money, in the years 1860, 1861, and 1862?

The author was frequently warned by the natives ere he left the North-West Frontier of India, that a general rising in the hills was contemplated, and his informant generally added, "It will not be set about before you leave the border;" and such proved to be the case. The author repeats this because it is *worthy of deep consideration.*

The intrusion of the Hindostanee fanatics, and their insolence towards us up to 1862 and 1863, which was the more immediate cause of the expedition being formed and sent into the Umbeylah Pass, arose entirely out of the disinclination that was shown by our Government, at first, to extinguish the colony. Having the Swatees behind them goading them on, as they are wont to do, the Bonairs and other tribes joined in the war; and had not the war terminated when it did, it is the author's firm belief that *all the hill tribes* would have risen, and would have been assisted by the restless spirits of Afghanistan. Well indeed was it for us that the war terminated when it did, for had the advice given to withdraw the force at the time, and re-commence hostilities in the mountains in the spring of 1864 been heeded, in all likelihood we should have heard of much more serious disasters all over the empire, than that which occurred in the Umbeylah Pass.

CHAPTER XVI.

March of an expeditionary Force into Hazara.—Disaffection of the European Troops of the late East India Company in Bengal. —The breaking-up of that splendid, and highly efficient force, which had performed services of incalculable benefit to the State, in all the wars of the Indian Empire.

WHEN it became safe and convenient for the author to quit for a time the all-important charge that had been allotted to him during the great struggles of 1857 and 1858, he commenced a tour through his district, as a convincing proof that our affairs on the border were no longer desperate.

On hearing that such was the author's intention, the Punjaub Government requested him to take a small force of horse and foot into the Hazara country. The Chiefs in that part had evinced towards the Government a feeling quite inconsistent with the respect that had been customary, under the impression that the British Government was tottering, or had come to an end. High-minded, and for ages thoroughly independent, these chieftains anxiously caught at the prospect (as was the case all over the country) of ridding themselves of the common enemy. The fall of Delhi, the turning point of the whole affair, had not served to convince the Hazara people that the British authority was about to be restored, simply because they could not bring themselves to believe that the troops of the King of Delhi had been forced into submission. In fact they had made up their minds not to believe it.

The author's visit to Hazara was intended therefore to be nothing more than a demonstration ; but still there can be no certainty in such matters as these, and the author's force was in readiness to act if necessary. The order then given, on entering the Hazara mountains, was, "Keep your powder dry, and your cutlery in working order."

In order to make the demonstration as suitable to the occasion as possible, the Peshawur Light Horse, and a detachment of the 87th Royal Irish Fusileers were selected, and formed part of the force. No European soldier had ever before been in the mountainous regions of Hazara, and the author was resolved that the people of that country should have a good opportunity of seeing the Majesty of England well represented, and in all its glory, although on a small scale.

To those military readers who knew the 87th about ten or twelve years ago, it will be unnecessary to explain the gigantic stature of the men, and the author considered, that when proceeding into such a country with such an object, that it was as well to let the people see a good specimen of the stuff of which the British army was composed. Sanction had been obtained from the Government to clothe all European soldiers on the frontier in a drab-coloured dress. For night duties in winter, these dresses are stuffed with cotton, and wadded all over. The appearance of the men of the 87th in their wadded jackets, was quite extraordinary. They had the appearance of giants, and everywhere they were looked upon by the mountaineers with reverential awe. This no doubt was of much benefit to the cause, as the people were repeatedly heard to say, that with such men, it was no wonder England could maintain, or recover its supremacy, indeed it was generally considered that these gigantic men of the 87th were only sent abroad in times of extreme trouble, as they had never seen the like of them before.

The march into Hazara was exceedingly interesting; it was not very likely that the author and his comrades would gain much by it in a military point of view; but still it was quite possible, although not very probable, that something might be done.

On the morning of the day, when the author crossed the Indus from Euzofzaie into Hazara, (notice having been given to the people of his approach), one of the leading chiefs of that part of the country was on the left bank of the Indus ready to receive him. A fine-looking country gentleman greeted him, with his two sons, nearly grown up, well mounted, and superbly dressed. They were accompanied by a strong escort of horsemen in chain armour, grim-looking devils, looking the very essence of defiance. The Hazara country is singularly beautiful, well watered, and mountainous, with highly cultivated plains intervening. A feudal system prevails throughout the country, which is subdivided into small principalities. The nobility of the country, extremely proud of their family antiquity, are thoroughly gentleman-like. It is really surprising to find in any part of Central Asia a state of things which so closely resembles that which we read of in days of yore of our own country, and certainly we cannot boast of greater family antiquity than is to be found in Hazara. The chiefs boast of their territories having been handed down to them from generation to generation in their primitive state with regal dignity.

On a plot of green grass not far from the Indus, (the great parent of streams as it is called) this Hazara noble had prepared a breakfast for the author and those with him. In company was a lady, the daughter-in-law of the author, and on this, as on many previous occasions, this lady's appearance served to tranquillise the minds of the chiefs, who are never certain (say or do as you will) that mischief is not brewing when British swords and bayonets are glistening about them.

The breakfast was in the rudest form, and near the charpoy (or couch) on which it was placed, was a cow to supply milk of undisputable freshness. The greeting had been demi-Asiatic, and demi-English, no cringing manner, no Asiatic affectation of servility, but a noble deportment on the part of the chief and his sons, which was well adapted to European society. The elephants, looking like porpoises in the ocean, were seen swimming the Indus in all their glory, whilst the company were pretending to eat their breakfast, as nothing could well be less pleasing to Europeans, than Asiatic gastronomy. In due course of time, . the howdahs being replaced on the elephants, and the author, with the Chiefs and escorts, being mounted, the cavalcade proceeded onwards towards Abbotabad, the newly-established head quarters of the British civil and military authorities in Hazara, a small post with a regiment or two of Sepoys. The establishment of this post had caused some uneasiness amongst the noblemen of the country, as it was the small end of the wedge that had been there inserted. The party had not proceeded many miles, when the author stopped short, and addressing himself to the Chief, exclaimed, "What a lovely spot! How I wish I could build a house here, and live in it for ever!" "Oh," said the chief, "that you shall have as soon as practicable. You have only to let me have your plan of a house, and tell me where to put it, and I will build it for you at my own expense. We will be neighbours and friends hereafter." It was in vain that the author assured the chief, that government officers were not allowed to receive such favours. He even wrote repeatedly to the author afterwards about the house.

The lovely spot that had attracted the author's notice, was near a mountain torrent, one of the tributaries of the Indus, which was seen rushing down from the midst of precipitous rocks, and noble timber, well cultivated ground being on either side of the stream; after it had got into the plain, the ground was undulating and picturesque, with magnificent crops of corn; and altogether the scenery was enchanting.

The Hazara mountains are very high and precipitous. On pitching the camp, after the first day's march, the chief and his sons galloped off with their men in armour, but at day-break on the following morning were at the author's tent door to escort him on his onward march. March after march was accomplished, and on each day a Durbar was held in the Commissioner's tent, which the several chieftains were invited to attend, and woe would it have been to them, if they had not accepted the invitations. They were all pretty much the same in the several districts, as has already been described of the noble on the bank of the river.

Having reached the border of the Maharajah of Cashmere's territory, the halt was sounded, and the force was encamped on the bank of a pretty river called the Naynsook, and afterwards moved back towards the plains of the Punjaub, having received unbounded civility and attention with ample supplies from the nobles in all parts of the country. It was on this march that the author formed his plan for making a great road through the Hazara Mountains, at the elevation of ten thousand feet above the sea level, to be worked out by European soldiers, a scheme which was ultimately sanctioned, but not without years of correspondence. The author almost despaired of this most valuable project, when he received a letter, enquiring as to whether the Europeans "*could do the job as cheap as natives.*" This was so foreign to the author's purpose, who had contemplated the most valuable and healthy recreation for his men, that he had scarcely patience to answer so mercantile a question, as to pounds, shillings, and pence ; which, as he thought, was a matter quite of secondary consideration. However, it was answered satisfactorily (it was supposed), as eventually a regiment of Highlanders escaped from their sedentary habits, punkahs, and workshops in the plains, and were found extending their powers as soldiers, in a cold climate, improving their lungs by scrambling up and down the mountain sides, and their muscles by the use of the spade and pickaxe.

These may appear to be trifling incidents, but they are not so, and they are valuable because they disclose to the world the feelings and sentiments of a Government towards its troops, of a financial character. No doubt the financier had to be consulted ; but what does that illustrious functionary know or understand about army efficiency? although, in such a country, army efficiency *should be the very first and most important consideration.*

After wading through the pages of this little work, it will not surprise the reader, to peruse a remark of the author on the value and importance of his own name in all matters of the nature above referred to. His various expeditions into the mountains beyond the British Frontier had brought him in contact with most of the chiefs and leaders in those regions; and he had now made himself known to the Hazara nobles, and he felt the power he possessed generally (although not permitted to use it) in all matters tending to the settlement of political questions. The affairs of the great mutiny at Peshawur had been, and probably ever will be, a subject of historical importance in Central Asia, and where and whenever the author took the field, his proceedings were watched by the people of the country with intense interest.

The author unhesitatingly declares, that, amongst other systems of a like nature, no more suicidal regulation could have been invented than that by which a limit of five years is put to all commands, and staff appointments throughout the Empire of India. On a frontier like that of the North-West, it would take an officer fully five years to place himself in a position to be of the slightest value to the State. He has so much to learn, and such acquaintances to make, that he could not discharge his duties at all satisfactorily, without serving a long and anxious apprenticeship. This must be a "solemn warning" again, and no doubt one deserving of the deepest consideration, as even the most inveterate "red tapist" of the bygone days of Indian rule, must admit that local experience can alone fit a man, even the ablest, for the proper discharge of his duties.

The heading of this chapter will have prepared the reader's mind for the next subject, which is to be brought under notice, viz., the "disaffection of the late East India Company's European soldiers."

The author was very seriously concerned in matters connected with that sad and lamentable affair, which sent off flying to Europe, ten thousand European soldiers, well acclimatized, strong, hearty, and able men, that could neither be replaced for years to come, nor without an immense sacrifice of public money.

The author touches on this subject with feelings of the deepest regret; he had ever entertained for the local European Forces of India the highest respect and esteem. He knew well their value and importance, and he deeply lamented the breaking up of the force, as much for the sake of the men themselves, as for the Government of the country which they had served so well and so bravely. If the reports of Parliamentary proceedings in the London newspapers are to be relied on, an incautious sentiment of the late Lord Palmerston was partly the cause of the breaking up of that force. But it was also stated, that no less a person than the Commander-in-Chief of the Indian army at the time, had contributed to the disaster by stating in a barrack-room, within the hearing of the soldiers, that on the transfer of the army from the East India Company to the Crown, the soldiers were entitled to bounty. The author could never bring himself to believe that such an incautious observation had fallen from any military officer in authority.

To acknowledge that the men were entitled to bounty, was of course to acknowledge, that they could accept a bounty or not, as they might think fit, or in other words, it was simply an admission, that they might refuse to serve her Majesty without a renewal of engagement.

No one who ever read the Attestation Oath of an East India Company's European soldier, could for a moment doubt his position as a soldier of the Crown of England; and when the case was referred to the law officers, they, without hesitation, declared that they were soldiers of the Queen of England, and were sworn to obey all orders of Her Majesty, her generals, and officers, and they were sworn to obey those also of the late East India Company.

Whether the Commander-in-Chief ever did make use of such an expression as is stated of him, the author never heard, but certain it is, that in communication with the men under his command of that branch, they were persuaded that he had done so; still, the author most industriously endeavoured to dissuade them from trusting in such a rumour. The author assured the soldiers that it was quite impossible for any officer to call in question the authority of her most gracious Majesty, as regarded British soldiers who were fighting under the flag of England, with a crown on their appointments, and whose officers bore her Majesty's commission.

Be this as it may, the Commander-in-Chief's supposed remark spread like wild-fire through the country, and aroused the disaffection of these misguided men. Singular enough it was on that identical spot where the Europeans acted in this manner, that the great mutiny of the native army broke out in earnest. It is strange, indeed, that Meerut should have been the scene of both these sad affairs. One Saturday evening a meeting of some of the leaders of the movement took place, at a village, a little way from the military cantonment of Meerut, and there it was resolved to commence on the following Monday morning, by refusing to obey their officers; in fact, the men determined to serve no longer, and they acted accordingly.

The officers acted with great spirit and determination, as they did on all occasions. The leaders of the movement were instantly confined on a charge of mutiny, and reports were sent off to the Commander-in-Chief of the army, at Simla, calling for his instructions. There was scarcely an officer throughout the country who had for a moment doubted the nature of the offence that these soldiers had committed. There could be no justification for such a demonstration on the part of soldiers; a respectful remonstrance is one thing, and an open declaration of war is another: a strike, therefore, of this sort, should not have been tolerated. However, the men were released from arrest, under the orders of the Commander-in-Chief, and an enquiry was directed to be made as to the *object* of the troops on this occasion.

There was a reason given (but only by rumour) for this line of proceeding being adopted towards these soldiers, but this reason the author dares not mention, solely because he is not in a position to prove it. What the author knows in regard to this transaction, is this, that had he been Commander-in-Chief of the army at that time, he would, in support of his authority, have pounced down upon the delinquents (let the collateral circumstances have been what they might), and would have punished the offenders to the extreme penalty of the law. And the author feels quite confident, when he makes this assertion, that he will be readily believed by all those who are aware of his antecedents. At the court of enquiry, which was ordered by Lord Clyde, a soldier stated as follows :—" You know well what we want ; we are not soldiers of the Queen, but of the Company, and we do not intend to serve any longer, unless we choose to re-engage on a bounty ;" (or words to the same effect).

The author had, at that time, a considerable force of the same European artillery under his command ; a finer body of men were nowhere to be seen, nor yet a better behaved, nor more loyal. On hearing of this outbreak at Meerut, correspondence was, as usual, intercepted, and by it, it appeared that the most resolute measures had been resolved on by the men, at Meerut and elsewhere. To save those under his command from contamination and disgrace, was of course the first duty and consideration of the author; and in this he was warmly supported by the artillery officers of the force.

The author trusts that a very gallant soldier of the late Company's artillery, who rendered the most important services on this occasion, will forgive him for making use of his name in connection with this subject. It was Lieutenant Colonel Olpherts, C.B., V.C., who commanded a splendid troop of horse artillery, at Peshawur, at that time. That gallant officer (which was a convincing proof of what might have been done elsewhere, if, at the outset, proper measure had been resorted to) instilled into the minds of his men, that they owed implicit obedience to the Crown of England; and they were loyal to a man. The sentiments of a Commander, who is looked up to by his men, generally prevail amongst them, and, as a body, they rarely take any course otherwise than that which is suggested to them by those they respect.

One day, in the very midst of all this, the author was waited upon by a sergeant-major, and three or four sergeants of horse artillery, with an invitation to a ball and supper, to be given by the artillery in barracks, in honour of her most gracious Majesty's birthday. There was something so cheering in this, and yet so extraordinary, that the author accepted the invitation, with heartfelt pleasure and satisfaction.

The ball accordingly came off, and the sergeant-major, who presided at the supper table, proposed the health of "The Queen," feelingly alluding to the sad events prevailing elsewhere, and warmly professing himself, in common with his comrades, to be deeply devoted to her Majesty, and her Majesty's service, being resolved, whatever might happen elsewhere, to stick to their duties as soldiers of the Crown of England. The author exultingly declares that in no single instance was there, in the Peshawur division, a case of disloyalty discovered on the part of these troops, but the merit is due to Colonel Olpherts and his men. This ball, at Peshawur, attracted very considerable notice at the time, and a report of it was read, with interest, in the London newspapers. The author received letters from England, congratulating him on the loyalty of his troops, and giving him the greatest credit for having encouraged, amongst his men, such feelings of devotion and loyalty. The author does not, however, take any credit whatever to himself for this display of loyalty that had been evinced on her Majesty's birthday. He was wholly unprepared for the invitation when he received it; it was due to the men themselves, and to the gallant officer at their head, who, no doubt, greatly assisted them on the occasion of this public demonstration. The ball-room was decorated with flags, pieces of ordnance, and mottos, all tending to prove the loyal feelings of the troops.

During the progress of events connected with this

very sad affair, the author received a letter from a General Officer, who, like himself, commanded a division of the Bengal army. From the tenor of his epistle it appeared that the General was in the midst of difficulties, and he enquired of the author as to the course he was pursuing with the Company's troops. The author informed him that there was no mutiny in his division, and added, "All the elements of mutiny have long since been blown away from the Peshawur division."

At the expiration of the mutiny of the native army, the author, on two occasions, earnestly implored of the Government to sanction the issue of twelve or six months' batta to these troops.

The great struggle of the mutiny was, of course, at its outbreak. It was stated that one hundred and fifty thousand men under arms had revolted, and the struggle under the walls of Delhi, with the ultimate fall of that important position, had determined the conduct of the surrounding independent states, and was *bonâ fide* the saving of the empire. To reward, then, in an especial and a peculiar manner, those troops who had saved their country, in so gallant, resolute, and determined a manner, at the most critical period of the insurrection, appeared to be a measure of justice, and indeed of necessity.

The number of European troops in India was at that time comparatively small, and the author, in recommending the measure, determined in his own mind, that the gratuity which he had proposed for the troops might have been gracefully allotted to them, not only for their services in the mutiny, but on their transfer to the more immediate authority of the Crown; a double object, which would have carried with it a feeling amongst the men of the deepest respect for the Government.

Days of rejoicing might have been appointed, with *fêtes* and amusements for the soldiery; and the author will not have much difficulty in convincing his military readers, that if such a course had been pursued, the sad and lamentable occurrences herein referred to would never have been heard or thought of. Nothing whatever was given to these troops by Government.

History has done ample justice to the Indian European army, which had for ages fought and bled in its country's cause; and it is sad indeed that it should have come to an end of so unworthy and unexpected a nature.

All such matters as these are "solemn warnings" for the future. Resolute measures, adopted towards the ringleaders of this movement at Meerut, would no doubt have preserved order, and must have saved the army.

There is no good to be derived from pusillanimous measures in mutiny. "Instant action," and that of the severest type, on such occasions, can alone save the troops, black or white, from their own disgrace and destruction.

CHAPTER XVII.

Sanitaria for European Troops in India.—Railways in India considered, as applicable to Military Purposes.—The Author quits the Frontier, after paying a farewell visit to his Troops, and calls, *en route* to England, at the seat of the Punjaub Government, where he is handsomely received by the Lieutenant-Governor.

THERE is no subject more worthy of deep consideration than the health of the European forces in India, and nothing more essentially required, than the proper application of measures resulting from long and anxious experience.

It would appear, at first sight, that medical men can alone satisfactorily dispose of such matters, and, without doubt, no enquiry into subjects of such a nature can be disposed of, without reference to the faculty. The author, ready and willing at all times to pay due respect to the medical gentlemen with whom he has been associated, always preferred to have their opinion on which to form his own judgment, rather than allow medical boards to settle such questions for him.

During one very sickly season at Peshawur, the author felt the advantages of this. He nominated himself, with two other officers of rank (not medical), as a board, to report to Government on the prevailing sickness ; and before it were summoned all the best medical men in the station, as evidences on the enquiry. Each medical officer being examined separately, their several opinions were recorded, and scarcely two of them agreed on any subject. There are old sayings, "Doctors differ," and again, "What should be done when doctors disagree ?" Why, glean from their opinions judiciously as much as are manifestly to the point, and then, by the application of common sense, draw out the conclusions. Medical boards (in the author's opinion) frequently do not arrive at such satisfactory conclusions, because the general feeling of the faculty have more or less to be considered by them. The recorded opinion of some great and leading functionary has to be more or less especially considered, and generally, as regards local circumstances, lengthened experience being wanted, most unsatisfactory conclusions are arrived at.

The great man of all, at the head of medical affairs, like his master, the Commander-in-Chief of the army, hastily perambulates the country, and as hastily forms his opinions. Travelling rapidly, with preconceived opinions of a general nature, which may be wholly inapplicable to particular localities, his reports are made out without due and sufficient experience, but, nevertheless, *his dictum is law.*

The military officer who has passed through all the seasons for many years, in a particular place, and has deeply considered the subject of the health of the troops in all its bearings, aided constantly by medical officers, whose hospitals he has visited, cannot well fail to be a good judge, in so important a matter; and he is continually paralysed in his efforts to do good, by the general measures adopted by Government, under the instructions and advice of the faculty itself. This may be well understood, without dwelling longer on the subject.

The Murree Sanitarium, of all other places, affords a striking example of the truth of these asseverations. The sums of money expended on the Murree depôt, with the mountain roads leading to it, exceed in amount what would be credited, even if the author had the figures at his disposal. One of the greatest errors of all, in this, as in all other matters in India, has been the admixture of civil and military affairs.

Murree is about eight thousand feet above the sea level, which, for the health of European troops in a body, is much too high. To young men, in fever cases and such like, when the organs of the body may be perfect, that elevation is generally suitable; but with any organic diseases (although the cool temperature, contrasted with the heat of the plains, may be agreeable), the rarefied air at such an elevation is fatal. In ascending mountains, from the very commencement, we are advancing towards a state of atmosphere to which the human frame must not be subjected. Some constitutions can bear up against the atmospheric changes much longer than others, but beyond a certain range, all must succumb to the rarefied condition of the atmosphere. In venturing into mountains, this must ever be borne in recollection, and the utmost precaution is needed.

The medical men, of course, being well aware of this, in their annual selection for this Murree and other hill depôts, carefully avoid sending men who have (as far as they can discover) heart complaints, and other organic diseases. Now, amongst soldiers accustomed to the heat of the plains, with all the damaging effects of a disorderly life, it is next to impossible to make universally proper selections, and continually men are sent to Murree, who on experience are found to be greatly injured, instead of benefited by the climate. The Murree depôt barracks are intended to contain about five hundred invalids, and most excellent they are; but annually, during the author's time, one tenth of that number, more or less, were recommended during the hot seasons to be hastily removed towards the plains, to save them from positive, or perhaps fatal injury. The elevation of the Murree depôt is, in fact, too great; and the author had to call upon the local government (after having, in its laudable efforts for the benefit of the troops, expended oceans of money) to establish a sanitarium for the Murree depôt.

Well does the author remember the astonishment of the Lieutenant-Governor of the Punjaub, when such a measure was proposed to him. However, there was no mistaking the fact; the heat of the plains had at that time become so intense, that to send men back to their own stations therein, from the cool temperature of the mountains, was impracticable, and so an intermediate sanitarium was really and truly imperatively needed. The mixing up of civil and military affairs was, in fact, concerned in this mischief. Whilst the Government was expending (it may be) millions of money, in establishing a sanitarium at Murree, the ostensible cause of the expenditure was the troops; but the civil and military officers of the Government thereby obtained an asylum for themselves and families, at Government expense.

The author very soon discovered in his own family the danger of a hill climate, and finding eight thousand feet too high, applied to the Government for permission to build a house at the elevation of about four thousand feet, which he was then, and is now, convinced, is the extreme height in which bodies of men can safely be placed. Be it remembered, that every description of constitution must be considered, when places for sanitaria for troops are selected. Not so with private families, who can resort to the hills at their own pleasure, unlike soldiers, who are sent there by a military order; besides which, private families are removed to and fro under very different arrangements.

The sanitary arrangements in the mountain stations of India, are generally bad in the extreme, and cholera is very likely to find an asylum in such places, simply from the extreme filth of the localities. In a place like Murree, the native population, who surround the military post, have habits (as everywhere else in India) of the most disgusting nature, and whichever way the wind blows, the stench is intolerable. The cleanliness of the depôt might have been preserved if it stood alone, but it certainly never can be whilst it is surrounded by a dense native population; so the admixture of civil and military at the Murree sanitarium, has been fatal to the health of the troops in one respect, whilst its elevation has been fatal, as above described, in another. In fact the Murree depôt, with its beautiful barracks, is a failure.

The author endeavoured, by all the legitimate means at his disposal, to get the bazaars of the place removed from the immediate vicinity of the barracks, where they are, or else to get the bazaars placed under the orders of the military Commandant. Liquor for sale used to abound in the bazaar, and drunkenness amongst the Europeans of the sanitarium at one time prevailed to such an extent, that the commanding officer of one of H.M. Regiments, who had men of his corps at the depôt, emphatically declared that Murree was the most drunken place in India. Improvements were made in that respect, but never satisfactorily, because the admixture of civil and military life in India, where the military is subservient to the civil (as it always is) never can possibly exist without detriment to the troops.

The Government at the time would not allow the author to build a house for himself at the elevation of four thousand feet above the sea level as he desired, because the distance from Murree would have been too great; but he had permission to build one nearer to Murree, and about one thousand feet below its level, where it at present stands.

Since that, at about three thousand five hundred feet above the sea level, a very eligible spot for a station has been selected by that very anxious and considerate Lieutenant-Governor, Sir Robert Montgomery, K.C.B., a very convincing proof as regards the Murree depôt that necessity existed, on experience, for such a remedial measure.

On the general question of utilizing the hills on the north-west provinces of India for European soldiery, the author emphatically pronounces the elevation of four thousand feet above the level of the sea to be ample and sufficient; and he adds that beyond that elevation, *with bodies of Europeans*, it is unsafe to fix them permanently.

The soldiers themselves, in general, hate the hills, and would much rather endure the heat of the plains than go there at all; besides which, it ought to be remembered, that if the change of temperature be too great, troops hastily brought down for service in the plains (which they must ever be liable to) could not fail to suffer.

In regard to railways in India as applicable to military purposes, the author has no hesitation in giving his opinion by stating that, used as they are at present for the transport of troops from one end of the empire to the other, the effect cannot fail to be, in the long run, injurious to the troops, as well as fatal to the security of the empire. If the author's project for the instruction and occupation of the troops in times of peace in the winter months, by having the armies in the field for exercise, was adopted; and if carriage for the army services was ever ready for "instant action," the objections to railways would be set aside. Rails no doubt are very convenient to the soldiery, as they must be to the Government, in transporting military stores, clothing, and supplies, and they must save the troops from much fatigue, whilst the injury contemplated by encouraging indolent habits would cease to exist, if the troops annually took the field as proposed. But let the Government of the country beware how they depend on rails in India for the transport of troops and military stores in times of trouble.

With an enemy all round, as must be the case in a general insurrection, or even when troops are hastily called for in any particular direction, the population of the country, at all times ready for mischief, and inimical to British rule, (although it is the fashion, unhappily, to think otherwise) would cause the rails to be destroyed, and would cut off the lines of communication. This they would assuredly be liable to do. What then would be the condition of the troops for services in the field, unaccustomed to marching, and to camp life, with the departments of the army

(Commissariat, Quartermaster-Generals, and such like) unused to field operations?

This is a question easily answered. The fact is, the troops would be all but worthless, and the expenditure of men would be extreme.

It must be remembered that the country affords no shelter nor quarters for European troops, as in England, and cattle to a large amount are required for the removal of camps and the munitions of war. The rails, even if permitted to exist, could never supply such requirements, and could afford no assistance whatever beyond their own range.

Beware then how dependence be placed on rails in India, for in the author's humble opinion, such dependence would sooner or later lead to the loss of the empire.

The natives cut the telegraph wires at the outbreak of the late mutiny, and so they would now the rails, or they would throw bodies of troops off them to cripple the Government in a great emergency.

Dictum sapienti sat est. No more need be written on a subject which speaks so manifestly for itself.

In the autumn of the year 1862, the author's time arrived for surrendering his very important and very interesting command. The five years' rule was made applicable in his case, notwithstanding his expressed desire to the contrary, and he had to "make way for better men."

The paternal anxiety for the welfare of the troops placed under his care and direction, caused him to resolve on making a tour through his district personally to take leave of them, and at the same time to ascertain if he could be of any further use.

The author, as is well known, had fought many a battle with pens, ink, and paper on their behalf, and he had accomplished many objects. Still, some matters that he had desired were left unaccomplished, which would have very materially improved the condition of the troops.

The establishment of a true and perfect military system throughout the country, so strongly referred to and advocated in different parts of this volume, is the chief and principal work that was left unaccomplished, and so it probably will, notwithstanding the unanswerable arguments in its favour that have universally been set forth.

In visiting the different corps under his command at this time, the author cannot help feelingly adverting, in particular, to his parting with the gallant Sutherland Highlanders (93rd of the line). This corps had been suffering severely from cholera in the cantonments of Peshawur, and the author removed it to a plain about seven miles from that station as a sanitary measure.

The locality selected, to all appearances, was admirably adapted to the purpose. The water was good, and there was no natural impediment to a free circulation of air. The ground for the encampment was clean and unpolluted, and the men were cheered up by change of scene and air.

The author followed the regiment to the spot on the day of its march out; he found that two men had been attacked with cholera on the line of march, which might have been expected. Of course any extra fatigue with those in whom the seeds of an epidemic may have been already sown, might produce, or perhaps accelerate such an evil.

On his arrival in camp, Major Middleton, who commanded the corps, informed the author that the men had expressed a wish to see him on parade, ere he quitted them for ever. Such were their soldier-like feelings towards their commander.

The author had made up his mind not to fatigue the men with a parade, but it would not do, so the parade took place. Amongst the officers present was that most valuable and devoted servant of the State, Doctor Munro, C.B.

The officers and soldiers were apparently much affected, when the author addressed the corps, as he was himself, at this parting interview.

In the evening of the same day, the author was entertained at dinner at the mess, when the officers were cheerful, contented, and happy. On mounting his horse, at the mess tent door, in the dead of the night, the author received an honest ebullition of feeling, by cheers, oft repeated, from a body of gentlemen, for whom he had ever entertained the highest respect and esteem, and he rode away from camp with feelings of the deepest regret.

Alas, alas! the time of joy and merriment was

destined to be of very short duration. In a very few hours, Major Middleton, commanding the corps, Colonel McDonnald, and other officers, were numbered with the dead. The cholera had returned with increased virulence, sweeping off numbers of valuable non-commissioned officers and men; gallant soldiers, doomed to suffer, not by swords and bullets, but by one of those special decrees of Providence, which are inscrutable: and, with this sad event, the curtain fell upon the author's career on the North-West Frontier of India.

The author then proceeded towards Calcutta, to embark for England, calling at Rawul Pindee, Jullunder, and Lahore, the capital of the Punjaub. At the first-named place, he was greeted by his old comrade and friend, Brigadier Tucker, C.B., who commanded the Station, and he was entertained by that gallant officer and by those officers under his command, with whom he had been long and happily associated. This parting entertainment was given in true British style, and the soldier-like bearing of the officers towards the author made a deep impression on his mind. A regiment of Dragoons, in camp, turned out spontaneously, in their shirt-sleeves, and with three hearty British cheers, took leave of their old commander, as he rode slowly and sorrowfully out of the Station.

His visit to Jullunder must not be overlooked. By the invitation of Major Mercer and the gallant 94th regiment, the author presented new colours to the corps. The 94th, a very beautiful regiment, in the highest state of order and discipline, had long served under his command, on the Peshawur frontier. He was proud of the regiment, and it can well be imagined how welcome to him was the opportunity thus afforded of bidding an affectionate farewell (under such pleasing and happy circumstances) to officers and men; the only thing the author regretted was the absence from the regiment, in England at the time, of its Senior Lieutenant Colonel Charles Mills, the son of one of the author's oldest friends, and a brother dragoon. He never can forget the pleasure as well as pain he experienced in parting with this corps.

At the capital of the Punjaub, Lahore, the author was warmly greeted by the Lieutenant Governor, Sir Robert Montgomery, K.C.B., who had never lost an opportunity of showing his respect for him. A little incident happened during this visit, which the author cannot and will not pass over without notice.

The Lahore Volunteer Corps had taken the field (a very useful lesson to that branch of the service in general). They were found by the author in a well-pitched camp, and everything strictly in accordance with military rule. The regiment, at Sir Robert Montgomery's desire, was paraded in front of their camp, for his inspection. Manœuvres were well executed, and the regiment had a strictly military appearance—steady under arms, and soldier-like.

The author was permitted to address the corps, and was enabled to express himself in very flattering terms. Of the speech of the Lieutenant Governor, Sir Robert Montgomery, on that occasion, the author is very proud, and reasonably so, because it emanated from one in the highest position, who was universally respected.

The Lieutenant Governor's speech, which follows, is transcribed, verbatim, from the *Lahore Chronicle*, the reporter of which journal was on the ground.

"*1st Punjaub Volunteer Rifles!*

"I will address a few words only to you :—

"If any proof was wanting of your zeal and earnestness in the Volunteer cause, you have given it in the steady course of drill you have gone through, and the sacrifice you have made in leaving your homes, and entering on a camp life.

"I feel highly gratified, as I feel sure you all do, at the praise bestowed on you by that most distinguished officer, Major General Sir Sydney Cotton, whose name and fame are known throughout the world, and to whom, we, at Lahore, and in the Punjaub, are so much indebted, for where should we have been in 1857, had not Sir Sydney Cotton commanded at Peshawur."

It is quite necessary now, that the author should comment on his own object in laying before the world, in this work, testimonials of a flattering nature relating to himself, which will have been found in its pages. It would have been even painful to his own feelings to do so, were it not for the imperative necessity that exists for resorting to such a measure.

The author is well aware that in writing a history of his own services on the North-West Frontier of India, he has laid himself open to the charge of being egotistical. The very nature of such a work must be egotistical; but if by "egotistical" is implied vain and empty boasting, he would deny the charge altogether, as not a word in this little volume could have been omitted without injury to the subjects which have been taken in hand. Facts are stubborn things. The recorded opinions of the author by those high civil and military officers, which have been introduced, are honourable and lasting testimonials, of which he never can be deprived.

The author has very freely offered his opinions on the prevailing systems of Indian government, which he considers prejudicial to the interests of the State, and, in so doing, it is certainly expedient that the public should be informed by what right he presumes to consider himself qualified to give such opinions, which could be of little or no value, unless supported by the recorded sentiments of the highest authorities as to his own merits and qualifications.

The success which may have attended the author's efforts, in the service of the country, as exhibited by the various testimonials now published, he does not place exclusively to his own credit. It is due to the support he ever received, during his arduous career, from men with whom he has happily been associated. There is no part of Her Majesty's dominions which have produced men of more real value and worth (whether in the civil or military services) than the North-West Frontier of India.

It would be quite impossible for the author to particularise any men or class of men now serving, to whom the country may look with confidence to the future, without making invidious distinctions; and it is sufficient for the author to state, that he feels deeply grateful for the support he received, and for the valuable co-operation he at all times met with during the many years that he served on the North-West Frontier.

It is not against men, but against systems, that the author has presumed to raise his voice, when bringing the subject of Indian Government under consideration.

CHAPTER XVIII.

The concluding Chapter, which is a General Summary.

In turning over in his mind the many circumstances that have been alluded to, and the many incidents that have been recorded in this brief summary of his services in the latter part of his career in India, the author considers it necessary, in his concluding chapter, to offer a few observations, of a general nature, on Indian government, with a view to a clear understanding as to his object in applying himself to a subject, in which, personally, he can now have no deeper interest than that which may be felt by any other of his fellow subjects.

The author (be it remembered) had devoted himself to the service of the Indian Government during nearly the whole course of his long military life, and indeed up to a very recent period, when it pleased the authorities to set him aside altogether, bringing to bear against him, instead of for him, the very experience he had acquired; his services (when again tendered for India) being rejected because his age was what it was. His physical and mental powers were not, nor could they be, called in question.

During the winter, between the years 1864 and 1865, the author had reason to think that he had been nominated for the command of the Madras army, but Lieutenant General Sir Gaspard Le Marchant succeeded to it. Of course a better man, and how could it be otherwise ordained? Something more, however, has to be explained with regard to this, and on a more fitting occasion the story will be told. It is too much of a private and personal nature for insertion here, but it is necessary to add, that in the sequel the author found himself not only disappointed, but a loser, by the transaction, of a very large sum of money.

He is, however, anxious now, at the termination of his career, to place in this manner, before the world, in unmistakable language, the result of his experience, which by no other process can be resorted to, in the hope that the "solemn warnings" that have been given may sooner or later be heeded.

It will not at all surprise the author to find that his views and sentiments are disregarded by official men. He is quite prepared to expect that those who commenced their career in civil, military, or political life, under systems of Government thoroughly at variance in principle, with those which are now advocated by the author, will even scornfully reject his suggestions. He is even prepared to find, when recommending the substitution of military for civil government in India, that such a preposterous proposition (as it may be considered) can alone emanate from a man who has taken leave of his senses.

The ordinary politician will have speedily made up his mind, that English institutions or English laws, must, of necessity, prevail in every quarter of the British Empire ; and that, in the sacred mission that has been allotted to us in India, we are called upon at once to confer the benefits of our institutions on those who have been emancipated by us, from despotic and overbearing rule, and are destined in times to come, to enjoy under an enlightened Government, a more just system than they have been accustomed to.

All this, in theory, may appear to be conclusive, but in practice it is, and will be found to be, beyond the reach of possibility.

An empire hastily and forcibly seized, and appropriated by a foreign power, cannot be at once prepared to receive so marvellous a change, especially at the hands of conquerors, who have recently laid waste and spoliated their country, casting into oblivion, and even into penury, the nobles and rulers of the land. In every city and province, men of those classes are to be found, restless and discontented, as might be expected.

Not only does the European in India appear as a spoliator, but he is a determined enemy to the religions of the country, and wherever he presents himself as such, he assails the tender feelings of the multitudes, and here the author does not hesitate to assert, that the periods which we have selected for the sudden establishment of British laws and institutions are a century or more in advance of those which the Kingdoms of India can be prepared for. Our institutions may eventually prevail, and it is to be hoped they will, but their introduction must be gradual, and will not be patiently submitted to by present generations. The natives hate our laws, although they acknowledge them to be equitable, but, if the truth must be told, they despise the authors of them. Dogs and infidels we are, and ever have been in their eyes, and so we shall continue until we have trained up future generations, and instilled into their minds principles, which are at present quite foreign to their nature. Even the mildness of our laws, they attribute to weakness, and the conciliatory measures we resort to, they view as unmistakable symptoms of fear.

Meanwhile, if we desire to be respected, and to hold the Government of the country in security, we must hold it with the strong arm of power—Military Government must prevail, and must prevail supreme.

No more convincing proof of this could be given, than was manifested by the great mutiny of the Indian Armies, and, indeed, ever has been manifested when we have been engaged in serious and difficult complications. If the world has been led to believe that the gigantic movement in 1857, was simply a rebellion of the army, it has been grossly misinformed: people at a distance from the scene of action, were led to believe that greased cartridges, the annexation of Oude, and such like considerations had caused the "outbreak;" and no doubt the priesthood made use of such means to accelerate the disaster, but the mutiny was a great national movement. All were in heart concerned in it, the army taking the lead, and all were keenly watching the turn of events, (even the independent States,) holding back from an open declaration against us, until the success of the troops had given them a certainty of success also. The time had not arrived for anything more than a severe struggle, and we weathered the storm; the rebels had no able leaders, and so by the blessing of Providence, time was afforded to us for placing on the stage all the available armies of England, and our empire was re-established.

One hundred and fifty thousand disciplined troops, it is said, broke out against our Government, the majority of them sacrificing the most lucrative employments, with pensions for their families unheard of in any other army in the world; and, notwithstanding these advantages, which they nowhere else could look for, the armies of Bengal *en masse* revolted simultaneously and almost universally, making a great and terrible effort to rid themselves of the common enemy. In the administration of the affairs of the Government, not an act of tyranny or oppression was laid to our charge, and yet the empire was in a blaze.

Cannot we read in these matters "solemn warnings" for the future? and are we not bound in justice to ourselves, to adopt a line of policy totally different to that which has brought us into such terrible difficulties?

Again, ought we not to remove from the people of the country, for their sakes as well as for ours, if we can, the power to rebel against us? There is no necessity for military despotism, there is no necessity for tyranny or oppression, because we assume an attitude, by military demonstrations, which may ensure respect. It has been proved beyond all doubt, that we cannot expect security by placing the power in the hands of the native police (the *élite* of a subdued population), nor yet in civil institutions, such as at present prevail all over the empire.

Military Government should not only prevail, but must be paramount. The civil officers of Government must act in concert with the military, and they must yield implicitly to military necessities. Financiers in India must be made subservient to the all important requirements of the troops, and not the troops to the views and desires of the financiers.

Erroneous notions of economy in state affairs are fatal, and have been fatal in countless instances, not only to the exchequer itself, but to the public security; some of our most valued economists, as statesmen, have gone down to the grave with the applause of the country, whose measures have brought down upon the empire, in the end, the most ruinous expenditure.

Rebellion may be transitory in our minor colonies, and may be easily overcome, which cannot be expected in the gigantic dominions of India. It must not, however, be supposed that because the military power in India is placed in the ascendant that the progress of improvement is to cease, or would be checked. On the contrary, the investment of money by private capitalists would most assuredly be promoted and encouraged by the strength and stability of the Government; and giving protection to the lives and property of those who invest their capital in foreign adventure, is assuredly not only a duty of the Government, but is essentially necessary to the interests of the State.

So long as the old civil institutions of India remain in the ascendant, private enterprise will be more or less discouraged.

It is essentially necessary now that every possible encouragement should be given to private capitalists to engage in great and important works in India. In these times the public at large may reasonably complain, when measures are adopted which are opposed in any manner to private enterprise, besides which the millions under our rule in India will be more surely emancipated from their ancient feelings and prejudices by the introduction of our improvements than by any other means that we can resort to, that is by turning the streams of wealth and science into a land, which for ages has been shut out from free institutions.

And now, as to erroneous notions of economy in India. Was it true economy that placed an unguarded

British arsenal of extraordinary magnitude at the disposal of the King of Delhi (without a European force to protect it) at the very seat of his ancient Government ready to his hand for the terrible conflict that ensued in 1857? Was it true economy that placed General Anson, Commander-in-Chief of the Indian army, with a considerable force of European troops in the Hymalayahs, and at no great distance from Delhi, without the means or possibility of moving, when by "instant action" the empire and the lives of thousands of white and black might have been saved? Was it true economy that had left all but bare and unprotected our frontier, when the Sikhs invaded it? And have any great and important improvements in military organisation been made since to avert such terrible calamities?

Similar questions might be submitted, which could only be answered in like manner, all tending to prove the inefficiency of the prevailing systems, and the extreme perils which in consequence hang over the very existence of the empire.

To such an extent do civil institutions prevail in India at present, that even Commanders-in-Chief drift into civil life. Locked up with civilians in council chambers, with their minds intent on civil as much as, or more than, on military affairs, they become little more than civilians themselves. Non-military feelings prevail, and ever will prevail, so long as the dominant power is vested in the hands of a civil ruler; and the Commander-in-Chief who appears before the council as the greatest economist in army matters, for good or evil, is the most highly estimated.

The Commander-in-Chief of a great and important army, as the member of a council by which he enjoys the bulk of his fortune, is seen twice in every year migrating from one end of the empire to the other *in the train* of a Civil Governor, to whose behests he is bound to pay the most deferential respect. He must either do that, or cease to hold a very lucrative appointment.

Looking to the very extensive territories, over which is scattered an army of such magnitude as that of Her Most Gracious Majesty in the East Indies, it will be readily understood how little time its Commander-in-Chief must have to spare in attending to its interests and efficiency, and it will be as readily understood how little can those interests be advanced by the periodical and hasty visits of a ruler who can rarely accomplish so much even as an annual inspection. It has already been explained that such hasty visits, *as regards local circumstances,* are generally not only not beneficial, but may be positively injurious.

In order that the Commander of an army should be of real value, he must be free to act on personal experience in all matters affecting the efficiency of the army, he must be amongst his troops at all seasons of the year, and must be wrapped up in military affairs. He must be content to relinquish the pleasing retreats of civilians in the summer seasons, and must devote his every energy, mental and bodily, to the main object of his mission.

A master mind is no doubt required to reorganise all our Indian military institutions, which the author maintains is essentially necessary to the security of the State. A half soldier and half civilian could never effect the object, nor yet a heaven-born soldier, such as occasionally flourishes in the world. He must be a real, practical, military man, with great local experience, and full of energy, who has passed through all the different grades of the profession in actual intercourse with the troops. Military officers who have passed their lives in the civil services of the State are even worse than civilians; they imagine because they are nominally soldiers, that they must possess military knowledge, but no man who has not real experience in military matters can arrive at prompt and just decisions thereon, and without promptitude of action an army and the interests of the country may, indeed must, be lost.

The breaking up of all the old stations of the armies of India, *which are simply occupied because they exist*, and by which our best troops are frittered away, must be one of the first considerations. These places are generally unhealthy for Europeans, and there being *no demonstration of power whatever under such a system*, the army's importance and value are lost.

Agra, Delhi, Lucknow, Allahabad, and such like posts, should be swept off the face of the earth, or be so thoroughly dismantled as to require no guarding. At the termination of the great mutiny, such a measure was manifestly just, as well as expedient; it was then seen that many of these sort of places were dangerous to the interests of the British Government; they were immediately resorted to by the disaffected, as they would be again and again, in times of trouble. Consequent on the removal of the troops from these localities, they should be congregated as *corps d'armée* in healthy parts of the country, prepared for "instant action," *en masse* or otherwise, as circumstances might require. The army then would be always as it, were in the field, and should be covered in only sufficiently for the preservation of the health of the soldiers, and liable at all times to be removed from one part of the country to another. Fixed localities for troops in India are at all times objectionable in a sanitary, as no doubt they must be in a political point of view, and the troops might do much in the cool seasons of the year in covering themselves, preparatory to the setting in of the hot weather. The lower ranges of hills in the upper provinces of Bengal might afford, in some instances, good scope for the favourable disposition of the troops. In all the presidencies of India, there are localities which might be made available, such as the Mysore country, the Deccan, the southern Mahratta country, and elsewhere, on elevated plateaus of about two thousand feet or more above the sea level; but as before stated, a master mind of great personal activity and energy, could alone solve the very difficult problem. A proper reorganisation might, however, be readily accomplished if the matter were placed in able hands.

This subject cannot be complete, or be referred to with any sort of utility, unless the attention of the reader be drawn to the many instances of discord which have prevailed between the civil rulers of India and the very distinguished military officers who have from time to time, *only nominally*, presided over the destinies of the army, all tending to prove, that the power has not been vested in those who could realise in their minds the vast and superlative importance of military organization.

Can the numerous instances be forgotten, in which our best soldiers, who had endeavoured to support military principles in India, have either had to resign their position as Commander-in-Chief, or have been removed from it. Sir Edward Paget, who saved the army from its own destruction (at the time of the first Burmese war), by crushing a mutiny at Barrackpore, had afterwards to resign his appointment, declining to sit in the civil council, from circumstances which had there occurred. And again, as regards the rule of the late East India Company, it is very necessary to add, in proof of the views entertained by that body on military discipline, that the conduct of Lord Amherst, who was at the same time Governor-General, was disapproved of by the Court of Directors, owing to the necessary punishments that had been inflicted on the Sepoys by Sir Edward Paget; and they were desirous, in consequence, of removing that nobleman from his Government. The Duke of Wellington (as a soldier), in support of military discipline, of course, objected to his Lordship's recall.

The author was with Lord Amherst at Barrackpore about the time of this occurrence.

Sir Edward Barnes was removed because he could not work in unison with the civil Government. Lord Dalhousie, a stout-hearted soldier of warm temperament, could not brook the treatment he received at the hands of the civil Government; and Sir Charles Napier was for ever at war with the nobleman at the head of the councils of India. Even Lord Combermere, who had resolved to support to the utmost of his power and ability the civil Government of the country, was at last severely condemned by the Court of Directors, as a disturber of the measures of that Government on the half batta question.

Disapproving of the half batta order, his Lordship placed on record in the Council his objections to it, which was no less than his *bounden duty* towards the army, whose destinies were supposed to be in his hands. His minute was couched in respectful terms. The Duke of Wellington (then at the head of affairs in England), on hearing of Lord Combermere's recorded objection to the half batta measure, wrote to him in a demi-official form, *and strongly advised him to abstain from interference.*

This half batta measure, in a financial point of view (as is well known), was all but valueless, while it was attended with the most serious embarrassment and inconvenience to the army. The auditors of accounts had to resort to the maps to ascertain the distance of two hundred miles from the several Presidencies of India, in order to determine the ordinary pay and allowances of the troops, which caused endless disputes, and *indeed jobbery, with bad feeling when the periodical reliefs of regiments took place.*

Lord Combermere was most harshly treated by the East India Directors for the part he had taken in the honest discharge of his duty on that occasion, but he lived long enough to see the measure cancelled by a future Government, as inexpedient and worthless. The author was Aide-de-Camp to Lord Combermere in India at the time, and was personally acquainted with these circumstances; and, strange as it may appear, he was so situated at most of the various periods of Indian history referred to in this volume, and possessed a personal and general knowledge of the matters that have been recorded.

In regard to military officers, it may be certainly stated that India has been at times ruled by them. The Marquis of Hastings, Lord William Bentinck, the Earl of Ellenborough (a civilian, although a thorough soldier in heart), and Lord Hardinge. True enough, but they served the State on civil principles of government, and were not free agents to carry out so radical a change in military affairs as the author proposes, even if they had desired it. The Marquis of Hastings was considered the ablest of all our rulers; Lord William Bentinck was the half batta man, and accepted office only on condition that the half batta measure would be introduced; of which the author was informed at the time by Lady William Bentinck. The Earl of Ellenborough certainly lost no opportunity in his power of advancing the interests of the army. (The author, during the time of his Lordship's government, was serving in Scinde with Sir Charles Napier). Lord Hardinge's reign was of very short duration, and he had not time to place our then frontier of the Sutlej in a respectable state of security.

The author was not in the Sutlej wars, but was at that time quartered with his regiment in the Deccan, and he alludes to that because he daily visited, during Lord Gough's operations, the native city of Poonah to receive the latest intelligence from the seat of war, and owing to the unsettled state of the country necessarily with loaded pistols. The ancient noblesse of the Peishwar were in the highest state of excitement with the momentary expectation that the *British Râj* would come to an end, the people of Poonah receiving hourly intelligence.

A glance at the map, by those unacquainted with Indian localities, may afford useful information as to the impending difficulties of our Indian Government, in a country where a common feeling against the British rule is unmistakably found to exist from one end of the empire to the other.

Another struggle or two for the existence of the

Indian empire may perhaps be needed, ere the minds of those who have long been accustomed to established systems can be aroused to a just appreciation of their danger. The many "solemn warnings" that have been received have not, in the author's humble opinion, made a sufficient impression, as army organization does not as yet hold a place in the councils of the State of *primary* importance.

It must not be supposed that the author advocates any increase in our European forces in India, but just the reverse; a proper organization would unquestionably rather lead to a diminution of that element. England cannot afford so great an expenditure of European troops as is incurred at present in India, and this forms an additional argument in favour of a radical change in the system, which could be accomplished were a military government instead of a civil to prevail. In times of peace, when troops are only required at home to garrison the towns and provinces, the absence of so large a force in India cannot be very severely felt; but let war break out in Europe or elsewhere, and the difficulty of our position in India, under present systems, will at once become transparent. Recruiting for the armies of India would then necessarily cease, as was the case during the Peninsular war.

We must not be discouraged in placing the affairs of our Indian empire in the hands of military officers, because the fate of the empire has in several instances depended upon men, who proved themselves to be unfit for an emergency. In the pages of this little work, are recorded two very memorable incidents, in which the empire was all but lost by the incapacity of military leaders; but in both cases the terrible disasters that ensued, were chargeable to the civil Government of the time. The disasters at Cabul were laid at the door of an inefficient military officer, whilst to the inefficiency of another military officer at Meerut, was attributed much of the disasters of the great mutiny of 1857. The ruling powers could not fail to be aware, as everyone else was aware, of the qualities of those men, and should never have sanctioned their being placed in such important places of trust. The officer in command at Meerut, had either caused himself to be removed from the frontier post of Peshawur to Meerut owing to his infirmities, or the Government had ordered him to be removed, as Meerut was considered then a place little liable to call forth the energies of a commander. But it so happened that Meerut turned out the very focus of mutiny, and hence we read one of the very many "solemn warnings" that have been providentially awarded to us.

Of the late East India Company, little else might have been expected. The seniority system which at that time prevailed, excluded efficient officers from places of high trust in the military services, whilst the Home Government, labouring under the very erroneous impression, that any one would do for India, frequently sent out officers notoriously unfit for active military duties.

The miserable specimens of decayed humanity, that appeared on the stage of India at times, were the cause of deep lamentation and danger; and yet, during the last fifty years of our rule (with which the author has been so intimately acquainted), our Indian empire has ever hung upon a thread.

Of later years, it must be admitted, that a better class of men have found their way to India as military rulers.

A general officer (it is true) may sit on his horse, and direct the great combinations of an army, even in the presence of an enemy, without being blessed with any considerable personal activity; but in India, an officer in command of troops, must at all times be prepared for "instant action," or a dashing exploit. Every general officer in command has light troops at his disposal; and must be prepared in cases of emergency to throw his leg across his horse, and at the head of his cavalry and horse artillery, be enabled to present himself, with great velocity, at any point where his presence may be required. Every man (it may be said) is not a Robert Rollo Gillespie, but every man ought to be, to whom the fate of a mighty empire may be entrusted. England can produce plenty of men of the right stamp, and so can India itself, as has been proved in countless instances in prolonged warfare; when men force their way to the front irrespective of military rules and private interest.

The story of Robert Rollo Gillespie and the 19th

Light Dragoons, who were quartered at Arcot, when the native troops broke out into mutiny at Vellore, cannot be forgotten, and the conduct of that dashing officer on the occasion, ought to be for ever before our eyes, and serve as a "solemn warning" for the future, when selections are made for Indian commands.

It has appeared to the author since his return to England after a very lengthened absence that very little is known or thought of our vast possessions in the East Indies, or of the character of the inhabitants of those countries, and it has surprised him very much to find that, even in the Houses of Parliament, so little attention seems to be paid to Indian affairs.

In a recent debate in the House of Commons, the author was very much surprised to find that the adoption of an heir to the throne of the Mysore country by the present Rajah had been approved of.

In the early part of the author's career, the present Rajah of Mysore had recently been placed on the throne by the British Government, when he frequently attended the Rajah's Durbars. It is well known to most people, that the Mussulman dynasty of Hyder Alli, by the death of Tippoo Sultan at the capture of Seringapatam, had ceased, and the Mysore territory was placed at the disposal of the British Government. It was understood at the time, that the Nyzam of Hyderabad, who had been engaged in concert with the British troops, and had a share in the capture of the country, laid claim to its sovereignty; and the only safe alternative the British Government had, was to bring out the old Hindoo family, of which the present Rajah is the representative—and he was placed on the musnud. Since that period, difficulties have arisen from the connexion we had formed, and it was very generally supposed, that on the death of the Rajah, the country would fall into the hands of the British Government. More especially as the Rajah had no heir of his own to succeed him; but it has pleased the authorities to sanction the adoption of an heir.

It must be manifest to every one, that the adopted heir to the throne of Mysore can, personally, have no just claim whatever.

The present Rajah has ever been friendly and apparently well-disposed towards the English. He is a mild Hindoo, but he has, like all other natives, his advisers about him.

The case of the Nana Sahib, who resided near Khawnpore, must be fresh in the memory of every-one. Up to the period of the mutiny in 1857, the Nana, like the Rajah of Mysore, was apparently on terms of friendship with the European ladies and gentlemen. He gave balls and entertainments to the English, and mixed in English society generally, when suddenly the opportunity was afforded him, and he massacred every European he could lay his hands upon. To conjure up then in Mysore, an heir to the throne, and place the power in the hands of a native who has no claims whatever to such a position, does indeed appear extraordinary, as no one can foresee what his character and policy may be.

At the present period of our rule in India, such acts of generosity on our part, instead of strengthening our Government (which it may be presumed is intended), have the very opposite tendency. Conciliatory measures are neither understood nor properly appreciated by the natives. They ever foster in their minds the latent hope of turning the position of power, in which we may be pleased to place them, to their own ultimate advantage, when a general effort is made throughout the empire to shake off our connection altogether. The author emphatically declares, from his knowledge of the native character, and of the precarious tenure of our authority in India, that we cannot afford, thus early in our imperial rule, to resort to such measures of generosity.

The Mysore country is, it must be remembered, in the very heart of the British dominions.

The author was in the habit, at one period of his life, of attending the Rajah's Durbars at Mysore, and had often received at his hands (as was customary in those days) Cashmere shawls, which were presented at court. It may appear strange, that a young officer of Cavalry, which the author then was, should have taken any interest in the Rajah; and he only alludes to the circumstance to shew that he was placed in a position to know something of the Mysore Government.

The "solemn warnings" that we have received from time to time (notwithstanding the apparent friendship of the natives in our intercourse with them) ought not to be disregarded; and those who appear to be most friendly, are, perhaps, the least to be depended upon, because they are not suspected, and the kindly feelings of John Bull may very likely be misplaced. Conciliatory measures towards the natives of India, tend to a result the very opposite to that which may be expected.

The intention of the author, when he commenced this narrative of his services on the North-West Frontier of India, was only to circulate it amongst his own friends, the members of the Government, and the different branches of the legislature, in the hopes that the stirring events, that would be adverted to, might awaken feelings in regard to India, which do not at present appear to exist; but this little work has become more lengthy than at first intended, and its circulation must be more extensive, at the urgent request of influential men, who apparently take a deep interest in Indian affairs.

It is the duty of every man (in the author's humble opinion) who is a sincere well-wisher of his country, to endeavour to serve it to the best of his ability, and to submit, if it be only for general consideration, opinions formed on long and anxious experience.

It may be considered here necessary to explain that the author is, at this moment, in possession of no political secrets, which might lead him to offer his opinions on the existing state of matters in India. He has no expectation of an immediate danger to our Indian empire, owing to the measures heretofore pursued, in the administration of its government; but there is no saying what an hour may produce in an empire of such magnitude, with a population so varied, so restless, and so recently subdued, and at the same time so inflammable, as to be liable to disruption, or agitation, from one extremity to the other.

Foreign complications may lead, at any moment, to a general conflagration in India. Wars in Europe or America, into which England may be drawn, whether she will or not, may lead to such a result, and even a threatening aspect of affairs on our North-West Frontier, may produce a general agitation in the provinces of Hindostan, and in Central and Southern India.

The author earnestly recommends the British Government not to look on, with cool indifference, at the advances of Russia, or even Persia, in Central Asia, which may lead to the necessity for the hasty reinforcement of troops to strengthen our Frontier, (which is certainly not, at present, well prepared, or sufficiently defended). For by denuding the provinces of Hindostan and the Punjaub of their ordinary garrisons, encouragement would be given to the disaffected.

Above all things, the Government must bear in

recollection that disaffection in the ranks of its native army may again and again prevail. The same systems of army discipline and organization remain, to a great extent, as existed antecedent to the great mutiny, and even the self-same troops remain embodied; troops, that at one time could not be trusted with arms in their hands, were unhappily re-armed, while smarting under the effects of the disgrace that had been inflicted upon them, and by the terrible punishments that were necessarily awarded to their comrades, relatives, and friends, in crushing the gigantic rebellion.

Long since the mutiny, and not many days before the author left the North-West Frontier of India, intercepted letters reached him from Hydrabad, in the Deccan, addressed by Sepoys, of one of these re-armed corps at Peshawur, to brother Mussulmans, in the Nyzam's territory, in which the most seditious expressions towards our Government were used, and calling on the Mussulmans generally to rise and make an effort to rid themselves of their common enemy. Of the feelings of the Nyzam and his subjects towards British rule, the author need say but little; but a glance at the map by those who are not intimate with the geography of India, must at once satisfy any reasonable person of the correctness of the author's assertion, that our Indian empire is liable to disruption or agitation from one end of it to the other.

The present native army of Bengal has in its

ranks much more energetic and intelligent races than were to be found in the ranks of the old army; the native officers, in Bengal, of the latter had risen, by seniority, from the ranks; they were generally worn out, and without any special qualifications, whilst the native officers of the new army are men full of vigour, and have risen by their superior merits and qualifications, and, in many instances, by hereditary distinctions. In cases of future rebellion, then, leaders may spring up much more dangerous in character than those who have appeared on the stage before.

The armed native police of the Trans-Sutlej territories, are (or recently were) composed, to a considerable extent, of the old Sepoys of Hindostan, well trained and well disciplined soldiers for good or evil, and certainly of a very dangerous character, if they chose to rebel against us. This police force is in possession throughout the main thoroughfares of the country, not only of the passages of the great rivers, as stated before, but of little fortifications, fourteen or fifteen miles apart, built of solid masonry, with a well of water in the centre, and looped for defence, the garrisons of which might hold out against Infantry for a considerable time, and against Cavalry altogether. A mistaken confidence in the natives, by the Civil Government of the Punjaub, could alone have led to so extraordinary a measure.

The natives of the upper class of the North-West

Frontier repeatedly assured the author, up to the very last moment of his sojourn there, that there will be, some day or other, a general rising of the Mussulmans of India, against our Government. Since the removal of the descendants of the Great Mogul, from Delhi, they look to the Nyzam in the Deccan, as the great head and chief of the Mussulman cause. The natives are keen observers of passing events, and will doubtless bide their time, awaiting opportunity suitable to their own purpose, when our hands are tied up with struggles elsewhere, even in the most distant parts of the universe.

"Put then your house in order, whilst you have the opportunity," is the concluding advice of an old and faithful servant of the Crown, to the Government of his country; and if he may presume to tender his advice, in addition, in a matter of detail, place at once, and without loss of time, on the plains of the Sind Sâgur district on the left bank of the river Indus, a *corps d'armée* of twenty thousand reliable troops of the three arms of the very best quality, under the command of an energetic, intelligent, and active soldier, who, setting aside all feelings of domestic comforts, heretofore so peculiar to officers of all services in the Indian armies, will devote himself exclusively to military life; and then, with transport boats ready for "instant action" across the river, the Government will be prepared for any frontier emergency (internal or external) without calling upon the provinces of Hindostan, and elsewhere, to part with the protection so essentially necessary to their own security.

This is the "solemn warning," in conclusion, by a Frontier Officer, whose principle is, and ever has been, readiness for

Instant Action.

APPENDIX.

APPENDIX.

THE ORGANISATION OF THE ARMIES OF INDIA.

The author now desires to offer for the consideration of his readers a remark on one subject, which may be useful; and in all respect to the present Government of India, he draws attention to the continuance of exclusive systems still prevailing in the administration of military affairs, which were generally supposed to have been abolished.

The great rebellion of the armies of India brought about, of necessity, a radical change in its Government.

It had been proved, beyond all doubt, that the monopoly of the late East India Company was not only unsuited to the spirit of the age, but absolutely dangerous to British power. The feelings of the soldiery, European and native, towards the Majesty of England, so glaringly exhibited, were sufficient proofs, if proofs were wanting, that so extraordinary a Government could no longer exist.

Without entering too deeply into subjects, which by force of circumstances have been disposed of, the late East India Company, with its authority in the East, fell to the ground, and the empire was placed under the direct control of Her Majesty's Government; but members of the late Court of Directors remain in the State Councils, although under a different designation, into which councils none of the officers of the most important element of the Indian empire (Royal army) have been admitted; and hence the interests of that army are not directly represented.

In re-constructing the affairs of a mighty empire, a fabric of such gigantic proportions, involving so many and such varied interests, the re-construction of the armies was, of all others, the most important consideration, because, as the author has before asserted, the actual power of the State (if it consulted its own interests) must be vested in military authority.

When the affairs of the great revolt had settled down, the Government, feelingly alive to this necessity, without loss of time wisely consulted the military officers in authority on the subject of the re-construction of the army.

It was part of the author's duty whilst in command of the Frontier Post of Peshawur, to submit for the consideration of the high authorities his scheme for the re-organisation of the army. A series of questions had been sent to him, seeking his opinions upon certain matters connected with this subject, which were, in all due respect, answered *seriatim*, but must have been drawn out by a civil officer of Government, or one who was not apparently acquainted with military life, and falling far short of the object in view; the author, in common with others, submitted a scheme of his own, the terms of which will be found hereinafter.

The amalgamation of all the armies employed in Her Majesty's service in India, was most strongly recommended by the author. There were some difficulties in accomplishing this, owing to the pecuniary affairs of the officers of the Indian service; but none that were insuperable, if officers, with military experience, had been permitted to handle them.

The amalgamation, however, was a work of necessity. Not only was the empire of India concerned in it, but the British empire in all quarters of the globe. To render available for the services of the State those able officers and soldiers who had been trained in military life in India, was one of the first and great objects of the amalgamation. No army in the world ever produced more efficient soldiers. Almost incessant wars had prevailed in India, and real soldiers can only be found where the opportunities are afforded them of practically learning their professional duties, whilst on the other hand the officers of the so-called Royal army serving in India had been placed for years, by the exclusive privileges of the Indian Company, in a position of manifest inferiority; and so it may be truly said, that in all respects the time had arrived for getting rid of such invidious distinctions. Officers of the Royal army were not even available for the ordinary staff appointments of India at that time.

This matter had apparently been settled, and it was generally understood, or supposed, that all distinctions in services had been removed, and that all (whilst serving under one Government) would enjoy the same privileges. This has been by no means accomplished, but in many matters just the reverse; and one or two may be particularised, viz., to the officers of the old Indian service, promotions are given permanently under local arrangements; and in order that by such promotions no immediate supercession should take place, the Royal officers who happen to be in India obtain local rank only. On quitting India the latter lose their rank, whilst the former retain their rank for ever. Now supposing (which may probably occur) that they come together in New Zealand, at the Cape of Good Hope, in Abyssinia, or elsewhere out of India, at a future period, the Royal officers will of course find themselves superseded by their Indian comrades, or great confusion will prevail. In an official gazette recently issued, a general list of officers of the Indian service appeared as members of the 2nd class of an Indian order of merit, established as it appears exclusively for those officers and the natives of India, whilst none of the Royal officers have been included in it, although labouring in the same cause, and fighting in the same battle-fields (and never otherwise) with their comrades of the Indian service.

Since the above was written, two Royal officers only (men of course it may be presumed of superior merit) have been admitted to the 2nd class of this order; but these, it would appear, are special, or exceptional cases.

The author wishes it to be clearly understood that he does not desire to call in question the justice of such measures as those; but the subject is certainly worthy of remark, and deserving of consideration.

The despatches (of which the two following are copies) were addressed to the Chief of the Staff in India, after the great mutiny of 1857, on the subject of the re-organisation of the Indian Armies, by the author:—

TO THE CHIEF OF THE STAFF.

Peshawur, 11*th June*, 1858.

SIR,—I have the honour to request that this despatch may be laid before His Excellency the Commander-in-Chief at your convenience, the subject of which, I am well aware, is of the highest importance to the interests of Government and the army, which unhappily has fallen into a state of unprecedented anarchy by the general mutiny of the native troops.

I trust it may not be considered presumptuous in me to offer remarks and suggestions on the re-organisation of the army, in which I am permitted to hold so important a command, seeing that a measure of such vital importance must shortly come under the consideration of Government.

Impressed then with the belief that the suggestions of experienced officers at such a moment will not be unacceptable to His Excellency, the Commander-in-Chief, and to the

Government, I hesitate not to record my sentiments, however valueless they may prove to be.

Having been connected with the armies of India in all its Presidencies, with but little intermission for nearly forty-eight years, commencing as Cornet in 1810 in a regiment of Light Dragoons, and passing through all the grades of the service to that of Major-General, and having been employed on the Staff as Military Secretary in Bengal, Deputy Adjutant General of Queen's troops both in Bombay and Madras, Deputy Quartermaster-General at Madras; also in a Divisional Command in Bengal, three Brigade Commands in Bengal, viz., Peshawur, Umballah, and Rawul Pindee, and one Brigade Command in Bombay, few officers in Her Majesty's service have ever had such an opportunity of observing the working of systems prevailing generally throughout India. On these grounds I venture to found my claims to the title of an experienced officer.

Consequent on the mutiny military authority must essentially prevail, and European troops must be employed mainly in the occupation of the country.

The recent mutiny in Bengal, and partially in the Bombay and Madras Presidencies, has opened our eyes at last to the fact that we must not rely with any confidence on the native troops of any creed or caste, as a body. The people of the vast empire of India, now under British rule, having been conquered by the sword, must by that weapon be held in subjection, and the sword must be firmly grasped in future by the hand of the European conqueror.

Throughout the length and breadth of the land the Government of India must henceforward be *essentially military*, but no one I think could reasonably expect that Great Britain would be able to furnish exclusively troops in a sufficient number for the military occupation of such a country.

The climate is much too hot for the European in many situations where military duties have to be performed, and the expenditure of troops would be vastly too great if the European alone endeavoured to take those duties. The natives of the country must therefore be called in to assist us, and a certain limited number must be armed and trained as soldiers, but by no means in the same numbers as heretofore. In fact, the native troops must be used as auxiliaries and nothing more, and they must be placed in such positions as to be powerless to do mischief. And here I would earnestly implore of the Government to take warning by the past. It is true that some native troops have, during the great crisis of the rebellion, remained faithful to the British Government; but the fidelity of these few is to be attributed more to local circumstances and to peculiar positions, rendering it difficult for them to act against us, than to any real attachment to the British Government. The mutiny may be considered as a great national movement, in which the whole army has taken the lead, and in which all are in heart concerned, the object being to expel from the country or to destroy the Christian conquerors, who are hated as such, universally, and indeed naturally despised, and looked down upon as enemies to their religion.

No confidence can hereafter be placed by the British Government in the native troops of India exclusively.

3. The newly raised troops of the Peshawur and Mooltan Frontier and of the adjacent countries, in and bordering on our territory, who have so well served us in our difficulties, and by adhering to, or espousing our cause, saved us at a most critical moment, are no more to be depended on than any others. I verily believe that these troops derived from much more energetic and intelligent races, would become still more formidable than the Hindostanees, if, by a sudden change in their sentiments towards us arising out of a fanatical cry, to which they are quite capable of responding, they might choose to desert our cause. Already do they feel their importance as the saviours of the tottering Govern-

ment; already do they feel the power which we have placed in their hands; and they have before their eyes the baneful example of rebellion, which has been shown them by their Hindostanee neighbours, tending to prove that our Government has hitherto been placed on an insecure foundation.

This very feeling will, in after times, deter many, who had formerly considered us invincible, to ponder well, ere they commit themselves by entering the service of so uncertain and insecure a Government.

4. Having adverted, therefore, to the fact, that the Hindostanee troops can never again be entrusted, as a body, and having endeavoured to show that no native of the country is deserving, at our hands, of any implicit confidence, I would suggest as a preliminary step towards re-organisation, that the whole of the native regular cavalry and infantry of the Bengal Army remaining embodied, whether armed or disarmed, whether apparently loyal or otherwise, be, *in limine*, discharged from the service of the British Government. This act would be eminently just on our part, the troops, as a body, having proved themselves to be, as at present constituted, not only unworthy of our confidence, but dangerous to us in the extreme.

The disbandment of the whole Native Army, as originally constituted, recommended.

5. With regard to the newly organised levies, they should be kept embodied, and treated with liberality, but at the same time so grafted on and amalgamated with European troops, that they would be powerless to do harm.

The newly raised troops to be kept embodied, but their organisation to be changed.

When once the terms are finally settled, no concessions are to be made to any natives whatever at their own seeking.

Their organisation must be changed as will be suggested hereinafter. And should it be deemed expedient, which, no doubt, it might be, to re-enlist in our service any portion of the old army of the country, the men should be hired on terms better suited than those of previous times, to our welfare and security, terms of such rigid discipline as would ensure ready and willing obedience to all such orders of superiors as are commonly issued to soldiers of all armies, without affording them the means of concealing their transactions, as heretofore, and of combining to mutiny against their employers; and whilst enforcing discipline with such troops, let our treatment of them be liberal; we must begrudge them nothing that is right to give them, but that once settled and determined on, let no concessions whatever be henceforward made when urged and solicited by themselves. Concede nothing to native troops, at their own requiring; they are incapable in such concessions of imputing to their employers aught but weakness.

Powers of Military Commanders to be increased. One Commander-in-Chief only of all the Indian armies recommended, with commanders of the forces, placed in convenient localities.

6. Of all the changes required in the great army of British India, there is none so much needed, indeed so imperatively called for, as the power to act on sudden emergencies by officers holding Commands, and it is most necessary that they should have the means nearer at hand to obtain instructions from the supreme military authorities, and the sanction of proposed measures without delay. The great machinery of military affairs is by much too complicated for such a country as India; I would therefore suggest that commanders of the forces, with vastly increased powers to act on their own responsibility, may be so located and within the reach of the troops as to remove all possibility of delay in carrying our measures of public utility.

In my humble opinion there should be but one Commander-in-Chief of all the armies of India, whose motto should be *ubique*, and he, as supreme military authority, should be vested with powers, in ordinary matters, to act without referring to the supreme Government of the country. It is impossible adequately to express or to explain the embarrassment caused and the evils to which the soldiers are liable, by the difficulty and delay which occur in obtaining authority for carrying out the most trifling measures of necessity. I would have commanders of the forces, but not Commanders-in-Chief at the subordinate presidencies, viz.: there should be one in Bengal, one at Madras, one at Bombay, and one in the Punjaub and adjacent provinces, all four reporting to the Chief of the Staff for the information of His Excellency the Commander-in-Chief.

The whole of the armies of India should be under one system, and under the same code of regulations, so that they might be transferred from one presidency to another, without difficulty or inconvenience.

Commanders of Forces to be empowered to order works to be undertaken and completed on a more extended and liberal scale than at present.

7. The rigid departmental rules, at present in force, which deprive the executive officer of the power of acting under or by the orders of the military authorities on the spot, except in the most paltry cases, are injurious to the soldiers. The Department superiors, to whom most matters must be referred, having no real interest in questions submitted for their consideration, and not being exactly aware of the nature of the exigencies of the troops, put aside matters of immediate necessity in the ordinary course of business, and by the delay which takes place, the object is frequently lost. Indeed, so long is the process and so hopeless the prospect of obtaining what is required, that wants are often endured, because the season must pass away ere authority for works can be obtained, and in consequence, are fatal to the interests of the troops.

The abolition of all distinctions between officers and soldiers of the armies of India, strongly advocated and recommended as a mea-

8. The amalgamation of the services is another measure of expediency as well as of necessity which should be at once resorted to, and the present is the most conve-

sure of imperative necessity, and highly advantageous to the interest of the Government of England and India.

nient opportunity for accomplishing it.

The Crown of Great Britain has erected under the names of Queen's and Company's services, a barrier which is a stumbling-block to all improvement, and causes embarrassment in carrying out measures of great public utility. In the re-organisation of the Indian Army, these services should be blended without breaking faith with officers already in that Army. The very feeling of jealousy which at present exists even between brothers and relations, as well as countrymen, engaged in the same duties, arising from this unnecessary and stupid distinction, is prejudicial to the interests, in a thousand ways, of the great Government under which we all are serving.

It is scarcely to be understood how it has happened, that the Crown of England should so long have permitted the existence of such a barrier, which to the nation at large is so highly prejudicial. India is or ought to be the great nursery or school of officers (Commanders and Staff,) for the services of the Crown.

The great field for the exercise of military talent and ingenuity in officers and soldiers, is alone to be found in her Majesty's Indian possessions, and to India mainly, the Crown should look for officers of military experience in her European Wars.

It is too late to train and make officers when war breaks out in Europe; and can officers be formed and made efficient within the limits of Great Britain and her smaller colonies, where the three arms of the service rarely or never in time of peace come together in the field? Certainly not. Hence, then, I maintain, as regards "European services," that the interests of the Crown are not consulted by the barrier which at present exists in regard to Indian Officers, and that as regards "Indian services" it is necessary that all European officers serving in the same army should be placed on the same footing, and thereby made available in common for all duties with the troops. In future engagements, therefore, all should enter on the same terms.

9. The Europeans and natives, must, in my opinion, be henceforward associated and placed in more immediate contact than heretofore, for the public safety.

Organization of the regular troops of India by a combination of Europeans with Natives in all regular corps of Horse and Foot recommended. British Artillery never again to be trusted to Natives.

The regular native army of Bengal, such as its regular cavalry and infantry, I consider as gone for ever; and the army must be re-modelled on principles totally different from those of former times, which have proved to be so thoroughly faulty.

It is scarcely necessary to make any allusion to the artillery branch of the service, which requires perhaps no re-organization, excepting that in no way in future should the natives of the country be intrusted with British Artillery, nor should any native of India be instructed in the use of such dangerous weapons. The native drivers are good horsemen, and the gunners most excellent, but they cannot be trusted; they have a religious veneration for their guns, and in proportion, as they are most valuable to the Government they serve, so are they most formidable when they choose to be rebellious. Considering that in times of peace, the regular native army of the state has hitherto been chiefly employed in police duties, such as escorting public and private property about the country; I would recommend that the army be reduced in numbers, whilst the police of the country be increased, and that the regular native soldiers be never permitted to travel and be scattered over the country as heretofore, in small parties. I would combine the regular native horse and foot altogether with the European corps, in proportion of two Europeans to one native. To the 40,000

European Infantry, which I would fix as the least amount of force required for the Bengal Presidency, I would attach 20,000 natives, trained, armed, and disciplined, precisely in the same manner; and being incorporated with the Europeans, they should be subject to the same rules and regulations of barrack discipline. With every due consideration for their religious prejudices and respect for their peculiar habits, I would keep them quite distinct in their quarters from the European soldiers, but the bugle which sounds the "assembly" for parade, should bring together by companies (only so far distinct,) the Europeans and natives of the corps.

These corps would consist then of 1500 men, 1000 Europeans, rank and file, and 500 natives. On parade, each corps should be formed up in two battalions, each battalion having the due proportion of two Europeans to one native. The natives should take their fair proportion of all regimental duties. On the regimental guards, the two should in general be associated, the native being placed on sentry on posts of exposure to heat for which the European is not calculated; I advocate this measure as one of vast utility, so found by experience throughout my command during the past twelve months of extraordinary difficulty. In Peshawur, the newly raised troops have universally been associated in this manner. They were first combined together from necessity, owing to the paucity of European troops, who had by night and day to guard against the insurrection, (for ever expected,) of the faithless Hindostanee troops in garrison. This system was first proposed to me by Brigadier Galloway, and it has succeeded admirably. To this measure I mainly attribute the rapid progress towards efficiency, which has been made in Peshawur by the newly raised corps of the country. The steadiness of these troops on the duties of the station is now perfectly wonderful. At first it was supposed that the native troops might not relish being brought so closely in contact with the European, but not only do they like it, but they are proud of their position, and strive to the utmost of their ability to bring themselves to the same perfection as Europeans; and the sergeants of guards, and even the European soldiers generally, take a pleasure in drilling and instructing their native comrades.

The Europeans, too, feel their value as helpmates in such a climate, and are kind to them. I have raised a corps of cavalry, which is one of the most valuable corps that I have seen in India, modelled on the same principle. I have had the Peshawur Light horse constantly under canvas since August last, and the corps is perfect in itself for field service. The corps consists of two troops of Europeans (eighty privates) each, and one of natives of the same strength. On service in the district, the cattle of the army must be protected by cavalry whilst grazing, and if baggage breaks down or strays by accident, it is the native soldier alone who can be detached on escort to bring it up, he alone can bear the exposure to such a climate. Foraging parties too in the heat of the day must be sent out, and hence the European is saved for services of different and greater importance. All power to rebel and do mischief is thus taken from the native soldier, and he has become a most valuable and necessary auxiliary; and I do not hesitate here to assert, because I know it to be a fact, that the white and black races so associated, would work together in the field, with one common rivalry for the public good, and I verily believe that the three troops of cavalry, constituted "as is the Peshawur light horse," are fully as valuable to the State, and would be fully as powerful, when in contact with the enemy in India, as the same number of Dragoons exclusively European.

The two fraternized in the most extraordinary manner. When serving with the Madras cavalry, which I did for many years in a regiment of Dragoons, I observed the same thing, the European and native troopers being continually on terms of good fellowship, and were ever friendly to each other; and when I advocate the measure of associating Europeans and natives, I do not hesitate to give it as my opinion, that 20,000 native soldiers, embodied and placed as part and parcel of the same corps with Europeans, would be in full as valuable to Government as even 40,000 of the same before, kept in battalions distinct from each other. The native companies of the regular forces should be classified, they should be enlisted for not less than seven years, and should be composed of Hindoos, Mussulmans, Ghoorkas, Seikhs, in fact all sorts, but they must be in separate companies. They should be completely officered like the European companies with European officers. The grade of native officers in such battalions should be for ever abolished. In each troop or company there should be a European Sergeant-Major or European Colour-Sergeant, the native non-commissioned officers of companies should be termed Havildars and Naiks as heretofore. The native non-commissioned officers should be selected and rise by merit and not by seniority, and to no higher grade than that should they ever rise in the regular army: and in order to encourage the well behaved and deserving non-commissioned officers, they might, for special services and general good conduct, be promoted into the Irregular corps, where, being perfect in drill, their services would be acceptable; or they might be removed into the civil branches of the service. Those natives who would choose to serve the Government on such terms, should be enlisted, and none other. They should be hired to serve everywhere, and to work as the soldiers of all nations work, with the spade and pickaxe.

It has been urged by some, that the natives when embodied with Europeans, might lose respect for them, owing to their dissipated habits. This is a mistake arising from a want of knowledge of European troops. Unfortunately, in isolated positions when the European soldiers are not properly looked after, some drunkenness prevails; but in well regulated corps, as all should be and generally are, a drunken soldier is never seen in a barrack square. Drunkenness is not now a prevailing crime as it used to be in the army. I can safely assert, that during the five or six years that I have been in the Peshawur cantonment, I have not seen half a dozen drunken European soldiers about the station, so vigilant are the military police and so strict are the regulations relative to drunkenness.

Organization of the Irregular Native Cavalry and Infantry recommended.

10. The Native Irregular Cavalry and Infantry must next come under consideration. I am of opinion that about 40,000 men would suffice for the service of the Bengal Presidency; the Infantry should be armed with firelocks and two grooved rifles, but the Enfield rifle should never be trusted to them. And as I would congregate troops very much more than heretofore in great military cantonments, and would keep them under strict and rigid discipline as in our military colonies, the Irregular forces should be chiefly therein cantoned, and distributed in due proportion to the other arms of the service. For instance, Trans Jhelum, I would have an army of 25,000 men, and these should garrison the whole of the posts and stations on the Sind Sâgur district, and the Peshawur, Kohat, and Hazara frontiers. The force should be composed of the three arms, with all services, and placed in the Sind Sâgur District, as the great frontier force of India, which has been found to be most healthy; and I would place the greater part of this body as near to the Indus as possible, say on the plains at Campbellpore, (if these plains are found on experience to be healthy). Campbellpore is admirably situated as a support to the frontier posts of Kohat, Peshawur, and Hazara, being nearly equi-

distant from these posts respectively. And I would keep only such troops at these advanced frontier posts, as are politically required to preserve order, looking to the great frontier force in the Sind Sâgur district as the base of all operations on the border, and available for service at a moment's notice in any direction at all seasons of the year, furnishing detachments for all these posts of the frontier, viz., Kohat, Peshawur, and Hazara, and the minor stations attached to them.

Proper arrangements should at once be made for the transport of these troops by boats, and sheds should be erected on all the great roads at convenient distances.

Of the constitution of the Native Irregular Cavalry and Infantry corps, as I think it is admitted by every one, that they have not at present nearly sufficient European officers, I would alter the present organization in that respect. It is proposed by many well acquainted with the subject, and I am inclined to consider that opinion is founded on wisdom, that instead of increasing very much the number of European officers with the corps as at present established, it would be far better to reduce the effective strength of corps in numbers of men, and to increase the number of European officers slightly; so that corps of cavalry should not exceed 300 men—two squadrons of two troops each, and corps of infantry should not exceed 500 rank and file in six companies. To each corps of Irregular Cavalry I would post a Commandant and second in command, with six officers doing duty besides the Adjutant; and, indeed, more European officers if found necessary.

To each corps of Irregular Infantry, a Commandant, a second in command, and twelve European officers doing duty; each company thereby having two European officers besides the Adjutant. I would not deprive these Irregular regiments of their native officers; they should remain as at present constituted in that respect; but the Commanders of regiments should have increased powers, and native officers as well as men should be subject at his hand to instant dismissal for breaches of discipline. It should not be necessary to raise these native officers from the ranks. On the contrary, the respectable natives of the country of the upper grades being desirous of serving the British Government, might be hired as native officers, bringing with them clansmen on whom they could depend, and over whom personally they might have some moral influence and control.

As regards classes and castes in these irregular corps, I am inclined to think, that as their numerical strength, regimentally, would be so small, and as I would keep the army cantoned generally in larger bodies than heretofore, it might be best that *each corps should be composed of one class or caste,* so that the counterpoise might be by regiments and not by troops and companies, as was suggested with regiments of their original strength.

Selection of officers for appointment to Irregular Corps.

11. In selecting the European officers for these duties, the greatest care should be taken. They should be well paid, and discouraged in every possible way from changing from one branch of the service to another.

The introduction of foreigners of colour as soldiers in the British service, disapproved of.

12. I do not think it ever would be necessary, if my proposal were carried out in full, to bring foreigners of colour into the Indian service; I think they would become a very great burden to the State when worn out, and perhaps very troublesome. Look at the Arabs in the Deccan, in the service of the Nizam. And if I mistake not, the corps composed of Malays, Caffres, and Sepoys in the British service in the Ceylon regiments in

former days, were not found to answer. Neither do I think that the natives of this country, situated as I have recommended, could ever combine together in general rebellion against the British Government.

The armies of India to be divided into *corps d'armée* told off into Brigades with staff complete as per field service.

These *corps d'armée* should take the field for exercise two months in each year.

13. I would divide the army into corps, each corps to consist of at least 20,000 men, and be numbered and kept entirely on field establishments. These *corps d'armée* as they should be termed, should be under the command of a Major-General, with the personal staff of Military Secretary, and two aides-de-camp, with a general staff of Assistant-Adjutant-General, Assistant-Quarter-Master-General and Deputies, so competent to the duties of the command and so complete, that business could meet with no hindrance. These *corps d'armée* should have their own Commissariat, Ordnance Commissariat, and Barrack Departments, and be divided into brigades, fully officered with staff as on field service. Camp equipage and carriage should always be kept up, so that the troops might move at a moment's notice; and every *corps d'armée* should take the field for exercise two months in every year at least, if not more. The present system of placing 12,000 men of the three arms (sometimes more and sometimes less) under one Brigadier with a single Brigade Major, should be at once discontinued. The Honourable the Court of Directors of the East India Company, who have established this system (probably looking to small expenditure, and that only), do not appear to have been aware or mindful of the necessities of armies. These old arrangements may cause a small draft on the Treasury for Commanders and Staff, but they are not economical, because practically (under such circumstances) troops cannot be efficient for immediate service.

Every soldier, to whatever arm he may belong, should be kept on the roll of a *corps d'armée,* where rigid and strict discipline being maintained, and all the military exercises being practised, none would be deteriorated by being temporarily on detached duties. It must be necessary of course sometimes to detach troops from these large bodies, but detachments should be relieved very frequently, and hence very little evil would happen to them. The great forts, such as Fort William, might or might not be an exception to this rule. It is impossible for any officer to enter into a detailed statement, pointing out all the necessary localities for these *corps d'armée,* in a political point of view; and therefore in writing on the subject, I can only recommend for the consideration of Government the general principles on which I would reorganise the army: the whole of my suggestions are intended to point very distinctly to the great principles on which such a country as India should henceforward be ruled with a view to its future security; *the general re-organisation being essentially military.*

Soldiers not to be employed in police duties or escorting prisoners: the police of this country to be increased in numbers, but not to be drilled and armed as soldiers, excepting in certain localities.

14. And now with regard to the general police of the country, which I would augment so as to discontinue altogether the practice of employing soldiers of the army in police duties, or such duties as would cause them to stroll or straggle all over the country.

In the first place, I would on no account arm and discipline police like soldiers, because by that measure the Government are training the police to be just as formidable as native soldiers of the regular army have been. The Peshawur and Frontier Districts must be exempted from this; the police must be armed in these places. Concluding that the British Government will never for the future allow the population of this country to be armed, it is wholly unnecessary to think of training policemen with arms, and to drill them as soldiers.

When the country becomes settled, therefore, and the people deprived of their arms, as they must be, and having settled down to peaceful occupations, it will be unnecessary to give the police of the country generally any other weapon than the tulwar, indeed even that might not be necessary. A few firearms at the police posts under the constable, or chief of police, would suffice to keep order in the country. I will leave to others to determine the amount of police force required, so as to avoid, in all ordinary cases, calling for the services of the troops as treasure escorts, &c., &c., by the civil authorities, as has been the practice heretofore.

A general list instead of Regimental lists recommended, for officers serving on the Staff and with Irregular Corps.

15. I think if the European officers *serving* on the Staff and other detached duties and in Irregular Corps were placed on one general list as in the Artillery, it would be far better to have them so than on regimental lists, because from those general lists selections being made for all regimental and staff duties, the officers best suited for the various occupations would find their way into their proper places; officers might be regularly appointed in the regular service and rise accordingly.

Recommending the abolition of the system by which troops such as the Punjaub Forces are kept under the civil authorities of Government and removed from the control of His Excellency the Commander-in-Chief.

16. The system at present prevailing of raising officers rapidly from the lower to the higher grades to meet the emergencies of the services according to their qualification, will I hope and trust speedily remove from the service that exceedingly objectionable arrangement, by which large bodies of troops are kept under the control and management exclusively of the civil officers of Government, entirely removed from the authority of the Commander-in-Chief of the army.

I have heard but two reasons given for the prevalence of such an extraordinary system, and which in times of war and difficulty could not possibly be sustained, which are, firstly —it enables local governments to place in authority over such troops younger and more efficient officers, and secondly —being under the immediate control of the local Civil Government, which is vested with powers at once to meet the wants and demands of the troops, the usual embarrassments which are experienced by the troops of the army are never felt. Does not this speak volumes as to the defects of the system under which the regular army suffers, when it is actually found necessary to organise and keep up forces, separate and distinct from the regular army for frontier services, the army embarrassments rendering it unserviceable in such positions? Indeed the army must and should be under one authority, and the army embarrassments must and should be removed. The present machinery of military matters is indeed, as before stated, much too complicated. During the greater part of the recent rebellion, fortunately for the troops of the Peshawur Frontier, the ordinary channels of communication with the far distant Government were closed, and the Chief Commissioner of the Punjaub, ever ready and prompt to meet the exigencies of the times, acted entirely on his own responsibility, and the most useful and necessary measures were sanctioned without a moment's delay. No sooner, however, were the roads thrown open, than the military machinery became again clogged, and matters were restored to their pristine embarrassments. I offer these remarks solely for the public good, not intending to reflect on any acts of my superiors, but simply to prove how much the present military administration needs reform.

17. I would urgently recommend also to the Government, to abolish a system by which some of its best and most valuable military

Recommending that officers of the army should not be taken from military duties and employed in the Civil services of the country.

officers are excluded from the power to do good in their own profession, by being locked up in Kutcheries and Commissariat offices, and employed in the various civil services of the country.

If the Government thinks that these officers, of whose valuable services the army is deprived, are, or ever can be, with all their talent, courage, and devotion, qualified to command troops as they should be commanded when brought out on a sudden emergency to serve with or lead them in the field, I, as an old soldier, can solemnly assure it that they cannot be so. To have the entire confidence of the troops. and that moral influence so essential to military government, officers must be identified with their men, and must be associated with them in peace as well as in war. They must know well their wants, and enter warmly into their feelings, and so maintain discipline by paternal and friendly intercourse, rather than by perpetually turning to the clauses of the Mutiny Act. There is much more required of an officer than courage in battle, and a clear head to discern. The admiration of the soldier towards any man who is daring in battle will be gained, it is true, for the moment, but the general confidence in him must still be wanting if he be a stranger to the troops. Let the army, then, have its own, and let the civil services of the country be otherwise provided for.

18. The unsettled state, at present, of the officers of the army in India, under that existing system, is enough to ruin the finest army in the world. Regimental officers being from the commencement of their career, taught as it were, by contagion, to look for pecuniary advantages, whether in civil or military life, have no *esprit de corps*, and escape from their men the first moment they get the opportunity.

Esprit de corps taken from officers by these various objectionable rules.

There is another vast evil prevailing, principally in the

Bengal presidency, to which I cannot help adverting, as tending in like manner to unsettle the minds of officers, and to take from them all interest in and affection for the soldiers of the service to which they belong, and that is the indiscriminate leave of absence which is given to officers, to visit the hills and Cashmere for six months in every year. Of all the inventions that could be hit upon to ruin and injure the younger officers, in particular, of the army, and to take away from them all feelings of affection towards the soldiers with whom they are enrolled and ought to be continually associated, none could be more effectual than this. Besides, large bodies of young officers congregating and away from military control, and leading a life of continued idleness for so long a period, resort to every description of immorality and debauchery, and are, in fact, utterly ruined, and thereby rendered unfit, to a very considerable extent, for the duties of their profession when they return to them.

Medical officers are indeed too incautious in granting medical certificates; and officers reported incapable of performing their military duties, are to be seen in droves, who are gaming and drinking all night in the hill stations, full of health and vigour, unblushingly laughing amongst themselves as to their adroitness in misleading the doctor.

This is by no means an incorrect picture of military life generally prevailing in the upper provinces of Bengal.

To save troops, the improvement of roads and bridges recommended. The introduction of European Sappers recommended, and also the discontinuance of the system of employing officers and soldiers of regiments of the line in overlooking Public Works.

19. I would here take leave to refer to several matters which bear very much on the question of reorganisation.

1st. The necessary strength of the army depends very much on the state of the roads and bridges, and means of transporting troops.

Government has expended vast sums of money in the construction of roads in the Punjaub which have remained unfinished the last two or three years.

The want of proper overseers, and trustworthy men in the Public Works, has caused a vast waste of public money.

I would recommend that a most efficient corps of Sappers, European and Native, be kept up with each *corps d'armée*, ready at all times to carry on under the executive engineer the great military works in progress; the former should be employed as overseers and chief artisans, and the latter as tradesmen.

The system heretofore prevailing of employing officers and soldiers of the line as overseers on the lines of roads is most objectionable. The former (young officers) are sent to overlook the construction of great works, of which they are entirely ignorant; and naturally idle, as many young officers are, they become more and more so when away from the duties of their profession and the control of their commanding officers. In many cases they are worse than useless to Government, and become totally ruined as officers by the bad habits they contract. The latter (the common soldiers) cannot be trusted with money, frequently turn out dishonest, rob the Government, and return to their corps with lost characters.

The soldiers generally, European and Native, should be, when available, employed as labourers in the public works, and in the great military gardens, which should be cultivated near to, but not in, the stations of the army, receiving for their services, working money.

The labour of soldiers, in cool weather, is most valuable to Government, much more so than that of Coolies, for the same money; and the system is in every way useful to the soldiers themselves; it assists them very much in providing for their families, prepares them, by practice, for throwing up field-works in time of war, and affords them healthy recreation.

20. Sheds should be erected, as before hinted at, along all the great military roads, for the shelter of troops in the heat of the day; and the land transport trains for the conveyance of troops in the hot weather, recently introduced from necessity in various parts of the country, should be vastly increased and improved, and they should be kept up until the railway is introduced, and river steam navigation improved throughout India. I would never move troops in the ordinary course of relief in tents; they should march from shed to shed in the ordinary routes, and the marches might be much longer with the same fatigue to the men.

The Land Transport trains to be improved and increased for the conveyance of troops all over the country.

21. A system of espionage so essential to good Government in a conquered country, should be established, and freely paid; and all breaches of regulations (such as being found with arms in possession, &c.,) should be considered capital offences, and summarily dealt with by order of military commanders. One of the greatest wants of an army, quartered, as it were, in an enemy's country, (for so we must view India, more or less, for a long time to come) is a good and sufficient intelligence department.

Intelligence departments recommended as most necessary in the re-organisation of the army.

The commanders of all the great military bodies should have a well organised establishment of this nature, with ample funds at their disposal to pay for secret intelligence. A strict surveillance may be kept, and, in such times as these, are kept, over the Post Office receipts and issues; and letters of a seditious nature may be often so intercepted; but the natives generally are much too cunning to expose their mutinous designs to such a risk of discovery. They have other modes of communicating which require the most shrewd and practised hands to trace and discover.

22. The construction of suitable barracks for the troops, European

Temporary Barracks recommended instead of Pucka Barracks.

and Native, in the great cantonments, is another subject of vast importance. It is wholly unnecessary to build such costly barracks as those recently constructed in the Punjaub. The kutcha barracks of an improved construction such as those built by Lieutenant Taylor of the Bengal Engineers, at Campbellpore, at the cost of 3000 Rs. for 50 European soldiers, are sufficiently good for any troops. The temporary buildings are much preferred (as being cooler than pucka buildings) by the soldiery, and then when it becomes necessary, from political motives, and from localities becoming unhealthy, to change quarters, the loss is not severely felt by Government. These temporary buildings ought to last ten years, at least, at the expiration of which time, in all likelihood, it may be considered expedient to take up new positions for the troops. And here I can venture to give as instances of the instability of military posts the three great stations of Peshawur, Rawul Pindee, and Sealkote, which have cost the Government so many lacs or perhaps crores of rupees; every one of which is either useless to Government or injurious to the troops.

Peshawur has proved to be so sickly as to be almost untenable. Rawul Pindee, although healthy, is so situated as to have no political object in itself, and is too far distant from the frontier to be a good support in time of need; and Sealkote is politically entirely useless. There, then, is a powerful argument in favour of temporary barracks as quarters for troops. In all the three above-named stations, the most costly buildings have been erected.

Native troops also must throughout be quartered in barracks, but of inferior construction, of course, to those of the Europeans. No soldier, white or black, should ever live out of barracks, and for the European officers everywhere should quarters be built by Government, in close proximity to their men. Of all the arrangements I have proposed for the maintenance of discipline, none is of greater importance than this. During the great mutiny, from first to last, I have never allowed the officers of corps, armed or disarmed, loyal or disloyal, to be absent from their men; their constant attendance has prevented combination. With 10,000 Hindostanee troops in the Peshawur district, and only 2000 Europeans, I have so successfully maintained order under such a system that although 2500 men have mutinied, not a European officer or soldier, woman or child, have fallen at the hands of the mutineers. I earnestly beg of the Government to take this suggestion most seriously under consideration.

Mess houses too for the European officers, of temporary materials, should be everywhere constructed with the officers' quarters on a moderate scale, and the quarters and mess houses should be sufficiently well furnished by Government; in fact, the officers should be thereby enabled to move at a moment's notice, without loss or encumbrance, and in every way should they be discouraged from keeping up useless baggage and furniture. The mess establishment of corps, at present cumbersome and exorbitant, should be entirely abolished in such a country as India; camp fashion, as it is termed, should be re-introduced as in former times, when messes, in my opinion, were as comfortable and as good as at present.

The mess house allowance would of course be discontinued, and when the troops are in the field, a liberal allowance for mess tents and carriage should be paid by Government; six or eight hundred rupees a month per corps, if the Government did not choose to provide mess tents, to be gradually diminished if the troops remained long under canvas.

The camp equipage for each *corps d'armée,* with carriage for the same, should be kept in cantonments at all times complete and ready for service. The regiments should be held answerable for tents only when using them. It was bad economy when, by a Government enactment, the carriage for camp equipage was discharged. I refer in particular to the embarrassment of the late Commander-in-Chief, when he could not move on Delhi from want of carriage.

A Citadel to be constructed in each military cantonment.

23. To every great military cantonment should be attached a sort of "Citadel" for the security of public property, which at all times should contain the arsenal and Treasury.

The citadel should be an entrenched camp, defensible and garrisoned by a portion of the *corps d'armée*, continually relieved. On the score of health it never would answer, in Asiatic climates, to huddle troops together in small spaces. The cantonments must be open, airy, and spacious, and when the troops are in the field, or danger apprehended, all valuable property, with the soldiers' families, &c., &c., should be placed for safety in the citadel, if such a term may be used.

Relative to the employment of Eurasians as troops in the service of Government.

24. I have collected and established in one company the half-caste native drummers of the disarmed Hindoostanee corps serving in the Peshawur division, and having trained them in the use of the two grooved rifle, and equipped them for field service, they are not only a reliable body, but are most useful, taking their duties in common with the European troops.

The principal duty of this company is to escort the batteries of artillery, whenever guns are required to leave the park.

I can report most favourably on the Eurasian company, and strongly recommend that persons of that class may meet with greater encouragement than they have hitherto done.

The double object of this measure, is to improve the condition of a class, which, as heretofore employed, had fallen into a state of degradation, and at the same time to obtain a reliable body of men, really attached to Government; considering them like Europeans, (one of the main objects being, to raise them as near as possible to the standard of European troops,) I have placed the Eurasians on the rolls for commissariat rations. Sir John Lawrence has opposed that part of the measure as unnecessary, although he warmly advocated their being enrolled as fighting men; but I know what their feelings are, they are most anxious to continue their present system of messing. I know well also the value to them of the rations, and I urgently recommend that they be rationed accordingly in common with the European troops.

Keeping a strict watch over the manufacture of Cannon and warlike stores and implements.

25. I recommend that a strict and watchful eye be kept in future over the manufacture of implements of war. I would exclude the native altogether from the ordnance foundries, and the manufactories of percussion caps and other warlike stores and implements; I would make it a capital offence for any native to manufacture such articles, or to have in their possession the implements by which they are made. Regardless of the danger attending the dissemination of such knowledge throughout India, in the art of war in all its branches, the Native Infantry soldiers have been taught by us to be gunners, and the people of the country have been taught to prepare weapons; and thus it appears, by incautious systems, we have been training the inhabitants to rise up in rebellion, well prepared for our destruction.

More European officers in India, and the pay of the lower grades recommended to be increased.

26. There are not at present nearly sufficient European officers in India or on its establishment, for the ordinary services of the country. I consider the ordinary pay and allowances of the lower grades of regimental European officers, to be wholly insufficient; many officers are in consequence, in such bad circumstances, as materially to interfere with their efficiency.

If the Government be pleased to build quarters for officers near to, and adjoining the soldiers' barracks, as I have recommended, it would be a great and necessary boon conferred on them, if the officers were allowed to occupy them as in Europe, without charge for rent; and I recommend very strongly, that the pay and allowances of all officers may be consolidated.

High ranges of hills not recommended for large bodies of European troops.

27. I do not recommend that European troops should be located and quartered in the high ranges of hills, excepting such as are specially recommended by experienced medical officers for change of air and recovery of health. There are many diseases, particularly those of an organic nature, which are not improved by the hills, and to the patients suffering under such diseases, the hills often are fatal. The climates of the mountains are, in fact, more or less unnatural; we ascend mountains gradually, until human life becomes extinct. The damp and rain of the Himalayahs at the elevation of seven or eight thousand feet, are very injurious in some cases, particularly with old soldiers suffering from chronic dysentery, the result of living long in tropical climates and leading a hard life. In heart complaints too, the hills are injurious, indeed fatal.

When bodies of troops, such as regiments, are placed in the hills, of course every description of disease to which the human frame is liable, will be found amongst them. To many the climate is fatal, whilst to others, of course, the cool atmosphere is beneficial; I would, therefore, recommend the hills for troops only, when the proper selections are made. The soldiers dislike the hills exceedingly, I recommend that the best selections may be made, in the most advantageous and healthy localities in the plains and lower ranges for the great cantonments.

Conclusion.

28. I feel confident, that with armies constituted and organized throughout India as I have suggested, the public safety would be maintained, and with forces infinitely less in numerical strength, than those heretofore in the service of Government. Very much more might be written on this most important subject.

I am quite unable now to enter into detailed particulars relative to the services of the Bombay and Madras presidencies, nor can I fix as to the amount of artillery and cavalry required in Bengal. My despatch, already perhaps too lengthy, contains, however, my views as to the general principles of "re-organisation" of the whole of the armies of India, subject to local modifications; my object in thus addressing my superiors at such a moment on such a subject, has, it appears to me, been sufficiently attained without entering into more minute particulars.

I have the honour to be, Sir,

Your most obedient servant,

(Signed) SYDNEY COTTON,

Major General,

Commanding Peshawur Division.

To Major General Sir W. R. Mansfield, K.C.B.,
Chief of the Staff.

Division Head Quarters, Peshawur,
29th December, 1858.

Sir,—In continuation of my despatch, addressed to you on the 11th June, 1858, in which I recommended to Government (amongst other things, consequent on the great mutiny of the Bengal army,) the concentration of large bodies of European and native troops, in healthy and centrical localities, in preference to the prevailing system, by which, it appears to me, our troops and military stores are unnecessarily distributed, and placed in isolated localities, to the danger of the interests of the state, as well as to the injury of the troops; I have now the honour to bring under the consideration of the Right Honourable the Commander-in-Chief in India, and of Government, certain suggestions, by which I would hope to introduce measures of reform, tending to strengthen our positions on the Peshawur Frontier, whilst the European Forces, now of such incalculable value to Government, would be economised.

2. It will not be found that I advocate measures, which would require of the Government a larger number of European troops for the services of the Peshawur division, than has already been sanctioned, but I hope to increase the strength and efficiency of those which have been allotted to us.

3. I am well aware of the difficulty in which I am placed when I recommend an alteration in, or discontinuance of, old and fixed establishments, which have become, by usage, apparently necessary to our existence; and when I endeavour to remove prejudices, which, notwithstanding recent events,

dispose men, even those who are best able to judge of such matters, to contemplate with alarm any radical changes in our present military system.

4. It has long been admitted by the civil and military authorities of the Punjaub and its environs, that the Peshawur district is unhealthy in the extreme, and that its climate is peculiarly unfavourable to Europeans, as it is to all other foreign troops; it is needless to attempt to exempt any portion of the Peshawur Valley from the effects of the general malaria; at certain times, certain parts of the valley have been more or less unhealthy; but no part whatever, is, or ever has been, exempt from the malarious fever of the country.

5. The measure of locating in the Peshawur valley, the large frontier force of this part of our Indian dominions, was originally opposed by the late Major-General Sir Henry Lawrence, under the full conviction, that if British troops were permanently fixed there, disastrous consequences must ensue; year after year has this expectation been realised in full; and during my service of nearly seven years on this frontier, I have witnessed the entire prostration of a force of upwards of 12,000 men, of all arms and colour, who have in the autumnal months of each year, become so entirely powerless, as to be useless to Government, should their service in the field have been required. The current year, (1858) owing, apparently, to the entire absence of rain, has been the only exception to the general rule.

6. Much as it is to be lamented, that barracks for European troops, of the most costly and extensive kind, have been erected in the cantonments of Peshawur and Nowshera, I am of opinion, that it would be a measure of real economy, at once to withdraw from the right bank of the Indus, every European and native soldier who is not actually and bonâ fide, required for the occupation of that country; concen-

trating and keeping up a powerful force as near as possible to the left bank of the River Indus;—this has been for a long time past my opinion, and caused me to direct the Engineer officers carefully to examine the country and plains near Attock, with a view to the selection of suitable ground for a large and extensive military position; no pains were spared in making this selection, and Government was pleased, on my recommendation, during the last year, to sanction the erection of temporary barracks at Campbellpore, experimentally, within twelve miles of the fort and ferry of the Indus, at Attock;—the experiment, as to the health of troops, has been tried, and Campbellpore is proved to be one of the healthiest places as yet discovered in India; whilst it is in other respects, as regards the Peshawur frontier, the most eligible spot for troops that could possibly be imagined. Campbellpore is also within four or five miles of the ferry over the Indus at Neelab (twelve miles down that stream from Attock). This ferry is one of the ancient routes across the Indus, by which trade was formerly carried on between Afghanistan, Central Asia, and the provinces of Hindostan.

During the current year, H.M. 98th Regiment, recently arrived from England, has been quartered in the new barracks at Campbellpore, in the enjoyment of health, almost, if not altogether, the most perfect that has ever been experienced in the most healthy countries in the world. The wonderful health of the troops, European and native, at Campbellpore, has been reported on by the medical officers to the head of their own department, as it has been in various ways and at various times by myself, to the Punjaub Government and to the highest civil and military authorities of the country.

7. I have been led to understand, by a recent despatch of the Secretary to the Punjaub Government, that the Chief Commissioner has contemplated, or perhaps has already re-

commended to Government, the surrender altogether of the Peshawur and Trans-Indus districts, and the withdrawal of our forces to the left bank of that river; thereby substituting the River Indus as our boundary instead of the mountain ranges of Afghanistan.

If, unhappily, at any time, a retrograde movement of that sort be sanctioned, and carried into effect, I am of opinion, that nothing but the most disastrous consequences must ensue. Having once placed ourselves under the mountain passes, and having well and truly established our supremacy throughout, and amongst the wild tribes inhabiting those mountains, which we certainly have done, at the cost of blood and treasure, it would appear to me, a vast sacrifice on our part, to relinquish the advantages we have gained; besides, a retrograde movement of any sort, would, in the eyes of the semi-barbarians of our present border, be an act of weakness for which they could not otherwise account, than by determining that our inability to hold our own caused us to fly from, and evacuate, a possession, which, it is well known, is considered by the people within, and beyond our border, of the utmost value.

None would indeed believe, that aught but dire necessity, could have caused us to surrender the advantage we have gained, and the British name by the movement would, unquestionably, be immeasurably deteriorated.

Moreover, it must be clear to every military man of consideration, that if at any time our frontier should be threatened and in danger of foreign invasion in this direction, we must instantly repossess ourselves of the fertile valley of Peshawur (if we had given it up), to prevent our enemies concentrating their forces in that quarter. An invasion by the mountain passes must be, to a certain extent, gradual, and situated as we are at present, the invading forces might be disposed of in detail; but let them have possession of the

Peshawur district, and their concentration and arrangements for attack would be made under the most favourable circumstances; besides which, in ordinary times, the Peshawur district would become in all likelihood as it has been before, the cockpit of all the discordant spirits and ruffians of Central Asia, causing our Government within the Indus incessant uneasiness and anxiety. The re-occupation of the Peshawur valley in case of necessity might perhaps too, be an operation of some difficulty; at all events when carried out, our troops would be placed in a sickly country under the most disadvantageous circumstances.

8. I will presume then, that on no account will our present frontier be surrendered. I would maintain the frontier as at present, keeping up the line of posts from the Hazara country by Topi in Euzofzaie on the right bank of the Indus, and following the present line by Hoti Murdan, the forts of Abaziai, Shubkudur, and Mitchnee to Peshawur, and thence on to Eymae-ka-Chabootra at the mouth of the Kohat Pass, and so on to Kohat, Bunnoo, Dera Ismail Khan, and Ghazee Khan, which brings the frontier of these parts to the vicinity of the Mooltan Cantonments.

In each of these posts, I would maintain such troops and munitions of war only as are absolutely necessary to assist the Civil Government in the preservation of peace and order along the border, withdrawing to the left bank of the Indus every European and native soldier, that is not necessary or absolutely required for that purpose. I would in like manner withdraw all the arsenals and military stores from these outposts, and would establish the great arsenal of the frontier as well as a force of 15,000 or 20,000 men of all arms, castes, and colours on the newly selected plains of Campbellpore. Having so brought together in the most centrical position that could be imagined not only as regards the frontier itself, but as regards the Peshawur division generally, this great and main reserve force, I would open the roads at once, and establish the most ready means of communication between Campbellpore and its outposts; a work now, I can assure the Government, of little labour, and of little expense compared with the vast and important object I have in view. The plains of Campbellpore are not only healthy, but most peculiarly well situated for all military purposes. They are so near the passages of the Indus at Attock and Neelab, that the troops there placed could by an easy night's march in the shortest nights and in the hottest weather, cross the Indus, should reinforcements at the more advanced positions be suddenly required.

9. I would here request the particular attention of the Right Honourable the Commander-in-Chief, and of Government, to the passage of the Indus at the Neelab Ferry, which is immediately opposite to the present cantonment of Campbellpore, and only four or five miles from it—being about twelve miles down the stream from Attock.

The current of the river at Attock, in passing through rocks with probably a considerable fall, rushes at times with extreme violence, causing a heavy swell with great danger to the ferry boats; whilst the river at Neelab, although not much wider, if any, is more open and still, and the current immeasurably less rapid. Neelab is placed at an elbow or bend in the river, which is of great advantage to the ferry boats, having very considerable back water towards its banks; so very particular is this difference between the ferry lines of Attock and Neelab, that it is only surprising that the latter should not have been more frequented by the traders.

In all likelihood, now that we have established ourselves at Campbellpore, the trade will be restored to that line, and it may be expected that the Attock passage may be less frequented—troops of the enemy surely, having a better passage of the river would never approach the ferry and guns of the fort at Attock; it would appear then that a post at Campbellpore is politically necessary on that account.

A glance at the accompanying sketch will show the centrical position of Campbellpore, and who can doubt but that with an army in health, vigour, and high discipline, in such a position, the powers of the Executive Government would be strengthened? The moral effect of collecting this force would indeed be most important to the interests of the British Government.

The countries of Central Asia, far and wide, would be held in awe, whilst our frontier would be firmly and finally secure in this direction.

10. Amongst the very many important advantages and considerations connected with Campbellpore as a location for troops, I would here desire to draw the attention of Government to its position as regards the Steam Navigation of the Indus, and the ferry passages across that river at Khala Bagh and Khooshalghur.—The New Steam Navigation Company propose to work their vessels up to within a couple of miles of Khala Bagh.—It is expected that these vessels will work against the stream at any season at the rate of eight knots an hour, they will carry a thousand men, with their baggage, or a thousand tons of goods. When fully laden the draft of water will be under four feet, and of course when half laden, which is the intention when the river is low, the draft of water will be very much less.

Should this project not be carried out in full, there is no doubt but that the navigation by steam will be effected by the Company to Khala Bagh. The road via Futty Jung to Khala Bagh is already made, and is capable of improvement, so that with great facility the troops at Campbellpore might perfect it for military purposes. The ferries of the Indus, at Khala Bagh and Khooshalghur are open to Campbellpore in like manner, and the approach to the British territory by those routes will be guarded by the force on the Campbellpore plains.

11. But in carrying out my proposed measure of concentration, it is necessary to explain that one of the main objects which I have in view is the constant drill and discipline of the troops. The strictest military discipline must prevail with all such concentrated forces, and I would constantly and from time to time relieve by the troops of the main reserve, the detached troops of the outposts, thereby depriving the native forces of the power to combine with foreigners against the British Government. By this arrangement their discipline would be kept perfect, and the health of all hands be preserved; besides, a British feeling, so essential to the interests of the Government, would be encouraged amongst the native troops by a constant intercourse with British soldiers.

12. I have already, in the despatch above alluded to, advocated in the strongest manner, the measure of placing the whole of the troops of this frontier of the British deminions under one commander, feeling convinced by that measure alone the machinery of military government can work well; and the powers of the civil government of the country would be vastly strengthened by resorting to that apparently most necessary expedient.

13. At Peshawur, I would keep up, of course, a considerable force of European and Native troops. Peshawur would become then the main outpost of the frontier, as it is at present the main reserve of the present line of posts. In an entrenched position, where the head quarters of the civil authorities are at present located, I would have a powerful brigade of the three arms, viz., one complete European regi-

ment of Infantry with a proportion of Native regular troops (two Europeans to one Native, as originally suggested, being attached to that corps), two complete regiments of Native Irregular Infantry, and one of Native Irregular Cavalry, one complete European Horse Battery of nine-pounders, and two companies of Sappers. I would also have the Mountain Train Buttery attached to the Peshawur force.

14. The passage through the Kuttuck Hills called the Meerkullen Pass should at once (as already ordered by Government) be made easy for military purposes, or else the road by the Pass Khanny-Khail somewhat to the eastward of Meerkullen might be made, which is rather more easy of access, and such means of transport down the Indus towards the Derajat, should be always available at Neelab, as would admit of reinforcements of troops and stores being speedily and at once despatched down the river from the great station and arsenal at Campbellpore.

15. It would be as needless for me here to dwell on the importance to Government of selecting healthy localities for troops as it is to argue on the advantages of concentration. The same number of troops placed in centrical positions with good roads and bridges on the lines leading therefrom, towards the various detached posts, must be of double value when so situated.

The garrison of the fort of Attock should belong of course to the Campbellpore force, the troops there being continually relieved, as elsewhere, from the parent station.

I would strongly recommend that no additional troops be placed at Rawul Pindee; that station has certainly the merit of being healthy, but it is too far distant from the Indus to be a good support to the troops on the Peshawur frontier; besides, it has really no political importance in itself besides being a connecting link between the troops on the frontier and the concentrated force which ought to be situated at Lahore, the capital of the Punjaub.

But it must here be remarked that if reinforcements should be required to the eastward, Campbellpore being exactly midway between Peshawur and Rawul Pindee, viz., 50 miles from each, can as easily reinforce the one as the other. The centrical situation of Campbellpore as head quarters and capital of the military command of the Peshawur division all must admit to be perfect.

16. The troops at Campbellpore should be placed in three divisions, on as many ridges, for which these plains are so remarkable. Each division should consist of a complete force of three arms, besides the forces at the outposts, being commanded by an energetic officer with a complete and efficient Staff to each division, at all times ready for field service, individually or collectively with the other divisions as may be required. These divisions should be quite separate in their organisation and management, but so near to each other as to admit of an assembly of the whole at all times for the purpose of exercise. The soil, water, and elevation of the several ridges are precisely the same, all having the same advantages. A portion of the central division should, as before recommended, be entrenched. The entrenchment should contain the great arsenals and military chest of the Peshawur division; and should be the place of residence of the Peshawur divisional commander and his head quarters.

The entrenched position should be the place of refuge for the families of the officers and soldiers in time of trouble, and the works of the entrenchment should be entirely got up by the troops themselves, who should be continually practised in the use of spade and pickaxe.

17. I would again venture to bring under the considera-

tion of Government the serious inconvenience which is attached to the military forces, by being continually employed in escort duties. It interferes most materially with the discipline and efficiency of the soldiers, and is therefore bad economy, if it is done only to save the expense attending any increase in the established police force of the country, which might be required for that purpose.

In my humble opinion, after due warning be given, it should be a capital offence for any inhabitants of the country, unless duly licensed, to have arms in their possession, or the means of making them, ammunition, or military stores. And if that be strictly carried out, it could not be necessary (when the country is settled) for the ordinary police force to carry fire arms; indeed, the police must not be trusted with fire arms. They might safely escort all ordinary goods with a talwar, having a few fire arms at the police chowkees, under charge of the European inspectors; the military forces only being employed in escorting treasures and military stores of any extraordinary value.

Your obedient Servant,

SYDNEY COTTON,

Major General,

Commanding Peshawur Division.

THE END.